crochet stitch motifs

THE HARMONY GUIDES

crochet stitch motifs

250 stitches to crochet

edited by Erika Knight

COLLINS & BROWN

C&B
CRAFTS

First published in the United Kingdom in 2008 by
Collins & Brown
10 Southcombe Street
London
W14 0RA

An imprint of Anova Books Company Ltd

ISBN 978-1-84340-426-2

A CIP catalogue for this book is available from the British Library.

9 8 7 6 5 4 3 2 1

Reproduction by Dot Gradations Ltd
Printed and bound by SNP Leefung Printers Ltd, China

This book can be ordered direct from the publisher.
Contact the marketing department, but try your bookshop first.

www.anovabooks.com

contents

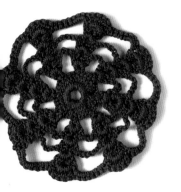

inspiration

Crochet offers a new dimension to craft, from scarves to sculpture. Discover the joys of working with motifs and the array of projects that can be made stitch by stitch.

The Harmony Stitch Guides are at the heart of needlecrafts. As indispensable reference books, resource manuals and companions, these authoritative guides inspire readers to create stiches, from the basic to the intricate, regardless of skill level.

The joy of crochet is its simplicity: there is only ever one stitch in work and just a few variations of the basic stitches to master, but the possibilities of using and combining those stitches together are endless.

This volume in the series is destined to be a classic because it boasts a wonderful collection of motifs. From rounds and squares to triangles and hexagons, rounds within squares and vice versa and even abstract forms, this really is a one-stop shop for inspiration.

Motifs can be worked in a myriad of yarns, colours and textures, for special design projects or just to add a little decoration. Take the opportunity to explore your creativity by indulging in yarns and colours you generally would not use. Working outside the box can often lead to uniquely successful results.

The 'Daisy Cluster Square' (page 55) is one of the prettiest and relatively simple to make. Worked in a single colour in pure cotton or linen blend yarn, it would make an unforgettable pattern for a throw or a cushion.

On the other hand, the 'Granny Square' or 'Traditional Square' (page 34) is one of the most popular and recognisable crochet motifs. Not only are the motifs quick and fun to create, they also make a striking contrast against bold colours. A multicoloured 'Granny Square' project with a classic and signature 'last row' border of strong black is crochet at its very best.

Indeed, many of the motifs featured in the book can be worked in a single or several colours to yield great effect. The only limits are your imagination. Create everything from garments and housewares to accessories and even soft modern art. Motifs can also be created in a range of sizes.

For a bed throw, work lots of motifs of the same design and join them together – either in the same colour or a stunning array of subtle darks with accents of Dijon and aubergine tones – for exciting contemporary styling.

Alternatively, tweedy textural yarns compliment sumptuous leather sofas and chairs.

Seek inspiration from the mathematics of nature: coral, stones, spiders' webs, the spiralling shell of a mollusc or even the innate beauty of formations of fungi. Seemingly ordinary objects take on a new dimension when they are converted to crochet stitches.

Motifs also take on a decidedly vintage appeal. A motif worked in fine classic mercerised cotton can be immersed in starch, baked and then made into a brooch or corsage for a coat, hat or bag. To enhance the home, try adding a bit of lacy romance to the fashionable 'girly' dressing table.

Crochet motifs are extremely versatile. Whether they're worked in gorgeous shiny ribbon or whisper-fine mohair, motifs in a range of textures can create glamorous design projects; or experiment in wool and felt for a rustic feel. 'Star to Star' (page 214) makes a lovely embellishment whether on a simple cushion or a little party cardigan. The 'Twelve-Petal Flower' motif (page 240) makes a brilliant little piece of jewellery by itself.

Another distinct favourite has to be the 'Gemini Spoke' (page 203) for decorating baby blankets or the 'Petit Point' (page 167) for the finishing touch to little baby shoes.

Irish crochet proffers pretty little 'leaf' motifs (page 29). I like to take these together with strands of double crochet and ribbon, to make personalised and decorative charms for handbags, mobile phones or key chains. They make wonderful little gifts for friends and family.

To be able to create something unique for ourselves, with just a ball of yarn and a little stick with a hook on the end, is immensely satisfying and rewarding, as we all crave a little individuality in our often stressful and occupied lives. With crochet in particular, there are no limitations to what you can create and construct by taking an approach which is less conventional. Once you are able to make a chain, work a few rows, go round and round to make a circle and use the basic stitches, you are then ready to go 'off-piste' and create your very own motifs.

Go 'free-form'! Create interesting and irregular shapes, forms and textures. Work motifs together in a random and 'organic' fashion – adding little bumps, flat round plates or dish shapes and extra 'bits' to create new designs. Crochet can also be used as a medium for self-expression via hangings and soft sculptures.

Whether you can already crochet or are just contemplating picking up that little hook for the very first time, this book contains something for every skill level – from starter to specialist – with technical know-how, tuition, resources and hopefully a dash of inspiration.

tools & equipment

It is sometimes hard to believe that beautiful, intricate-looking crochet is created using only two essential tools – a crochet hook and the yarn itself.

Crochet Hooks

Crochet hooks are usually made from steel, aluminum or plastic in a range of sizes according to their diameter. As each crochet stitch is worked separately until only one loop remains on the hook, space is not needed to hold stitches.

Steel

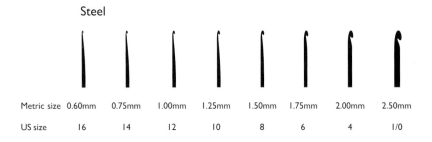

Metric size	0.60mm	0.75mm	1.00mm	1.25mm	1.50mm	1.75mm	2.00mm	2.50mm
US size	16	14	12	10	8	6	4	1/0

Aluminum

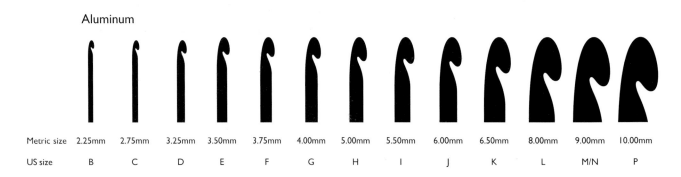

Metric size	2.25mm	2.75mm	3.25mm	3.50mm	3.75mm	4.00mm	5.00mm	5.50mm	6.00mm	6.50mm	8.00mm	9.00mm	10.00mm
US size	B	C	D	E	F	G	H	I	J	K	L	M/N	P

Crochet Yarns

Traditionally crochet was worked almost exclusively in very fine cotton yarn to create or embellish household items such as tablecloths, doilies, cuffs and frills. The samples in this book were worked in a fine mercerised cotton, but may take on a totally different appearance if different yarns are used. Lacier stitches probably look their best in smooth threads, but some of the all-over stitches can be more interesting when worked in tweedy or textured yarns. Crochet yarns can now be found in leather, suede and even fine jewellery wire.

Holding the Hook and Yarn

There are no hard and fast rules as to the best way to hold the hook and yarn. The diagrams below show one method, but choose whichever way you find the most comfortable.

Due to the restrictions of space it is not possible to show diagrams for both right and left handed people. Left handers may find it easier to trace the diagrams and then turn the tracing paper over, thus reversing the image or alternatively reflect the diagrams in the mirror. Read left for right and right for left where applicable.

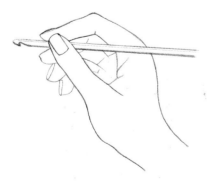

The hook is held in the right hand as if holding a pencil.

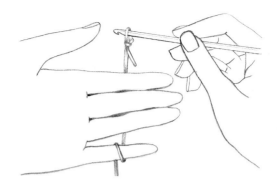

To maintain the slight tension in the yarn necessary for easy, even working, it can help to arrange the yarn around the fingers of the left hand in this way.

The left hand holds the work and at the same time controls the yarn supply. The left hand middle finger is used to manipulate the yarn, while the index finger and thumb hold on to the work.

the basics

The patterns in this book use the following basic stitches. They are shown worked into a starting chain but the method is the same whatever part of the work the stitch is worked into.

Slip Knot

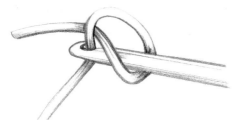

Almost all crochet begins with a slip knot. Make a loop then hook another loop through it. Tighten gently and slide the knot up to the hook.

○ Chain Stitch (ch)

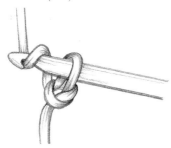

1 Yarn over and draw the yarn through to form a new loop without tightening up the previous one.

Yarn Over (yo)

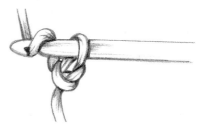

Wrap the yarn from back to front over the hook (or hold the yarn still and manoeuver the hook). This movement of the yarn over the hook is used over and over again in crochet and is usually abbreviated as 'yo'.

2 Repeat to form as many chains as required. Do not count the slip knot as a stitch. **Note:** Unless otherwise stated, when working into the starting chain always work under two strands of chain loops as shown in the following diagrams.

● Slip Stitch (sl st)

This is the shortest of crochet stitches and unlike other stitches is not used on its own to produce a fabric. It is used for joining, shaping and, where necessary, carrying the yarn to another part of the fabric for the next stage.

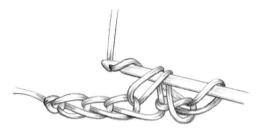 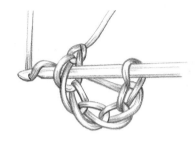

1 Insert the hook into the work (second chain from hook in diagram), yarn over and draw the yarn through both the work and loop on the hook in one movement.

2 To join a chain ring with a slip stitch, insert the hook into the first chain, yarn over and draw through the work and the yarn on the hook.

+ Double Crochet (dc)

1 Insert the hook into the work (second chain from hook on starting chain), *yarn over and draw yarn through the work only.

2 Yarn over again and draw the yarn through both loops on the hook.

3 1dc made. Insert hook into next stitch; repeat from * in step 1.

⊤ Half Treble Crochet (htr)

1 Yarn over and insert the hook into the work (third chain from hook on starting chain).

2 *Yarn over and draw through the work only.

3 Yarn over again and draw through all three loops on the hook.

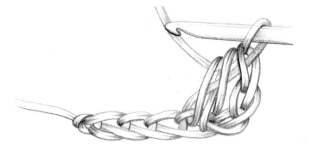

4 1hdc made. Yarn over, insert the hook into the next stitch; repeat from * in step 2.

⊤ Treble Crochet (tr)

1 Yarn over and insert the hook into the work (fourth chain from hook on starting chain).

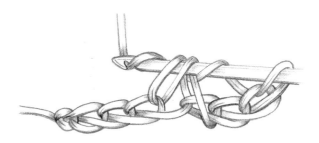

2 *Yarn over and draw through the work only.

3 Yarn over and draw through the first two loops only.

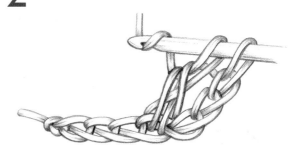

4 Yarn over and draw through the last two loops on the hook.

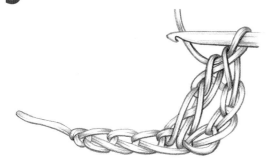

5 1dc made. Yarn over, insert hook into next stitch; repeat from * in step 2.

Double Treble (dtr)

1 Yarn over twice, insert the hook into the work (fifth chain from hook on starting chain).

2 *Yarn over and draw through the work only.

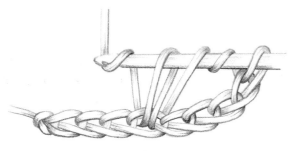

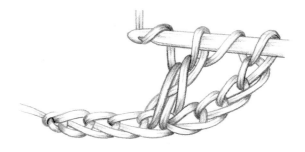

3 Yarn over again and draw through the first two loops only.

4 Yarn over again and draw through the next two loops only.

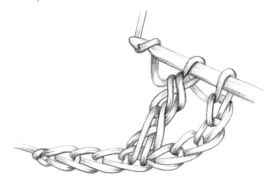

5 Yarn over again and draw through the last two loops on the hook.

6 1dtr made. Yarn over twice, insert the hook into the next stitch; repeat from * in step 2.

Longer Basic Stitches

Triple treble (trtr), quadruple treble (quadtr), quintuple (quintr) etc. are made by wrapping the yarn over three, four, five times etc. at the beg and end as for a double treble, rep step 4 until two loops remain on hook, finishing with step 5.

Solomon's Knot

A Solomon's Knot is a lengthened chain stitch locked with a double crochet stitch worked into its back loop.

1 Make 1 chain and lengthen the loop as required. Wrap the yarn over the hook.

2 Draw through loop on the hook, keeping the single back thread of this long chain separate from the 2 front threads.

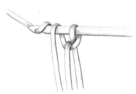

3 Insert the hook under the single back thread. Wrap the yarn over the hook.

4 Draw a loop through and wrap again.

5 Draw through both loops on the hook to complete.

6 It is necessary to work back into the 'knots' between the lengthened chains in order to make the classic Solomon's Knot fabric.

making fabric

These are the basic procedures for making crochet fabrics – the things that crochet patterns sometimes assume you know. These principles can be applied to all the patterns in this book.

Starting Chain

To make a flat fabric worked in rows you must begin with a starting chain. The length of the starting chain is the number of stitches needed for the first row of fabric plus the number of chains needed to get to the correct height of the stitches to be used in the first row. Each pattern in this book indicates the length of starting chain required to work one repeat of the design.

Working in Rows

A flat fabric can be produced by turning the work at the end of each row. Right handers work from right to left and left handers from left to right. One or more chains must be worked at the beginning of each row to bring the hook up to the height of the first stitch in the row. The number of chains used for turning depends upon the height of the stitch they are to match:

    double crochet = 1 chains

    half treble crochet = 2 chains

    treble crochet = 3 chains

    double treble = 4 chains

    When working half treble crochet or longer stitches the turning chain takes the place of the first stitch. Where one

chain is worked at the beginning of a row starting with double crochet it is usually for height only and is in addition to the first stitch.

Basic Tr Fabric

Make a starting chain of the required length plus two chains. Work one treble crochet into the fourth chain from the hook. The three chains at the beginning of the row form the first treble crochet. Work one treble crochet into the next and every chain to the end of the row.

    At the end of each row turn the work so that another row can be worked across the top of the previous one. It does not matter which way the work is turned but be consistent. Make three chains for turning. These turning chains will count as the first treble crochet.

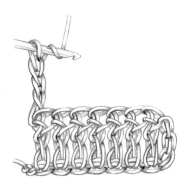

Miss the first treble crochet in the previous row, work a treble crochet into the top of the next and every treble crochet including the last double crochet in the row, then work a treble crochet into the third of three chains at the beginning of the previous row.

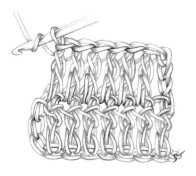

Cast Off

To cast off the yarn permanently break off the yarn about 5 cm (2 in.) away from the work (longer if you need to sew pieces together). Draw the end through the loop on the hook and tighten gently.

Joining in New Yarn and Changing Colour

When joining in a new yarn or changing colour, work in the old yarn until two loops of the last stitch remain in the old yarn/colour. Use the new colour/yarn to complete the stitch.

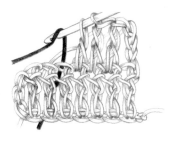

Continue to work the following stitches in the new colour or yarn, as before.

When working whole rows in different colours, make the change during the last stitch in the previous row, so the new colour for the next row is ready to work the turning chain.

Do not cut off any yarns which will be needed again later at the same edge, but continue to use them as required, leaving an unbroken 'float' thread up the side of the fabric.

If, at the end of a row, the pattern requires you to return to the beginning of the same row without turning and to work another row in a different colour in the same direction, complete the first row in the old colour and cast off by lengthening the final loop on the hook, passing the whole ball through it and gently tighten again. That yarn is now available if you need to rejoin it later at this edge (if not, cut it).

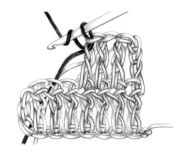

Placement of Stitches

All crochet stitches (except chains) require the hook to be inserted into existing work. It has already been shown how to work into a chain and into the top of a stitch, however stitches can also be worked into the following places.

Working into Chain Spaces

When a stitch, group, shell, cluster, bobble etc. is positioned over a chain or chains, the hook is often inserted into the space under the chain.

It is important to notice if the pattern instructions stipulate working into a particular chain as this will change the appearance of the design.

If necessary, information of this kind has been given as notes with the diagram.

A bobble, popcorn or cluster that is worked into a chain space is shown in the diagram spread out over more than one stitch, therefore on the diagrams they will not be closed at the base.

Working Around the Stem of a Stitch

Inserting the hook around the whole stem of a stitch creates raised or relief effects.

Working around the front of the stem gives a stitch that lies on the front of the work.

Working around the back of the stem gives a stitch that lies on the back of the work.

Working Between Stitches

Inserting the hook between the stems of the stitches produces an open effect.

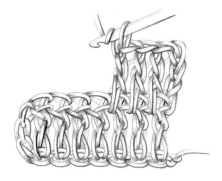

Ensure that the number of stitches remains constant after each row.

Working Under the Front or Back Loop Only

Inserting the hook under one loop at the top of the stitch leaves the other loop as a horizontal bar.

Under front loop.

Under back loop.

Working in Rows

If you work consistently into the front loop only you will make a series of ridges alternately on the back and front of the work. Working into the back loop only makes the ridges appear alternately on the front and back of the work.

If however you work alternately into the front loop only on one row and then the back loop only on the next row, the horizontal bars will all appear on the same side of the fabric.

Working in Rounds

Working always into the front loop only will form a bar on the back of the work and vice versa.

Starting Chains and Pattern Repeats

The number of starting chains required is given with each pattern. It may be given in the form of a multiple, for example: **Starting chain: Multiple of 7 sts + 3**. This means you can make any length of chain that is a multiple of 7 + 3, such as 14 + 3ch, 21 + 3ch, 28 + 3ch etc.

In the written instructions the stitches that should be repeated are contained within brackets [] or follow an asterisk *. These stitches are repeated across the row or round the required number of times. On the diagrams the stitches that have to be repeated can be easily visualised. The extra stitches not included in the pattern repeat are there to balance the row or make it symmetrical and are only worked once. Obviously turning chains are only worked at the beginning of each row. Some diagrams consist of more than one pattern repeat so that you can see more clearly how the design is worked.

Working in Colour

Capital letters A, B, C etc. are used to indicate different yarn colours in both written instructions and diagrams. They do not refer to any particular colour. See page 19 for instructions on changing colour within a pattern.

Increasing and Decreasing

If you are working crochet to make something which requires shaping, such as decreasing for the neckline of a garment or increasing to add width for a sleeve, you need to know something about shaping.

Increasing is generally achieved by working two or more stitches in the pattern where there would normally be one stitch. Conversely, decreasing is achieved by working two or more stitches together or missing one or more stitches. However it can be difficult to know exactly where these adjustments are best made and a visual guide would make the work easier!

On the diagrams below we show you some examples of shapings which cover a variety of possibilities. We recommend that you use this method yourself when planning a project. First pencil trace the diagram given with the stitch. If necessary repeat the tracing to match the repeat of the pattern until you have a large enough area to give you the required shape. Once this is correct ink it in so that you can draw over it in pencil without destroying it. Now over this draw the shaping you want, matching as near as possible the style of the particular pattern you are using.

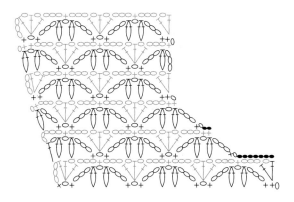

Tension

Whenever you are following crochet pattern instructions, whatever form they take, probably the most important single factor in your success is obtaining the 'tension' or 'gauge' that the pattern designer worked to. If you do not obtain the same tension as indicated your work will not turn out to be the measurement given.

The tension is usually specified as a number of stitches and a number of rows to a given measurement (usually 10 cm (4 in). The quick way to check is to make a square of fabric about 15 cm (6 in.) wide in the correct pattern and with the correct yarn and suggested hook size, lay this down on a flat surface and measure it – first horizontally (for stitch tension) and then vertically (for row tension). If your square has too few stitches or rows to the measurement, your tension is too loose so try smaller hook size. If it has too many stitches try a size larger hook. (Hint: Stitch tension is generally more important than row tension in crochet.)

Note that the hook size quoted in instructions is a suggestion only. You must use whichever hook gives you the correct tension.

Line showing required decrease slope

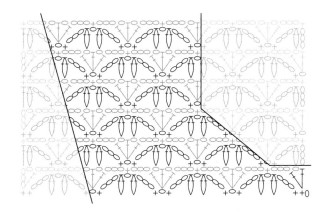

Line showing required increase slope

stitch variations

Different effects can be created by small variations in the stitch-making procedure or by varying the position and manner of inserting the hook into the fabric.

Filet Crochet

This is a particular technique of crochet based on forming designs from a series of solid and open squares called 'blocks' and 'spaces'. These are more often used in crochet lace patterns made with cotton, but can be worked in knitting yarn.

To work a space make 2 chains, miss 2 chains (or 2 stitches on the preceding row) and work 1 double into the next stitch. To work a block, work 1 double into each of the next 3 chains or stitches. When a block follows a space, it will look like 4 doubles; this is because the first double belongs to the adjacent space.

Groups or Shells

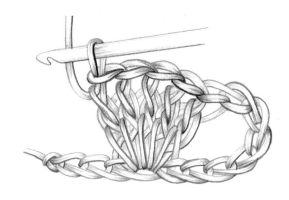

These consist of several complete stitches worked into the same place. They can be worked as part of a pattern or as a method of increasing.

On diagrams the point at the base of the group will be positioned above the space or stitch where the hook is to be inserted.

Clusters

Any combination of stitches may be joined into a cluster by leaving the last loop of each temporarily on the hook until they are worked off together at the end. Working stitches together in this way can also be a method of decreasing.

It is important to be sure exactly how and where the hook is to be inserted for each 'leg' of the cluster. The legs may be worked over adjacent stitches or stitches may be missed between legs.

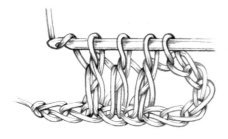

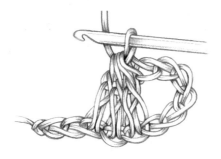

1 Work a treble crochet into each of the next three stitches leaving the last loop of each treble crochet on the hook.

2 Yarn over and draw through all four loops on the hook. On diagrams each leg of the cluster will be positioned above the stitch where the hook is to be inserted.

Bobbles

When a cluster is worked into one stitch it forms a bobble.

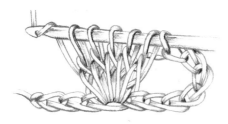

1 Work five treble crochet into one stitch leaving the last loop of each on the hook.

2 Yarn over and draw through all the loops on the hook. More bulky bobbles can be secured with an extra chain stitch. If this is necessary it would be indicated within the pattern.

Popcorns

Popcorns are groups of complete stitches usually worked into the same place, folded and closed at the top. An extra chain can be worked to secure the popcorn. They're great for adding textural interest to a garment.

1 Work five treble crochet into one stitch. Take the hook out of the working loop and insert it into the top of the first treble crochet made, from front to back.

2 Pick up the working loop and draw this through to close the popcorn. If required, work one chain to secure the popcorn. On diagrams the point at the base of the popcorn will be positioned above the space or stitch where it is to be worked.

Puff Stitches

These are similar to bobbles but worked using half treble crochet. As half treble crochet cannot be worked until one loop remains on the hook, the stitches are not closed until the required number have been worked.

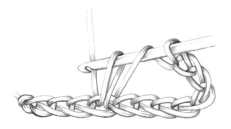

1 Yarn over, insert the hook, yarn over again and draw a loop through (three loops on the hook).

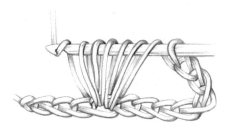

2 Repeat this step twice more, inserting the hook into the same stitch (seven loops on the hook); yarn over and draw through all the loops on the hook.

3 As with popcorns and bulky bobbles an extra chain stitch is often used to secure the puff stitch firmly. This will be indicated within the pattern if necessary.

A **cluster** of half treble crochet stitches is worked in the same way as a puff stitch but each 'leg' is worked where indicated.

When working a large piece it is sensible to start with more chains than necessary as it is simple to undo the extra chains if you have miscounted.

Picots

A picot is normally a chain loop formed into a closed ring by a slip stitch or single crochet. The number of chains in a picot can vary. When working a picot closed with a slip stitch at the top of a chain arch, the picot will not appear central unless an extra chain is worked after the slip stitch.

1 Work four chains.

2 Into the fourth chain from the hook work a slip stitch to close.

3 Continue working chains or required stitch.

Crossed Stitches

This method produces stitches that are not entangled with each other and so maintain a clear 'X' shape.

Miss two stitches and work the first double into the next stitch. Work one chain then work the second double into the first of the missed stitches, taking the hook behind the first double before inserting. See individual pattern instructions for variations on crossed stitch.

Irish crochet

Of all forms of crochet lace, Irish crochet is the most revered and sought after. This type of lace is comprised of separately crocheted motifs which are assembled into a mesh background.

Irish Crochet

True Irish crochet is made by first working motifs and then creating a net or mesh background incorporating the motifs and forming the fabric which holds them in position. This is done by placing the motifs in the required position face down on paper or a scrap of fabric and temporarily securing them. The background or filling, is then worked progressively, joining in the motifs. After the work is completed the paper or fabric is carefully removed.

Historically crochet is believed to have been introduced into Ireland in the early part of the 19th century by nuns, probably from Italy or France. It was evolved by them and convent-educated girls into an artform in itself, reaching levels of complexity and delicacy not seen in other styles of crochet work.

Stitches and techniques were developed which are particular to Irish crochet. The use of padding threads which are held at the edge of the work, so that subsequent rows or rounds are worked over them to give a three-dimensional effect is one example; another is the Clones Knot and both of these are described below.

Because of the difficulty of giving general instructions for the construction of true Irish crochet and particularly since the various motifs can each be incorporated into almost any crocheted net background, we have simplified the following selection to give you a taste of Irish style crochet.

Padding Threads

Padding threads are used to give a three-dimensional appearance to some Irish crochet motifs. The thread used is usually the same as the thread used for the motif and the number of threads worked over determines the amount of padding. In this book we have usually worked over three thicknesses of thread.

The example below is for padding threads at the beginning of a motif, but they can also be used in other areas of motifs (see Tristar on page 83).

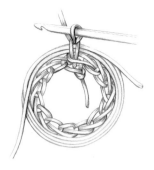

1 Make the required number of chains and join with a slip stitch.

2 Wind a length of thread three or four times around the end of a pencil or finger and hold against the chain.

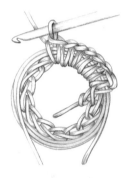

Working into Base of Stitch

Insert the hook under two strands at the base of the stitch. The diagram below shows work viewed from the back.

3 The stitches are then worked over the chain and 'padding' threads. When the motif is complete, the ends of the padding thread are pulled through several stitches and cut.

   Instructions and diagrams of individual patterns indicate where it is appropriate to use padding threads. On the diagrams the padding thread is indicated with a thicker line.

Clones Knot

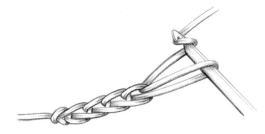

1 Draw up a chain to required length and hold it in place.

2 *Yarn over, twist hook over, then under the loop, then pull the yarn back under the loop with the hook; repeat from * until the loop is completely covered.

3 Yarn over, draw the hook through all loops on the hook.

4 To secure the knot work 1 double crochet into the last chain stitch before the Clones Knot.

stitch gallery

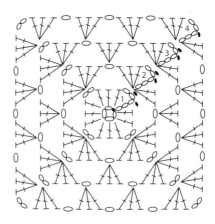

Traditional Square 1

Base ring: 4ch, join with sl st.

1st round: 5ch (count as 1tr and 2ch), [3tr into ring, 2ch] 3 times, 2tr into ring, sl st to 3rd of 5ch.

2nd round: Sl st into next sp, 5ch (count as 1tr and 2ch), 3tr into same sp, *1ch, miss 3tr, [3tr, 2ch, 3tr] into next sp; rep from * twice more, 1ch, miss 3 sts, 2tr into same sp as 5ch at beg of round, sl st to 3rd of 5ch.

3rd round: Sl st into next sp, 5ch (count as 1tr and 2ch), 3tr into same sp, *1ch, miss 3tr, 3tr into next sp, 1ch, miss 3tr**, [3tr, 2ch, 3tr] into next sp; rep from * twice more and from * to ** again, 2tr into same sp as 5ch, sl st to 3rd of 5ch.

4th round: Sl st into next sp, 5ch (count as 1tr and 2ch), 3tr into same sp, *[1ch, miss 3tr, 3tr into next sp] twice, 1ch, miss 3tr**, [3tr, 2ch, 3tr] into next sp; rep from * twice more and from * to ** again, 2tr into same sp as 5ch, sl st to 3rd of 5ch.

Cast off.

Traditional Square II

Worked as Traditional Square I.

Work 1 round each in colours A, B, C and D.

Although bamboo needles are beautiful and light to use, they can often be sharp and split the yarn. Consider using an alternative such as Addi Turbo Needles – made of 'Turbo' finish brass. These needles are fast, quiet and easy-to-use.

Double Crochet Square I

Base ring: 4ch, join with sl st.
1st round: 5ch (count as 1tr and 2ch), [3tr into ring, 2ch]
3 times, 2tr into ring, sl st to 3rd of 5ch. (4 groups of 3tr)
2nd round: Sl st into next sp, 7ch (count as 1tr and 4ch),
*2tr into same sp, 1tr into each tr across side of square**,
2tr into next sp. 4ch; rep from * twice more and from *
to ** again, 1tr into same sp as 7ch, sl st to 3rd of 7ch. (4
groups of 7tr)
3rd round: As 2nd round. (4 groups of 11tr)
4th round: As 2nd round. (4 groups of 15tr)
Cast off.

Double Crochet Square II

Worked as Double Crochet Square I.
Work 1 round each in colours A, B, C and D.

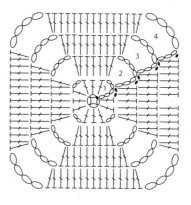

Painter's Palette

Base ring: 4ch, join with sl st.

1st round: Work 8dc into ring, sl st to first dc.

2nd round: 5ch, 1htr and 3ch, miss dc at base of 5ch, htr into next dc, *3ch, htr into next dc; rep from * 5 more times, 3ch, sl st to 2nd ch of 5ch.

3rd round: 1ch, work 1dc into each htr and 4dc into each sp around, sl st to first dc.

Cast off.

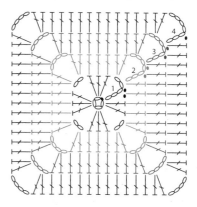

DOUBLE CROCHET SQUARE II

PAINTER'S PALETTE

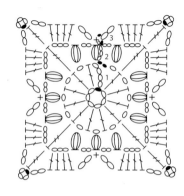

French Square

Special Abbreviation: Puff st = [yo, insert hook into sp, yo and draw loop through] 4 times, yo and draw through all loops on hook.

Base ring: 6ch, join with sl st.

1st round: 4ch (count as 1tr and 1ch), [1tr into ring, 1ch] 11 times, sl st to 3rd of 4ch. (12 spaces)

2nd round: Sl st into next sp, 3ch, work puff st into same sp (counts as puff st), *2ch, work puff st into next sp, 3ch, 1dtr into next tr, 3ch, work puff st into next sp, 2ch**, puff st into next sp; rep from * twice more and from * to ** again, sl st to top of first puff st.

3rd round: 1ch, 1dc into same place, *2ch, miss next 2ch sp, 4tr into next 3ch sp, 2ch, 1dtr into next dtr, 3ch, insert hook down through top of last dtr and work sl st, 2ch, 4tr into next 3ch sp, 2ch, miss next 2ch sp, 1dc into next puff st; rep from * 3 more times, omitting dc at end of last rep, sl st to first dc.

Cast off.

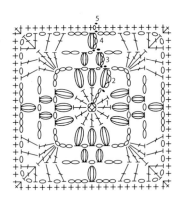

Italian Square

Special Abbreviation: Puff st = [yo, insert hook into sp, yo and draw loop through] 4 times, yo and draw through all loops on hook.

Base ring: 4ch, join with sl st.

1st round: 3ch (count as 1tr), 11tr into ring, sl st to top of 3ch. (12 sts)

2nd round: 3ch, work htr3tog into same place as 3ch (counts as puff st), *[1ch, work puff st into next st] twice, 5ch**, puff st into next st; rep from * twice more and from * to ** again, sl st to top of first puff st.

3rd round: Sl st into next sp, 3ch, work htr3tog into same sp (counts as puff st), *1ch, puff st into next sp, 2ch, 5tr into next 5ch sp, 2ch**, htr4tog into next sp; rep from * twice more and from * to ** again, sl st to top of first puff st.

4th round: Sl st into next sp, 3ch, work htr3tog into same sp (counts as puff st), *3ch, miss 2ch, [1tr into next tr, 1ch] twice, work [1tr, 1ch, 1tr, 1ch, 1tr] into next tr, [1ch, 1tr into next tr] twice, 3ch, miss 2ch**, work puff st into next sp; rep from * twice more and from * to ** again, sl st to top of first puff st.

5th round: 1ch, 1dc into each ch and each st all around, but working 3dc into second/centre tr of each corner group at each corner, ending sl st to first dc.
Cast off.

Christmas Rose Square

Special Abbreviation: Bobble = work 4tr into same sp leaving last loop of each on hook, yo and draw through all loops on hook.

Base ring: Using A, 6ch, join with sl st.

1st round: 5ch (count as 1tr and 2ch), [1tr into ring, 2ch] 7 times, sl st to 3rd of 5ch. (8 spaces)

2nd round: Sl st into next sp, 3ch, work tr3tog into same sp (count as bobble), [5ch, work bobble into next sp] 7 times, 5ch, sl st to top of first bobble. Cast off.

3rd round: Using B join into same place, 1ch, 1dc into same place, *2ch, working over the 5ch sp so as to enclose it work 1tr into next tr of first round, 2ch, 1dc into top of next cluster; rep from * all around omitting dc at end, sl st to first dc.

4th round: Sl st into next sp, 1ch, 1dc into same sp, *3ch, 1dc into next sp; rep from * all around omitting dc at end, sl st to first dc.

5th round: Sl st into next sp, 3ch (count as 1tr), [1tr, 2ch, 2tr] into same sp, *2ch, 1dc into next sp, [3ch, 1dc into next sp] twice, 2ch**, [2tr, 2ch, 2tr] into next sp ; rep from * twice more and from * to ** again, sl st to top of 3ch.

Cast off.

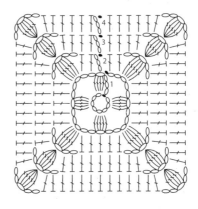

Baltic Square

Special Abbreviation: Popcorn = work 5 tr into same sp. Remove hook from working loop and insert it into the top of the first tr made from front to back, pick up working loop and draw through to close popcorn.

Base ring: 8ch, join with sl st.

1st round: 3ch, 4tr popcorn into ring (counts as 5tr popcorn), [5ch, 5tr popcorn into ring] 3 times, 5ch, sl st to top of first popcorn.

2nd round: 3ch (count as 1tr), *work [2tr, 2ch, 5tr popcorn, 2ch, 2tr] into next 5ch sp**, 1tr into next popcorn; rep from * twice more and from * to ** again, sl st to top of 3ch.

3rd round: 3ch (count as 1tr), 1tr into each of next 2 sts, *2tr into next sp, 2ch, 5tr popcorn into next popcorn, 2ch, 2tr into next sp**, 1tr into each of next 5tr; rep from * twice more and from * to ** again, 1tr into each of last 2tr, sl st to top of 3ch.

4th round: 3ch (count as 1tr), 1tr into each of next 4tr, *2tr into next sp, 2ch, 5tr popcorn into next popcorn, 2ch, 2tr into next sp**, 1tr into each of next 9tr; rep from * twice more and from * to ** again, 1tr into each of last 4tr, sl st to top of 3ch.

Cast off.

Cranesbill Lace Square

Special Abbreviation: Bobble = work 4tr into same sp leaving last loop of each on hook, yo and draw through all loops on hook.

Base ring: 6ch, join with sl st.

1st round: 3ch, tr2tog into ring (counts as bobble), [3ch, bobble into ring] 7 times, 3ch, sl st to top of first bobble.

2nd round: Sl st to centre of next 3ch sp, 1ch, 1dc into same sp, [5ch, 1dc into next sp] 7 times, 2ch, 1tr into first dc.

3rd round: *5ch, [bobble, 3ch, bobble] into next sp**, 5ch, 1dc into next sp; rep from * twice and from * to ** again, 2ch, 1tr into tr which closed 2nd round.

4th round: *5ch, 1dc into next sp, 5ch, [1dc, 5ch, 1dc] into corner 3ch sp, 5ch, 1dc into next 5ch sp; rep from * 3 more times, ending last rep into tr which closed 3rd round, sl st to first ch.
Cast off.

We know you're hooked on crochet, so why not use metal hooks for better accuracy – they last a lifetime too!

next sp**, 1tr into next sp; rep from * to **, sl st to top of 3ch.

8th round: 3ch (count as 1tr), 1tr into each tr all around with [3tr, 2ch, 3tr] into each 2ch corner sp, ending sl st to top of 3ch. Cast off.

9th round: Using C, join into same place, 1ch, 1dc into same st as 1ch, *[1dc into next st, picot] twice, 1dc into each of next 3 sts, work [picot, 1dc into next st] twice, [1dc, 7ch, 1dc] into corner 2ch sp, [1dc into next st, picot] twice, 1dc into each of next 3 sts, [picot, 1dc into next st] twice, 1dc into next st; rep from * 3 more times omitting dc at end of last rep, sl st to first dc.

10th round: Sl st across to top of next 3ch picot, 1ch, 1dc into same picot, *5ch, miss next picot, 1dc into next picot, 5ch, (dc, 5ch, dc) in next 7ch sp, [5ch, miss next picot, 1dc into next picot] twice, 5ch, 1dc into next picot; rep from * 3 more times omitting dc at end of last rep, sl st to first dc. Cast off.

Rose Square

Special Abbreviation: Picot = 3ch, sl st down through top of last dc made.

Base ring: Using A, 12ch, join with sl st.

1st round: 1ch, 18dc into ring, sl st to first dc. (18 sts)

2nd round: 1ch, beginning into same st as 1ch [1dc, 3ch, miss 2 sts] 6 times, sl st to first dc.

3rd round: 1ch, work a petal of [1dc, 3ch, 5tr, 3ch, 1dc] into each of next six 3ch sps, sl st to first dc.

4th round: 1ch, [1dc between 2dc, 5ch behind petal of 3rd round] 6 times, sl st to first dc.

5th round: 1ch, work a petal of [1dc, 3ch, 7tr, 3ch, 1dc] into each of next six 5ch sps, sl st to first dc. Cast off.

6th round: Using B, join between 2dc, 1ch, [1dc between 2dc, 6ch behind petal of 5th round] 6 times, sl st to first dc.

7th round: Sl st into next sp, 3ch (count as 1tr), *[4tr, 2ch, 1tr] all into same sp, 6tr into next sp, [2tr, 2ch, 4tr] all into

Saturn Motif

Special abbreviation: Bobble = work 3tr into same sp leaving last loop of each on hook, yo and draw through all loops on hook.

Base ring: Using A, 8ch, join with sl st.

1st round: 1ch, 12dc into ring, sl st to first dc. (12 sts)

2nd round: 3ch, 1tr into same place as 3ch (counts as tr2tog), [3ch, tr2tog into next st] 11 times, 3ch, sl st to first bobble.

3rd round: Sl st into each of next 2ch, 1ch, 1dc into same place as 1ch, [4ch, 1dc into next 3ch sp] 11 times, 4ch, sl st to first dc.

4th round: 1ch, *[2dc, 3ch, 2dc] all into next 4ch sp; rep from * 11 more times, sl st to first dc. Cast off.

5th round: Join B into next 3ch sp, 3ch, tr2tog into same sp (counts as first bobble), 4ch, bobble all into same sp, *[bobble, 4ch, bobble] all into next 3ch sp; rep from * 10 more times, sl st to first bobble.

6th round: 1ch, 1dc into same place as 1ch, *[2dc, 3ch, 2dc] all into next 4ch sp, miss next bobble**, 1dc into next bobble; rep from * 10 more times and from * to ** again, sl st to first dc.

Cast off.

Thai Orchid

Special Abbreviation: 3 picot cluster = work 4ch, sl st into first ch, [3ch, sl st into same ch as first sl st] twice.

Base ring: Make 6ch, sl st into first ch to form a ring.

1st round: With yarn A 1ch, work 12dc into ring, sl st into first dc.

2nd round: With yarn A 3ch (count as 1tr), 1tr into same st as last sl st, work 2tr into each of next 11dc, sl st into 3rd of 3ch at beg of round.

3rd round: With yarn A 1ch, 1dc into same st as last sl st, 1dc into each of next 23tr, sl st into first dc.

4th round: With yarn B 1ch, 1dc into same dc as last sl st, 5ch, miss 2dc, [1dc into next dc, 5ch, miss 2dc] 7 times, sl st into first dc.

5th round: With yarn B 1ch, 1dc into same st as last sl st, *into next 5ch sp work [1htr, 3tr, 3 picot cluster, 3tr, 1htr], 1dc into next dc; rep from * 7 more times omitting 1dc at end of last rep, sl st into first dc.

6th round: With yarn C 1ch, 1dc into same st as last sl st, *7ch, 1dc into centre picot of 3 picot cluster, 7ch, 1dc into next dc; rep from * 7 more times omitting 1dc at end of last rep, sl st into first dc.

7th round: With yarn C sl st into first 7ch sp, 1ch, [work 8dc into next 7ch sp, 3 picot cluster, 8dc into same 7ch sp] 8 times, sl st into first dc.

Cast off.

Roulette Wheel

Special Abbreviation: 3 loop cluster = 7ch, sl st into first of these ch, [6ch, sl st into same ch as last sl st] twice.

Base ring: 8ch, join with a sl st.

1st round: 1ch, 18dc into ring, sl st to first dc.

2nd round: 6ch (count as 1htr, 4ch), miss first 3dc, 1htr into next dc, [4ch, miss 2dc, 1htr into next dc] 4 times, 4ch, sl st to 2nd of 6ch at beg of round.

3rd round: 1ch, work [1dc, 1htr, 3tr, 1htr, 1dc] into each of the six 4ch sps, sl st to first dc. (6 petals)

4th round: Working behind each petal, sl st into base of each of first 4 sts, [5ch, miss next 6 sts, sl st into base of next tr] 6 times, working last sl st to base of same tr as sl st at beg of round.

5th round: 1ch, work [1dc, 1htr, 1tr, 5dtr, 1tr, 1htr, 1dc] into each of the six 5ch sps, sl st into first dc.

6th round: Working behind each petal, sl st into base of each of first 6 sts, [6ch, miss next 10 sts, sl st into base of

next dtr] 5 times, 3ch, miss next 10 sts, 1dtr into base of next dtr.

7th round: Sl st into sp made by dtr just formed, into same sp work [1dc, 6ch, 1dc], 6ch, *into next sp work [1dc, 6ch, 1dc], 6ch; rep from * 4 more times, sl st to first dc.

8th round: Sl st into each of first 3ch of 6ch sp, into same sp work [1dc, 6ch, 1dc], 6ch, 1dc into next 6ch sp, 6ch, *into next 6ch sp work [1dc, 6ch, 1dc], 6ch, 1dc into next 6ch sp, 6ch; rep from * 4 more times, sl st to first dc.

9th round: Sl st into each of first 3ch of 6ch sp, into same sp work [1dc, 6ch, 1dc], 6ch, [1dc into next 6ch sp, 6ch] twice, *into next 6ch sp work [1dc, 6ch, 1dc], 6ch, [1dc into next 6ch sp, 6ch] twice; rep from * 4 more times, sl st to first dc.

10th round: Sl st into each of first 3ch of first 6ch sp, into same sp work [1dc, 3 loop cluster, 1dc], 6ch, [1dc into next 6ch sp, 6ch] 3 times, *into next 6ch sp work [1dc, 3 loop cluster, 1dc], 6ch, [1dc into next 6ch sp, 6ch] 3 times; rep from * 4 more times, sl st to first dc.

Cast off.

3 loop cluster

base of st

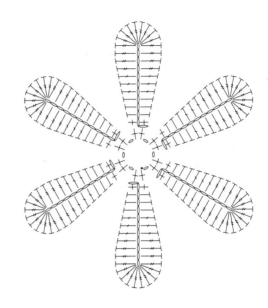

Dandelion

Petals: 12ch, 1dc in 2nd ch from hook, 1htr in each of next 3ch, 1tr in each of next 3ch, 1dtr in each of next 3ch, 10dtr in last ch – work along opposite side of ch, 1dtr in each of next 3ch, 1tr in each of next 3ch, 1htr in each of next 3ch, 1dc in next ch. Cast off. Make 5 more petals. After 6th petal, do not Cast off, work 2dc across base of petal, *1ch, 2dc across base of next petal; rep from * 4 more times, 1ch, join with sl st to first dc of first petal. Cast off.

Centre motif: Make 4ch, join with sl st.

1st round: 3ch (count as 1tr), 17tr into ring, sl st to top of 3ch. Cast off.

Sew together on wrong side.

Spring Zinnia

Paisley: 70ch, 2tr in 4th ch from hook, *miss 2 chs, sl st in next ch, 3ch, 2tr in same sp (shell); rep from * 15 times, miss next 2ch, hook in next ch and in base of first shell, yo and draw through all loops, 3ch, 2tr in same sp, miss 2 ch, sl st in next ch, **3ch, 2tr in same sp, miss 2 ch, sl st in next ch; rep from ** 3 times. Cast off.

Flower: 8ch, join with sl st to form ring.

1st round: 3ch (counts as tr), tr in ring, *4ch, sl st in first ch for picot, 2tr in ring; rep from * 7 times, 4ch picot, join with sl st to top of 3ch. Attach another strand of yarn and 5ch, for stem *with single strand 5ch and join with sl st in base of 4th shell from bottom of paisley, 2ch, tr in 2nd ch, dtr in each of next 2chs, tr in next ch, sl st in stem; rep from * with second strand attaching to base of shell opposite the 4th shell. End with sl st in stem. Cast off. Sew 7 picots of flower to paisley on wrong side leaving bottom 2 picots free.

Think outside the skein! Since you can crochet with almost any yarn or continuous length fibre, why not experiment with different materials such as torn tees, leather cords or even plastic bags? The results may just surprise you.

Floribunda

Base ring: Using A, 6ch, join with sl st.

1st round: 1ch, 16dc into ring, sl st to first dc. (16 sts).

2nd round: 6ch (count as 1tr and 3ch sp), miss first 2 sts, [1tr into next st, 3ch, miss 1 st] 7 times, sl st to 3rd of 6ch.

3rd round: 1ch, work a petal of [1dc, 1htr, 5tr, 1htr, 1dc] into each of next eight 3ch sps, sl st to first dc. Cast off.

4th round: Using B join between 2dc, 1ch, [1dc between 2dc, 6ch behind petal of 3rd round] 8 times, sl st to first dc.

5th round: 1ch, work a petal of [1dc, 1htr, 6tr, 1htr, 1dc] into each of next 8 sps, sl st to first dc. Cast off.

6th round: Using C join into 2nd tr of petal of 5th round, 1ch, 1dc into same place as 1ch, 6ch, miss 2tr, 1dc into next tr, [6ch, 1dc into 2nd tr of next petal, 6ch, miss 2tr, 1dc into next tr] 7 times, 3ch, 1tr into first dc.

7th round: 3ch (count as 1tr), 3tr into sp formed by tr which closed 6th round, *4ch, 1dc into next sp, [6ch, 1dc into next sp] twice, 4ch**, [4tr, 4ch, 4tr] into next sp; rep from * twice more and from * to ** again, ending [4tr, 4ch] into last ch sp, sl st to top of 3ch.
Cast off.

Sow Thistle Square

Special Abbreviation: Cluster = yo, insert hook in st and draw up a loop, yo and draw through 2 loops. (Yo, insert hook in next st and draw up a loop. Yo, draw through 2 loops) twice, yo and draw through all loops on hook.

Base ring: Using A, 4ch, join with sl st.

1st round: 4ch (count as 1tr and 1ch), [1tr, 1ch] 11 times into ring, sl st to 3rd of 4ch. Cast off.

2nd round: Using B join into same sp, 3ch, tr2tog into same sp (counts as cluster), [3ch, cluster into next sp] 11 times, 3ch, sl st to top of first cluster. Cast off.

3rd round: Using A join into 3ch sp, 1ch, 1dc into same sp, [5ch, 1dc into next sp] 11 times, 2ch, 1tr into first dc. Cast off.

4th round: Using B join into sp formed by tr, 1ch, 1dc into same place, *5ch, 1dc into next sp, 1ch, [5tr, 3ch, 5tr] into next sp, 1ch, 1dc into next sp; rep from * 3 more times, omitting dc at end of last rep, sl st to first dc. Cast off.

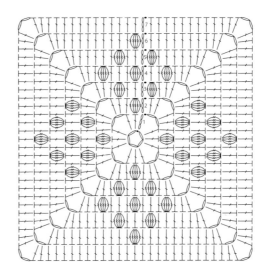

Diamond Cluster Motif

Special Abbreviation: 5dtr bobble = leaving last loop of each st on hook, work 5dtr into next tr, yo and draw through all loops on hook.

Base ring: 6ch, join with sl st.

1st round: 3ch (count as 1tr), 2tr into ring, [2ch, 3tr into ring] 3 times, 2ch, sl st to top of 3ch. (4 blocks of 3tr)

2nd round: 3ch, *5dtr bobble into next tr, 1tr into next tr, [2tr, 2ch, 2tr] into next 2ch sp, 1tr into next tr; rep from * to end omitting 1tr at end of last rep, sl st to top of 3ch.

3rd round: 3ch, *1tr into top of bobble, 1tr into next tr, 5dtr bobble into next tr, 1tr into next tr, [2tr, 2ch, 2tr] into next 2ch sp, 1tr into next tr, 5dtr bobble into next tr, 1tr into next tr; rep from * to end omitting 1tr at end of last rep, sl st to top of 3ch.

4th round: 3ch, *5dtr bobble into next tr, 1tr into next tr, 1tr into top of next bobble, 1tr into next tr, 5dtr bobble into next tr, 1tr into next tr, [2tr, 2ch, 2tr] into 2ch sp, 1tr into next tr, 5dtr bobble into next tr, 1tr into next tr, 1tr into top of next bobble, 1tr into next tr; rep from * to end omitting 1tr at end of last rep, sl st to top of 3ch.

5th round: 3ch, *1tr into top of next bobble, 1tr into next tr, 5dtr bobble into next tr, 1tr into each of next 5 sts, [2tr, 2ch, 2tr] into next 2ch sp, 1tr into each of next 5 sts, 5dtr bobble into next tr, 1tr into next tr; rep from * to end omitting 1tr at end of last rep, sl st to top of 3ch.

6th round: 3ch, *5dtr bobble into next tr, 1tr into each of next 9 sts, [2tr, 2ch, 2tr] into next 2ch sp, 1tr into each of next 9 sts; rep from * to end omitting 1tr at end of last rep, sl st to top of ch.

7th round: 3ch, *1tr into each of next 12 sts, [2tr, 2ch, 2tr] into next 2ch sp, 1tr into each of next 11 sts; rep from * to end omitting 1tr at end of last rep, sl st to top of 3ch. Cast off.

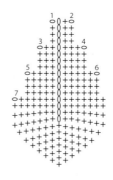

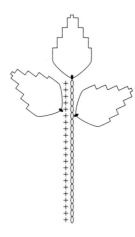

Trefoil I

Leaf (make 3 alike)
Base chain: 17ch.
1st row (right side): Miss 2ch (count as 1dc), 1dc into each ch to last ch, work 3dc into last ch for point, then work back along underside of base chain with 1dc into each ch to end, turn.
2nd row: 1ch (counts as 1dc), miss 1 st, 1dc into each st up to st at centre of point, work 3dc into centre st, 1dc into each st to last 3 sts and tch, turn.
3rd, 4th, 5th, 6th and 7th rows: As 2nd row.
Cast off.

Stem
Make 22ch (or as required), sl st to point of centre Leaf (2nd) as diagram, work back along base chain in dc and at same time join in side Leaves (first and third) at, say, 6th and 7th sts as follows: *insert hook through point of first leaf and base chain, make 1dc, sl st to point of 3rd Leaf to match; rep from * once more. Continue to end of base chain in dc. Cast off.

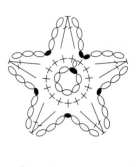

tr2tog

Daisy Time

Special Abbreviation: Tr2tog = work 1tr into each of next 2dc until 1 loop of each remains on hook, yo and draw through all 3 loops on hook.

Base ring: 6ch, join with sl st.

1st round: 1ch, work 15dc into ring, sl st into first dc.

2nd round: [3ch, tr2tog over next 2dc, 3ch, sl st into next dc] 5 times placing last sl st into first dc of previous round. Cast off.

Captain hook! Experiment with hooks of different sizes until you feel comfortable and are able to achieve the desired result.

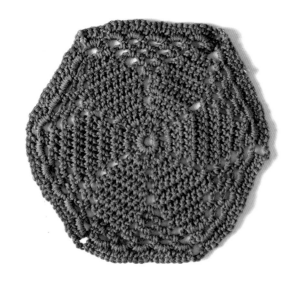

Flower Hexagon

Base ring: 6ch, join with sl st.

1st round: 4ch, [1tr into ring, 1ch] 11 times, sl st to 3rd of 4ch.

2nd round: 3ch, 2tr into next sp, 1tr into next tr, 2ch, *1tr into next tr, 2tr into next sp, 1tr into next tr, 2ch; rep from * 4 more times, sl st to top of 3ch.

3rd round: 3ch, 1tr into same place as last sl st, 1tr into each of next 2tr, 2tr into next tr, 2ch, *2tr into next tr, 1tr into each of next 2tr, 2tr into next tr, 2ch; rep from * 4 more times, sl st to top of 3ch.

4th round: 3ch, 1tr into same place as last sl st, 1tr into each of next 4 tr, 2tr into next tr, 2ch, *2tr into next tr, 1tr into each of next 4tr, 2tr into next tr, 2ch; rep from * 4 more times, sl st to top of 3ch.

5th round: 3ch, 1tr into each of next 7tr, *3ch, 1dc into next 2ch sp, 3ch, 1tr into each of next 8tr; rep from * 4

more times, 3ch, 1dc into next 2ch sp, 3ch, sl st to top of 3ch.

6th round: Sl st into next tr, 3ch, 1tr into each of next 5tr, *3ch, [1dc into next 3ch sp, 3ch] twice, miss next tr, 1tr into each of next 6tr; rep from * 4 more times, 3ch, [1dc into next 3ch sp, 3ch] twice, sl st to top of 3ch.

7th round: Sl st into next tr, 3ch, 1tr into each of next 3tr, *3ch, [1dc into next 3ch sp, 3ch] 3 times, miss next tr, 1tr into each of next 4tr; rep from * 4 more times, 3ch, [1dc into next 3ch sp, 3ch] 3 times, sl st to top of 3ch.

8th round: Sl st between 2nd and 3rd tr of first group, 3ch, 1tr into same place, *3ch, [1dc into next 3ch sp, 3ch] 4 times, 2tr between 2nd and 3rd tr of next group; rep from * 4 more times, 3ch, [1dc into next 3ch sp, 3ch] 4 times, sl st to top of 3ch.

9th round: Sl st into next 3ch sp, 3ch, 3tr into same sp, [4tr into next 3ch sp] 4 times, *3ch, miss 2tr, [4tr into next 3ch sp] 5 times; rep from * 4 more times, 3ch, join with a sl st to top of 3ch.

Cast off.

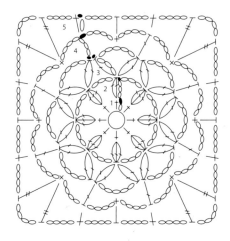

Daisy Cluster Square

Special Abbreviation: Bobble = yo, insert hook in st and draw up a loop, yo and draw through 2 loops. [Yo, insert hook in same st and draw up a loop. yo, draw through 2 loops] twice, yo and draw through all loops on hook.

Base ring: Wrap yarn around finger.

1st round: 1ch, 8dc into ring, sl st to first dc. (8 sts)

2nd round: 3ch, tr2tog into first st (counts as cluster), [3ch, cluster into next st] 7 times, 3ch, sl st to top of first cluster.

3rd round: 3ch, 1tr into first st (counts as tr2tog), *miss 3ch, [tr2tog, 5ch, tr2tog] all into next cluster; rep from * 6 more times, tr2tog into first clutter from 2nd row, 5ch, sl st to top of 3ch.

4th round: Sl st into next cluster, 7ch (counts as 1tr and 4ch), [1dc into next 5ch sp, 4ch, miss 1 cluster, 1tr into next cluster, 4ch] 7 times, 1dc into next 5ch sp, 4ch, sl st to 3rd of 7ch.

5th round: 1ch, 1dc into same place as 1ch, *4ch, miss 4ch, [1dtr, 4ch, 1dtr] into next dc, 4ch, miss 4ch, 1dc into next tr, 4ch, miss 4ch, 1htr into next dc, 4ch, miss 4ch, 1dc into next tr; rep from * 3 more times, omitting dc at end of last rep, sl st to first dc.

Cast off.

Viola

Special Abbreviation: Sdc (Spike double crochet) = insert hook lower than usual (as indicated), yo, draw loop through and up to height of current row, yo, draw through both loops on hook (see also page 10).

Base ring: Using A, 4ch, join with sl st.

1st round: 1ch, 6dc into ring, sl st to first dc. (6 sts)

2nd round: 1ch, 2dc into each dc, sl st to first dc. (12 sts)

3rd round: 1ch, 1dc into first st, [2dc into next st, 1dc into next st] 5 times, 2dc into last st, sl st to first dc. (18 sts)

4th round: 1ch, 1dc into first st, [2dc into next st, 1dc into each of next 2 sts] 5 times, 2dc into next st, 1dc into last st, sl st to first dc. (24 sts) Cast off.

5th round: Using B join into same place, 1ch, then starting in same st as 1ch work *1Sdc inserting hook into base ring, [1Sdc over next st inserting hook to left of last dc, but 1 round higher] twice, 1htr into next st, 3tr into next st, 1htr into next st, 1Sdc over next st inserting hook through top of 2nd round, 1Sdc over next st inserting hook through top of 1st round; rep from * twice more, sl st to first Sdc. Cast off.

6th round: Using C join into same place, 1ch, then starting in same st as 1ch work *1Sdc inserting hook between threads of previous Sdc and through top of first round, 1Sdc over next st inserting hook between vertical threads of previous Sdc and through top of 2nd round, 1htr into next st, 1tr into next st, 2tr into next st, 3tr into next st, 2tr into next st, 1tr into next st, 1htr into next st, 1Sdc over next st inserting hook between threads of 2nd of 5 previous Sdcs and 1 round higher; rep from * twice more, sl st to first Sdc. Cast off.

7th round: Using D join into same place, 1ch, starting in same st as 1ch *1Sdc inserting hook between threads of previous Sdcs and through top of 2nd round, 1dc into next st, [1htr, 1tr] into next st, [1tr into next st, 2tr into next st] 4 times, 1tr into next st, [1tr, 1htr] into next st, 1dc into next st; rep from * twice more, sl st to first Sdc. Cast off.

8th round: Using B, join into next st, 1ch, 1dc into same st as 1ch, *[5ch, miss next st, 1dc into next st] 9 times, miss next st**, 1dc into next st; rep from * and from * to ** again, sl st to first dc. Cast off.

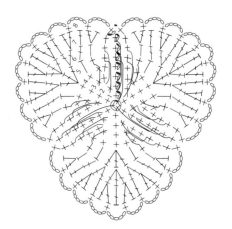

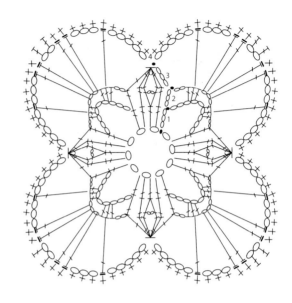

Garden Balsam

Special abbreviation: Cluster = [yo, insert hook in next st, yo and draw up loop, yo and draw through 2 loops on hook] as many times as indicated, yo and draw through all loops on hook.

Base ring: 10ch, join with sl st.

1st round: 3ch (count as tr), 4tr into ring, [9ch, 5tr into ring] 3 times, 9ch, sl st to top of 3ch.

2nd round: 3ch, 1tr into each of next 2tr, *2ch, 1tr into same tr as last tr, 1tr into each of next 2 tr, 2ch, into next 9ch sp work [3tr, 3ch, 3tr] for corner, 2ch**, 1tr into each of next 3 tr, rep from * 3 times more, ending last rep at **, sl st to top of 3ch.

3rd round: 3ch (count as tr), cluster over next 5tr, *5ch, miss 1 tr, 1tr into next tr, 3ch, into next 3ch sp work [2tr, 2ch, 2tr], 3ch, miss 1 tr, 1tr into next tr, 5ch, miss 1tr, [cluster over next 6 tr, draw; rep from * twice more, 5ch, miss 1 tr, 1tr into next tr, 3ch, into next 3ch sp work [2tr, 2ch, 2tr], 3ch, miss 1 tr, 1tr into next tr, 5ch, sl st to top of first cluster.

4th round: 1dc in each ch and in back loop of each tr, working 2tr into 2ch sp at each corner, sl st to first dc. Cast off.

Spandrel Motif

Base ring: Using A, 4ch, join with sl st.

1st round: 1ch, 1dc into ring, [4ch, 1trtr into ring, 4ch, 1dc into ring] 4 times omitting dc at end of last rep, sl st to first dc. Cast off.

2nd round: Join B into same place, 11ch (count as 1dtr and 7ch), miss 4ch, 1dc into next trtr, *7ch, miss 4ch**, 1dtr into next dc, 7ch, miss 4ch, 1dc into next trtr; rep from * twice more and from * to ** again, sl st to 4th ch of 11ch. Cast off.

3rd round: Join C into same place, 4ch (count as 1dtr), 2dtr into same place as 4ch, *1ch, 1dc into next 7 ch sp, 1ch, work [2trtr, 2ch, 2trtr] into next dc, 1ch, 1dc into next 7 ch sp, 1ch**, 3dtr into next dtr; rep from * twice more and from * to ** again, sl st to top of 4ch. Cast off.

4th round: Rejoin B into same place, 1ch, 1dc into same place as 1ch, 1dc into next and each ch and each st all around, except 3dc into each 2ch sp at corners, ending sl st to first dc. Cast off.

5th round: Rejoin A into next dc, 6ch (count as 1dtr and 2ch), miss first 2dc, *1dtr into next dc, 2ch, miss 1dc, 1tr into next dc, 2ch, miss 1dc, 1htr into next dc, 2ch, miss 1dc, 1dc into next dc, 2ch, miss 1dc, 1htr into next dc, 2ch, miss 1dc, 1tr into next dc, 2ch, miss 1dc, 1dtr into next dc, 2ch, miss 1dc**, 1dtr into next dc, 2ch, miss 1dc; rep from * twice more and from * to ** again, sl st to 4th ch of 6ch.

6th round: 1ch, into first st work a trefoil of [1dc, 5ch, 1dc, 7ch, 1dc, 5ch, 1dc], *[2dc into next 2ch sp, 1dc into next st] twice, work a picot of [3ch, insert hook down through top of dc just made and work sl st to close], [2dc into next 2ch sp, 1dc into next st] 4 times, picot, 2dc into next 2ch sp, 1dc into next st, 2dc into next 2ch sp**, trefoil into next st; rep from * twice more and from * to ** again, sl st to first dc.
Cast off.

Clockwork

Base ring: 8ch, join with sl st.

First motif: 3ch (count as 1tr), 1tr in ring, *3ch, sl st in top of last tr (picot), 2tr in ring; rep from * until 12th picot is completed, join with sl st in top of 3ch. Cast off.

Second motif: 8ch, join with sl st, 3ch, 1tr in ring, 2ch, drop loop from hook, insert hook in any picot of first motif and in dropped loop, draw loop through, 1ch, complete picot on 2nd motif, 2tr in ring of 2nd motif, join with picot to next free picot on first motif, continue as in first motif until 12th picot is completed (including the 2 joined picots), join with sl st in top of 3ch. Cast off.

Rep 2nd motif, joining first 2 picots to 7th and 8th picot of previous motif.

2nd row – first motif: Follow directions for 2nd motif of 1st row, but join the first 2 picots of this motif to the 4th and 5th picots of the first motif in 1st row.

2nd row – second motif: Work as before, joining first 2 picots to 10th and 11th picots of next motif in 1st row and the 4th and 5th picots to 4th and 5th picots of first motif of 2nd row.

Continue, 1 picot of each motif remains free between joinings.

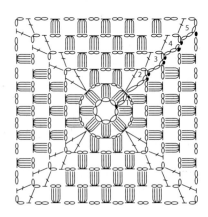

Puff Stitch Square

Special Abbreviation: Puff st = htr5tog. (see page 14)
Base ring: 8ch, join with sl st.
1st round: 2ch, htr4tog into ring (counts as 1 puff st), 2ch, work [puff st, 2ch] 7 times into ring, sl st to first puff st.
2nd round: 5ch (count as 1tr and 2ch), 1tr into same puff st, *2ch, [puff st into next sp, 2ch] twice**, work a V st of [1tr, 2ch, 1tr] into next puff st; rep from * twice more and from * to ** again, sl st to 3rd of 5ch.
3rd round: Sl st into next ch sp, 5ch (count as 1tr and 2ch), 1tr into same sp, *2ch, [puff st into next sp, 2ch] 3 times**, V st into next sp at corner; rep from * twice more and from * to ** again, sl st to 3rd of 5ch.
4th round: As for 3rd round, but work 4 puff sts along each side of square.
5th round: As for 3rd round, but work 5 puff sts along each side of square.
Cast off.

Take some time familiarizing yourself with new yarn, particularly unconventional fibres like hemp, raffia and cotton. These yarns have no elasticity so achieving the correct tension often requires a bit more focus.

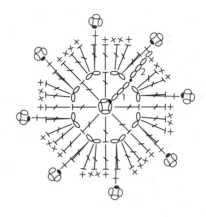

Halley's Comet

Special Abbreviation: Sdc (Spike double crochet) = insert hook below st indicated 1 row down, i.e. into top of first round, yo, draw loop through and up to height of current round, yo, draw through both loops on hook (see also page 10).

Base ring: Using A, 4ch, join with sl st.

1st round: 5ch (count as 1tr and 2ch), [1tr into ring, 2ch] 7 times, sl st to 3rd of 5ch. (8 spaces)

2nd round: 3ch (count as 1tr), 3tr into next sp, [1tr into next tr, 3tr into next sp] 7 times, sl st to top of 3ch. Cast off. (32 sts)

3rd round: Join B into same place, 1ch, 1Sdc over first st, work a picot of [3ch, insert hook down through top of dc just made and work sl st to close], *1dc into next st, 2dc into next st, 1dc into next st**, 1Sdc over next st, picot; rep from * 6 more times and from * to ** again, sl st to first Sdc.

Cast off.

Trefoil II

1st round: Make 16ch, sl st into first ch (first loop formed), [15ch, sl st into same ch as last sl st] twice.

2nd round: 1ch, work [28dc into next loop, 1 sl st into same ch as sl sts of first round] 3 times.

3rd round: Sl st into each of first 3dc, 1ch, 1dc into same st as last sl st, 1dc into each of next 23dc, [miss 4dc, 1dc into each of next 24dc] twice, 17ch, work 1dc into 2nd ch from hook, 1dc into each of next 15ch, sl st into first dc. Cast off.

Daisy Wheel Square

Base ring: 8ch, join with sl st.

1st round: 1ch, 12dc into ring, sl st to first dc. (12 sts)

2nd round: 6ch (count as 1dtr and 2ch), miss first st, [1dtr into next st, 2ch] 11 times, sl st to 4th of 6ch.

3rd round: 5ch (counts as 1tr and 2ch), *[1dc into next sp, 2ch] twice, [3tr, 2ch, 3tr] into next sp, 2ch; rep from *3 more times, omitting 1tr and 2ch at end of last rep, sl st to 3rd of 5ch.

4th round: 1ch, *[1dc into next sp, 2ch] 3 times, [3tr, 2ch, 3tr] into corner sp, 2ch; rep from *3 more times, sl st to first dc.

5th round: 1ch, work 2dc into each sp and 1dc into each st all around, but working 3dc into each corner sp, sl st to first dc. Cast off.

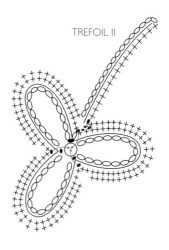

TREFOIL II

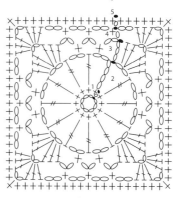

DAISY WHEEL SQUARE

Cluster Wheel

Base ring: 6ch, join with sl st.
1st round: 4ch (count as 1tr and 1ch), (3tr into ring, 1ch) 5 times, 2tr into ring, sl st to 3rd of 4ch.
2nd round: Sl st into next ch sp, 3ch (count as 1tr), [2tr, 1ch, 3tr] into same sp, *1ch, [3tr, 1ch, 3tr] into next 1ch sp; rep from * 4 more times, 1ch, sl st to top of 3ch.
3rd round: Sl st in next 2 sts, sl st into next ch sp, 3ch (count as 1tr), [2tr, 1ch, 3tr] into same ch sp, *1ch, 3tr into next ch sp, 1ch, [3tr, 1ch, 3tr] into next ch sp, rep from * 4 more times, 1ch, sl st into top of 3ch.
Cast off.

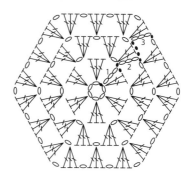

CLUSTER WHEEL

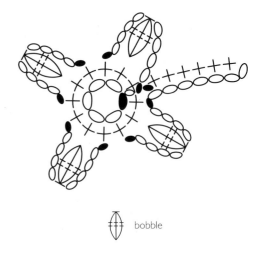

 bobble

Four Petal

Special Abbreviation: Bobble = 3dtr into next dc until I
loop of each remains on hook, yo and draw through all 4
loops on hook.
Base ring: 5ch, join with a sl st.
1st round: Ich, 12dc into ring, sl st into first dc.
2nd round: *4ch, I bobble into next dc, 4ch, sl st into
each of next 2dc; rep from * 3 more times, missing I sl st
at end of last rep, 7ch, Idc into 2nd ch from hook, Idc
into each of next 5ch, sl st into first dc on first round.
Cast off.

Different yarns have individual qualities and attributes.
Understanding the characteristics of your yarn and allowing
them to show is essential in achieving the best results.

Flower Square

Base ring: 4ch, join with sl st.

1st round: *2ch, 4tr into ring, sl st into ring; rep from * 3 times more. (4 petals)

2nd round: Sl st into back of 2nd tr, * keeping yarn at back of work, 4ch, sl st into back of 2nd tr of next petal; rep from * twice more, 4ch, sl st to first sl st.

3rd round: [1 sl st, 5tr, 1 sl st] into each loop.

4th round: *6ch, 1 sl st into back of sl st between petals; rep from * 3 times more.

5th round: 3ch (count as 1tr), [2tr, 3ch, 3tr] into first loop, *1ch, [3tr, 3ch, 3tr] into next loop; rep from * twice more, 1ch, sl st to top of 3ch.

6th round: Sl st across next 2tr and into next 3ch sp, 3ch (count as 1tr), [2tr, 3ch, 3tr] into same sp, *1ch, 3tr into next 1ch sp, 1ch, [3tr, 3ch, 3tr] into next 3ch sp; rep from * twice more, 1ch, 3tr into next 1ch sp, 1ch, sl st to top of 3ch.

7th round: Sl st across next 2tr and into next 3ch sp, 3ch (count as 1tr), [2tr, 3ch, 3tr] into same sp, *[1ch, 3tr into next 1ch sp] twice, 1ch, [3tr, 3ch, 3tr] into next 3ch sp; rep from * twice more, [1ch, 3tr into next 1ch sp] twice, 1ch, sl st to top of 3ch.

Cast off.

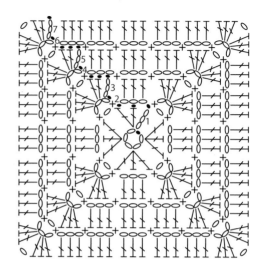

Vintage Square

Base ring: 5ch, join with sl st.

1st round: 3ch (count as 1tr), 2tr into ring, [1ch, 3tr into ring] 3 times, 1ch, sl st into top of 3ch.

2nd round: Sl st into each of next 2 tr, *[1dc, 3ch, 1dc] into next sp for a corner; 3ch; rep from * 3 times more, sl st to first dc.

3rd round: Sl st into corner sp, [3ch (count as 1tr), 1ch, 3tr] into same sp, *3tr into next 3ch sp, 3ch (count as 1tr), [2tr, 1ch, 3tr] into same sp, *3tr into next 3ch sp, [3tr, 1ch, 3tr] into next corner sp; rep from * twice more, join 3tr into next 3ch sp, sl st to top of 3ch.

4th round: Sl st into each of next 2tr, *[1dc, 3ch, 1dc] into next corner sp, [3ch, skip 3tr, 1dc between last tr and next tr] twice, 3ch, skip 3tr, rep from * 3 times more, sl st to first dc.

5th round: Sl st into next corner sp, [3ch (count as 1tr), 2tr, 1ch, 3tr] into same sp, *[3tr into next 3ch sp] 3 times, [3tr, 1ch, 3tr] into next corner sp; rep from * twice more, [3tr into next 3ch sp] 3 times, sl st to top of 3ch.

6th round: Rep 4th round, working 4 [3ch] sps between corner sps.

7th round: Rep 5th round, working 3tr into each 3ch loop along sides between [3tr, 1ch, 3tr] at corners.

Cast off.

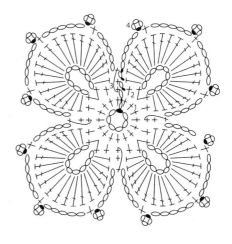

Moorish Medallion

Special Abbreviation: Sdc (Spike double crochet) = insert hook 2 rounds below st indicated, i.e. into top of first round, yo, draw loop through and up to height of current round, yo, draw through both loops on hook (see also page 13).

Base ring: 6ch, join with sl st.

1st round: 1ch, 16dc into ring, sl st to first dc. (16 sts)

2nd round: 1ch, 1dc into same place as 1ch, 1dc into next dc, *[1dc, 9ch, 1dc] into next dc**, 1dc into each of next 3dc; rep from * twice more and from * to ** again, 1dc into next dc, sl st to first dc.

3rd round: 1ch, 1dc into same place as 1ch, *miss next 2dc, [2htr, 17tr, 2htr] into next 9ch sp, miss next 2dc, 1dc into next dc; rep from * 3 more times, missing 1dc at end of last rep and ending sl st to first dc.

4th round: 1ch, 1Sdc over first st, *5ch, miss 5 sts, 1dc into next st, work picot of [3ch, sl st into 3rd ch from hook], [5ch, miss 4 sts, 1dc into next st, 3ch, sl st into 3rd ch from hook] twice, 5ch, miss 5 sts, 1Sdc over next st; rep from * 3 more times, missing Sdc at end of last rep and ending sl st to first sdc.

Cast off.

Frozen Star

Special Abbreviation: Cluster = trtr4tog.

Base ring: 12ch, join with sl st into ring.

1st round: 1ch, 24dc into ring, sl st to first dc. (24 sts)

2nd round: 6ch, trtr3tog over next 3 sts (counts as trtr4tog), [7ch, trtr4tog over same st as last leg of previous cluster and next 3 sts] 7 times, 7ch, sl st to top of first cluster.

3rd round: 1ch, 1dc into same place as 1ch, *[3ch, skip 1ch, 1dc into next ch] 3 times, 3ch, skip 1ch, 1dc into top of next cluster; rep from * 7 more times, skipping dc at end of last rep, sl st to first dc.

4th round: Sl st to centre of next 3ch sp, 1ch, 1dc into same sp, *3ch, 1dc into next sp; rep from * to end, skipping dc at end of last rep, sl st to first dc.

5th round: As 4th round.

6th round: Sl st to centre of next 3ch sp, 1ch, 1dc into same sp, *[3ch, 1dc into next sp] 4 times, 3ch, skip next sp, [dtr3tog, 5ch, trtr4tog, 4ch, sl st to top of last cluster, 5ch, dtr3tog] into next sp, 3ch, skip next sp, 1dc into next sp; rep from * 3 more times, skipping dc at end of last rep, sl st to first dc.

Cast off.

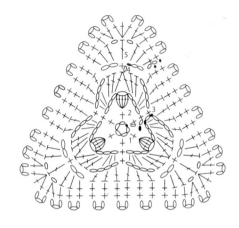

Popcorn Trefoil

Special Abbreviations: Cluster = tr2tog.

Popcorn = see page 26.

Base ring: Using A, 5ch, join with sl st.

1st round: 1ch, 6dc into ring, sl st to first dc. Cast off.

2nd round: Join B in same st, 1ch, 1dc into same place as 1ch, *3ch, 5tr Popcorn into next st, 3ch**, 1dc into next st; rep from once more and from * to ** again, sl st to first dc.

3rd round: 1ch, 1dc into same place as 1ch, *4ch, 2tr into next 3ch sp, tr2tog inserting hook into same ch sp for first leg and into next ch sp for 2nd leg, 2tr into same ch sp, 4ch**, 1dc into next dc; rep from * once more and from * to ** again, sl st to first dc. Cast off.

4th round: Using C join into corner cluster, 1ch, 1dc into same place as 1ch, *2ch, skip 2tr, going behind ch sps of 3rd round, [tr into next ch sp of 2nd round] twice, 2ch, skip 2tr**, 1dc into corner cluster; rep from * once more and from * to ** again, sl st to first dc. Cast off.

5th round: Using B join into last 2ch sp of 4th round, 1ch, *[1dc, 1htr, 1tr] into 2ch sp, 1ch, 1tr into next dc, 1ch, [1tr, 1htr, 1dc] into next 2ch sp, 1dc into each of next 6tr; rep from * twice more, sl st to first dc.

Cast off.

6th round: Using A join into same place, 1ch, 1dc into same place as 1ch, 3ch, 1dc into each of next 2 sts, 3ch, *2dc into next ch sp, 3ch, 3dc into tr at corner, 3ch, 2dc into next ch sp, 3ch**, [1dc into each of next 2 sts, 3ch] 6 times; rep from * once more and from * to ** again, [1dc into each of next 2 sts, 3ch] 4 times, 1dc into next st, sl st to first dc.

Cast off.

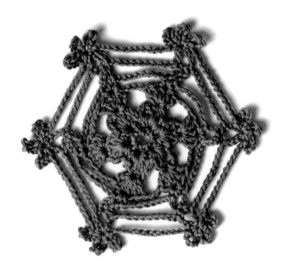

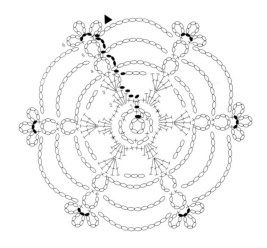

Snowflake 1

Base ring: 6 ch, join with sl st.

1st round: 1 ch, into ring work [1dc, 2 ch] 6 times, join with sl st to first dc.

2nd round: 1 ch, into each 2-ch sp work [2dc, 1htr, 3tr, 1htr, 2dc], join with sl st to first dc. (6 petals)

3rd round: 3 sl sts to centre tr, 3 ch (count as 1 tr), 4tr into same st, *3ch, 5tr in centre of tr of next petal; rep from * 4 more times, 3 ch, join with sl st to 3rd of first 3ch.

4th round: Sl st to centre tr, 1ch, [1dc, 7ch, 1dc] into same st, *8 ch, sk 4 tr, [1dc, 7ch, 1dc] into next tr; rep from * 4 more times, 8 ch, join with sl st to first dc.

5th round: Sl st to 4th ch of 7ch loop, 1ch, [1dc, 7ch, 1dc] into same st, *10 ch, [1dc, 7ch, 1dc] into 4th ch of next 7ch loop; repeat from * 4 more times, 10 ch, join with sl st to first dc.

6th round: 3 sl sts to 4th ch of 7ch loop, 1ch, into same st work (1dc, 6ch, [1 sl st, 6ch] twice, 1dc), *12 ch, into 4th ch of next 7ch loop work (1dc, 6ch, [1 sl st, 6ch] twice, 1dc); rep from * 4 more times, 12 ch, join with sl st to first dc.

Cast off.

Two-Tone Hexagon

Base ring: Using A, 6ch, join with sl st.

1st round: 3ch (count as 1tr), 2tr into ring, *3ch, 3tr into ring; rep from * 4 more times, 3ch, sl st to top of first 3ch. Cast off.

2nd round: Join B to any 3ch sp, 5ch (count as 1trtr), [2trtr, 2ch, 3trtr] into same sp, *[3trtr, 2ch, 3trtr] into next 3ch sp; rep from * 4 more times, sl st to top of 5ch. Cast off.

3rd round: Join A to same place as sl st, 3ch (count as 1tr), 1tr into each of next 2trtr, *[2tr, 2ch, 2tr] into next 2ch sp, 1tr into each of next 6trtr; rep from * 4 more times, [2tr, 2ch, 2tr] into next 2ch sp, 1tr into each of next 3trtr, sl st to top of 3ch. Cast off.

4th round: Join B into any st, 3ch (count as 1tr), 1tr into previous st, *skip 1 st, 1tr into next st, 1tr into the skipped st; rep from * all around, sl st to top of 3ch. Cast off.

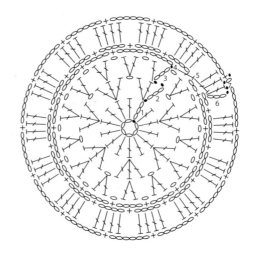

Begonia Wheel

Base chain: 6ch, join with sl st.
1st round: 3ch (count as 1tr), 13tr into ring, sl st to top of 3ch.
2nd round: 3ch (count as 1tr), 2tr into first st, *1ch, skip 1tr, 3tr into next tr; rep from * 5 more times, 1ch, skip 1tr, sl st to top of 3ch.
3rd round: Sl st into next tr, 3ch (count as 1tr), 1tr into same tr, *1ch, 2tr into next 1ch sp, 1ch, skip 1tr, 2tr into next tr; rep from * 5 more times, 1ch, 2tr into next 1ch sp, 1ch, sl st to top of 3ch.

4th round: [4ch, 1dc into next 1ch sp] 13 times, 2ch, 1tr into base of first 4ch.
5th round: [4ch, 1dc into centre of next 4 ch sp] 13 times, 2ch, 1tr into tr at end of previous round.
6th round: 3ch (count as 1tr), 3tr into same sp, 4tr into each of next 13 sps, sl st to top of 3ch.
7th round: Sl st to centre of first tr group, 1ch, 1dc into same place, [6ch, 1dc into centre of next tr group] 13 times, 6ch, sl st to first dc.
Cast off.

4th round: Using A, 5ch, 5dtr into same sl st, *[6dtr, 2ch, 6dtr] into next 2ch sp, 6dtr into sl st at top of next cl; rep from * twice more, [6dtr, 2ch, 6dtr] into next 2ch sp, sl st to top of 5ch. Cast off A.

5th round: Join C to last sl st of 4th round, 1ch, 1dc in same st, 1dc into each of next 5dtr, 1tr into 1ch sp between group of dtr on 3rd round, *1dc into each of next 6dtr, 3dc into 2ch sp at corner; [1dc into each of next 6dtr, 1tr into 1ch sp between group of dtr on 3rd round] twice; rep from * twice more, 1dc into each of next 6dtr, 3dc into 2ch sp at corner, 1dc into each of next 6dtr, 1tr into 1ch sp between group of dtr on 3rd round, join with a sl st to first ch.

6th round: 3ch (count as 1tr), 1tr into each st all around, working 3tr into centre st of each corner, sl st to top of 3ch. Cast off.

Tricolour Square

Special abbreviation: Cluster = work dtr into each of next 6tr leaving last loop of each dtr on hook, yo and draw through 7 loops on hook.

Base ring: Using A, 8ch, join with sl st.

1st round: 4ch (count as 1dtr), 5dtr into ring, *3ch, 6dtr into ring; rep from * twice more , 3ch, sl st to top of 4ch.

2nd round: 4ch, work dtr into each of next 5dtr leaving last loop of each dtr on hook, yo and draw through 6 loops on hook (count as 1st cluster), *5ch, 1 sl st into 2nd of 3ch, 5ch, work cluster over next 6dtr; rep from * twice more, 5ch, 1 sl st into 2nd of 3ch, 5ch, sl st to top of first cluster. Cast off A.

3rd round: Join B to top of cl, *[3dtr, 1ch, 3dtr, 2ch, 3dtr, 1ch, 3dtr] into next 3ch sp of first round, 1 sl st into top of next cl; rep from * 3 times more, working last sl st into same place as yarn was joined and joining A at the same time. Cast off B.

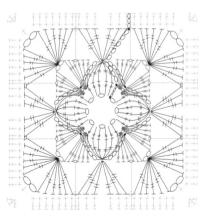

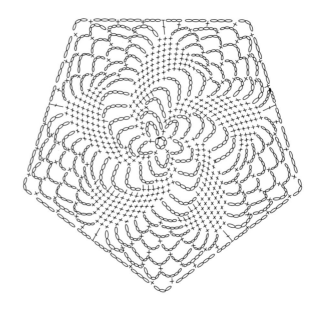

Spiral Pentagram

Base ring: 5ch, join with sl st.

1st round: [6ch, 1dc into ring] 5 times.

Note: mark last dc of each round with contrasting thread.

2nd round: [6ch, 3dc into next 6ch sp] 5 times.

3rd round: [6ch, 3dc into next 6ch sp, 1dc into each of next 2dc] 5 times. (5 blocks of 5dc each)

4th round: [6ch, 3dc into next 6ch sp, 1dc into each dc of next block skipping last dc] 5 times. (5 blocks of 7dc each)
Cont as given on 4th round for 3 more rounds finishing with 5 blocks of 13dc each.

8th round: *5ch, 1dc into centre of next 6ch sp, 5ch, skip 1dc, 1dc into each dc of next block skipping last dc; rep from * 4 more times.

9th round: *[5ch, 1dc into next sp] twice, 5ch, skip 1dc, 1dc into each dc of next block skipping last dc; rep from * 4 more times.

Continue as given on 9th round for 3 more rounds, but work 1 more 5ch sp in each segment on each round at same time as number of dc in each block reduces, finishing with 6 sps and 3dc in each of 5 segments.

13th round: 5ch, 1dc into next sp, *[3ch, 1dc into next sp] 5 times, 3ch, 1tr into 2nd of next 3dc, 3ch, 1dc into next sp; rep from * 4 more times, skipping dc at end of last rep, sl st to first dc.

Cast off.

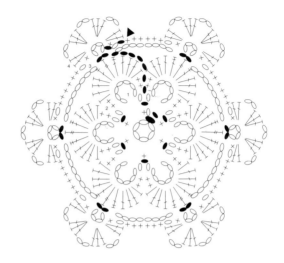

Snowflake II

Special abbreviation: Htr = yo twice, insert hook in st, yo and draw through two loops, yo and draw through last 3 loops.

Base ring: 6 ch, join with sl st.

1st round: 1 ch, [1 dc into ring, 7 ch] 6 times, join with sl st to first dc (6 loops).

2nd round: *1 ch, into next 7ch sp work [2dc, 1htr, 3tr, 1htr, 1tr, 1htr, 3tr, 1htr, 2dc], 1 ch, sl st to next dc; rep from * 5 times more.

3rd round: 7 sl sts to centre dtr, *4ch, sl st into same dtr; 8 ch, sl st on top of next dtr; rep from * around.

4th round: sl st into 4ch loop, *1ch, work 1dc, 2tr, 2ch, [3tr, 2ch] twice, 2tr, 1dc into same sp, 1 ch, 6dc into next 8ch sp; rep from * around, join with sl st to first dc.

Cast off.

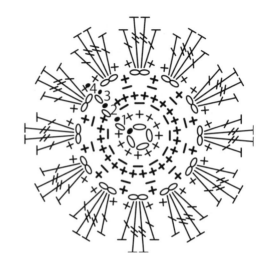

Primula Circle

Base ring: 4ch, join with sl st.

1st round: 1ch, 12dc into ring, join with a sl st to first ch.

2nd round: 1ch, 2dc into same place, inserting hook into back loop of each st work 2dc into each st to end, sl st to first ch. (24dc)

3rd round: 1ch, 1dc in same st, 2ch, *skip 1dc, 1dc into back loop of next dc, 2ch; rep from * to end , sl st to first of 3 ch.

4th round: [1dc, 1tr, 2dtr, 1tr, 1dc] into each 2ch sp, sl st to first dc.

Cast off.

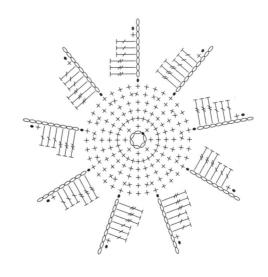

Incan Star

Note: Pattern is worked in a spiral, do not join at the end of rounds 1–6.

Base ring: 6ch, join with sl st.

1st round: 8dc into ring.

2nd round: 3dc in each st. (24sts)

3rd and 4th rounds: 1dc in each st.

5th round: *1dc in next dc, 2dc in next dc; rep from * around. (36sts)

6th round: 1dc in each st.

7th round: *9ch, sl st in 2nd ch from hook, 1dc in next ch, 1tr in each of next 3 ch, 1dtr in each of next 3 ch, skip next 3 sts of previous round, sl st in next st; rep from * around, join with sl st.

Cast off.

When approaching a new design, consider the previous successes you have had, the yarn you are working with, and your goal for the project. Careful planning will be rewarded, as often even the simplest stitch can be charming and effective.

Traditional Hexagon I

Special Abbreviation: Cluster = tr3tog.

Base ring: 6ch, join with sl st.

1st round: 3ch, tr2tog into ring (counts as tr3tog), [3ch, tr3tog into ring] 5 times, 1ch, 1htr into top of first cluster.

2nd round: 3ch, tr2tog into sp formed by htr (counts as tr3tog), *3ch, [tr3tog, 3ch, tr3tog] into next sp; rep from * 4 more times, 3ch, tr3tog into last sp, 1ch, 1htr into top of first cluster.

3rd round: 3ch, tr2tog into sp formed by htr (counts as tr3tog), *3ch, [tr3tog, 3ch, tr3tog] into next sp**, 3ch, tr3tog into next sp; rep from * 4 more times and from * to ** again, 1ch, 1htr into top of first cluster.

4th round: 3ch (counts as 1tr), 1tr into sp formed by htr; *3tr into next sp, [3tr, 2ch, 3tr] into next sp**, 3tr into next sp; rep from * 4 more times and from * to ** again, 1tr into next sp, sl st to top of 3ch.

5th round: 1ch, 1dc into same place, 1dc into each tr and each ch all around, ending sl st to first dc.

Cast off.

Traditional Hexagon II

Worked as Traditional Hexagon I.
Work 1 round each in colours A, B, C, D and E.

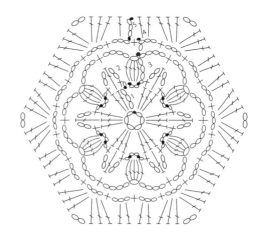

Two-Tone Popcorn Hexagon

Special Abbreviations: 4tr Popcorn = 4tr into next st, drop loop off hook, insert hook into top of 3ch, pick up dropped loop and draw through loop on hook.

5tr Popcorn = 5tr into next st, drop loop off hook, insert hook into first of these tr, pick up dropped loop and draw through loop on hook.

Base ring: Using A, 6ch, join with sl st.

1st round: 3ch (count as 1tr), 2tr into ring, [2ch, 3tr into ring] 5 times, 2ch, sl st to top of 3ch. (6 spaces)

2nd round: 1ch, 1dc into same place, *2ch, 1tr into next tr, 2ch, 1dc into next tr, 1ch, sl st into each of next 2 ch, 1ch, 1dc into next tr; rep from * 5 more times skipping last dc and ending sl st to first dc. Cast off.

3rd round: Using B, join into 2ch sp from 1st round, 3ch, 4tr popcorn into same sp (counts as 5tr popcorn), *4ch,

skip 1dc and 2ch, 1dc into next tr; 4ch, skip 2ch and 1dc, 5tr popcorn into next 2ch sp from 1st round; rep from * 5 more times, skipping last popcorn and ending sl st to top of first popcorn.

4th round: 1ch, 1dc into same place, *[3ch, 1dc into next sp] twice, 3ch, 1dc into next popcorn; rep from * 5 more times skipping last dc and ending sl st to first dc. Cast off.

5th round: Using A, join into next chsp, 3ch (count as 1tr), 1tr into same sp, *[3tr, 2ch, 3tr] into next sp**, 2tr into each of next 2 sps; rep from * 4 more times and from * to ** again, 2tr into next sp, sl st to top of 3ch. Cast off.

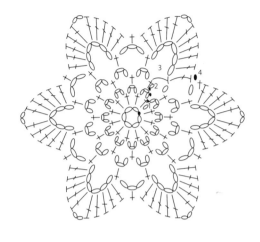

Eastern Star

Base ring: 6ch, join with sl st.

1st round: 1ch, [1dc into ring, 3ch] 12 times, sl st to first dc.

2nd round: Sl st into each of next 2ch, 1ch, 1dc into same 3ch sp, [3ch, 1dc into next 3ch sp] 11 times, 1ch, 1htr into top of first dc.

3rd round: *6ch, 1dc into next 3ch sp**, 3ch, 1dc into next 3ch sp; rep from * 4 more times and from * to ** again, 1ch, 1tr into htr which closed previous round.

4th round: *[5tr, 2ch, 5tr] into next 6ch sp, 1dc into next 3ch sp; rep from * 5 more times ending last rep in tr which closed previous round, sl st to next st.

Cast off.

Two-Colour Star

Special Abbreviation: Cluster = tr3tog.

Note: For dedcription of changing colour see page 7; for tr2tog and tr3tog (see page 15).

Base ring: Using A, 4ch, join with sl st.

1st round: 3ch (count as 1tr), 14tr into ring, sl st to top of 3ch. (15 sts)

2nd round: 3ch (count as 1tr), 1tr into same place as 3ch, 2tr into next and each tr all around, sl st to top of 3ch. (30 sts)

3rd round: 3ch (count as 1tr), *1tr into next st, tr2tog over next 2 sts, 1tr into each of next 2 sts, change to B, 2tr into same place as last tr with A, 2tr into next st, change to A**, 1tr into same place as last tr with B; rep from * 3 more times and from * to ** again, sl st to top of 3ch.

4th round: 3ch (count as 1tr), *tr2tog over next 2 sts, 1tr into each of next 2 sts, change to B, 2tr into next st, 1tr into each of next 2 sts, 2tr into next st, change to A**, 1tr into next st; rep from * 3 more times and from * to ** again, sl st to top of 3ch.

5th round: 3ch (count as 1tr), *tr2tog over next 2 sts, 1tr into next st, change to B, 2tr into next st, 1tr into next st, 2tr into each of next 2 sts, 1tr into next st, 2tr into next st, change to A**, 1tr into next st; rep from * 3 more times and from * to ** again, sl st to top of 3ch.

6th round: 3ch, tr2tog over next 2 sts (counts as tr3tog), *change to B, 3tr into next st, [1tr into each of next 2 sts, 2tr into next st] twice, 1tr into each of next 2 sts, 3tr into next st, change to A**, tr3tog over next 3 sts; rep from * 3 more times and from * to ** again, sl st to top of first cluster. Cast off B.

7th round: Cont using A only 1ch, 1dc into same place as 1ch, 1dc into next and each st all around, sl st to first dc, turn.

8th round (wrong side): 1ch, 2dc into same place as 1ch, 1dc into next and each st all around, except 2dc into each of 4 sts corresponding to remaining points of Star, ending sl st to first dc.

Cast off.

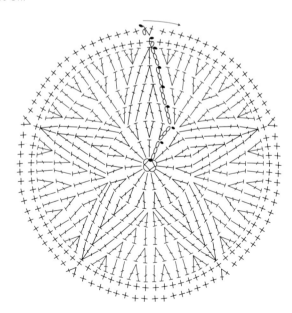

picot

—— base of st

Tristar

Special Abbreviation: Picot = 3ch, sl st into first of these ch.

1st round: 10ch, sl st into first ch, [9ch, sl st into same ch as last sl st] twice. (3 loops formed)

2nd round: *1ch, working into next 9ch sp work [2dc, 1htr, 1tr, 1htr, 2dc], 1ch, sl st into same ch as sl sts of first round; rep from * twice more.

3rd round: Sl st into each of first 9 sts of first loop, [16ch, skip first 8 sts on next loop, sl st into next tr] twice, 16ch, sl st into same tr as last sl st at beg of round.

4th round: 1ch, 1dc into same tr as last sl st of previous round, 19dc into first 16ch sp, [1dc into same tr as next sl st of previous round, 19dc into next 16ch sp] twice, sl st to first dc. (60dc)

5th round: 8ch (count as 1tr, 5ch), skip next 3dc, [1tr into next dc, 5ch, skip 3dc] 14 times, sl st to 3rd of 8ch at beg of round.

6th round: Sl st into first 3ch of first 5ch sp, 1ch, 4dc into first sp, 7dc into each of next 14 sps, 3dc to same sp as first 4dc, sl st into first dc.

7th round: [6ch, skip next 6dc, sl st into next dc] 14 times, 6ch, sl st to same dc as last sl st of previous round.

8th round: 1ch, into each 6ch sp work 2dc, [1 picot, 2dc] 3 times, sl st to first dc.

Cast off.

Scalloped Circle

Base ring: 6ch, join with sl st.
1st round: 3ch (count as 1tr), 23tr into ring, join with a sl st to top of 3ch.
2nd round: 5ch (count as 1tr and 2ch), 1tr into sl st, 1ch, *miss 2tr, [1tr, 2ch, 1tr] into next tr, 1ch; rep from * 6 times more, sl st to 3rd of 5ch.
3rd round: Sl st into next 2ch sp, 3ch (count as 1tr), [1tr, 2ch, 2tr] into same sp, *1dc into next 1ch sp, [2tr, 2ch, 2tr] into next 2ch sp; rep from * 6 times more, 1dc into next 1ch sp, sl st to top of 3ch.
4th round: Sl st into next 2ch sp, 3ch (count as 1tr), [2tr, 1ch, 3tr] into same sp, *1dc in sp before next dc, 1dc in sp after the same dc, [3tr, 1ch, 3tr] into next 2ch sp; rep from * 6 times more, 1dc in sp before next dc, 1dc in sp after the same dc, sl st to top of 3ch.
Cast off.

Five-Point Star

Note: Pattern is worked in a spiral, do not join at the end of each round.
Base chain: 2ch.
1st round: 5dc in 2nd ch from hook.
2nd round: 3dc in each dc. (15 sts)
3rd round: [1dc in next st, ch 6, sl st in 2nd ch from hook, 1dc in next ch, 1htr in next ch, 1tr in next ch, 1dtr in next ch, 1dtr in bottom of base dc, skip 2dc] 5 times, sl st in first dc.
Cast off.

Citrus Ring

Base ring: 4ch, join with sl st.

1st round: 4ch (count as 1tr and 1ch), *1tr into ring, 1ch; rep from * 6 times more, sl st in 3rd of 4ch.

2nd round: 2ch, [1tr, 1dtr, 1tr, 1htr] in same sp, *[1htr, 1tr, 1dtr, 1tr, 1htr] in next sp; rep from * around, sl st to top of 2ch.

Cast off.

FIVE-POINT STAR

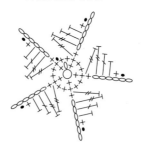

CITRUS RING

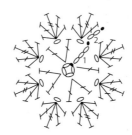

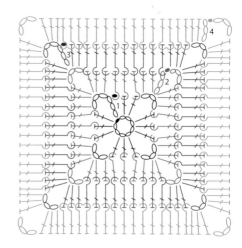

Russian Square

Special Abbreviations: Tr/rf = insert hook around the post of the stitch indicated from the front, around the back and to the front again and complete the tr as usual.
Tr/rb = insert hook around the post of the stitch indicated from the back, around the front and to the back again and complete the tr as usual. See raised stitches, page 264.

Base ring: Using A, 8ch, join with sl st.

1st round: 6ch (count as 1tr and 3ch), [3tr into ring, 3ch] 3 times, 2tr into ring, sl st to 3rd of 6ch. Cast off.

2nd round: Using B, join into a different corner 3ch sp, 3ch (count as 1tr), 2tr into same corner sp, *1tr/rf around each of next 3 sts**, [3tr, 3ch, 3tr] into next corner sp; rep from * twice more and from * to **
again, [3tr, 3ch] into last corner sp, sl st to top of 3ch.

Cast off.

3rd round: Using C, join into a different corner sp, 6ch (count as 1tr and 3ch), 3tr into same corner sp, *1tr/rb around each of next 3 sts, 1tr/rf around each of next 3 sts, 1tr/rb around each of next 3 sts**, [3tr, 3ch, 3tr] into next corner sp; rep from * twice more and from * to ** again, 2tr into last corner sp, sl st to 3rd of 6ch. Cast off.

4th round: Using D, join into a different corner sp, 3ch (count as 1tr), 2tr into same corner sp, *[1tr/rf around each of next 3 sts, 1tr/rb around each of next 3 sts] twice, 1tr/rf around each of next 3 sts**, [3tr, 3ch, 3tr] into next corner sp; rep from * twice more and from * to ** again, [3tr, 3ch] into last corner sp, sl st to top of 3ch. Cast off.

Spider Square

Special Abbreviation: Cluster = tr3tog.

Base ring: 6ch, join with sl st.

1st round: 1ch, [1dc into ring, 15ch] 12 times, sl st to first dc.

2nd round: Sl st along to centre of next 15ch sp, 3ch, tr2tog into same sp (counts as tr3tog), *4ch, tr3tog into same sp, [4ch, 1dc into next sp] twice, 4ch, tr3tog into next sp; rep from * 3 more times, missing tr3tog at end of last rep, sl st to first cluster.

3rd round: Sl st into next 4ch sp, 3ch, tr2tog into same sp (counts as tr3tog), *4ch, tr3tog into same sp, [4ch, 1dc into next 4ch sp, 4ch, tr3tog into next 4ch sp] twice; rep from * 3 more times, missing tr3tog at end of last rep, sl st to first cluster.

Cast off.

Don't get dizzy – mark the first stitch of a circle or spiral and move the marker up as you work your way round. This way you won't lose count.

Mosaic Tile

Base ring: Using A, 6ch, join with sl st.

1st round: 4ch, [1tr, ch1] 11 times into ring, sl st to 3rd of 4ch, draw B through loop, drop A.

2nd round: [1dc into next sp, 2ch] 12 times, sl st to first dc, draw A through loop, drop B.

3rd round: *[1dc into next sp, 2ch] twice, [2tr, 2ch] twice into next sp for corner; rep from * 3 times more, sl st to first dc, draw B through loop, cast off A.

4th round: *(1dc, 3ch) into each sp to corner; [1dc, 3ch] twice into corner sp; rep from * 3 times more, sl st to first dc.

Cast off.

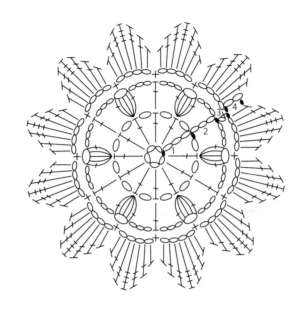

Flower Crystal

Special Abbreviation: Popcorn = 5tr into next st, drop loop off hook, insert hook into first of these tr, pick up dropped loop and draw through.

Base ring: 5ch, join with sl st.

1st round: 4ch (count as 1tr, 1ch), [1tr, 1ch] 11 times into ring, sl st into 3rd of 4ch.

2nd round: 6ch (count as 1tr, 3ch), 1 popcorn into next tr, 3ch, [1tr into next tr, 3ch, 1 popcorn into next tr, 3ch] 5 times, sl st into 3rd of 6ch at beg of round.

3rd round: 1ch, 1dc into same st as last sl st, 4ch, 1dc into top of next popcorn, 4ch, [1dc into next tr, 4ch, 1dc into top of next popcorn, 4ch] 5 times, sl st into first dc.

4th round: Sl st into first 4ch sp, 2ch (count as 1htr), [1tr, 1dtr, 1trtr, 1dtr, 1tr, 1htr] into same sp, [1htr, 1tr, 1dtr, 1trtr, 1dtr, 1tr, 1htr] into each of next 11 4ch sps, sl st to top of 2ch.

Cast off.

Snowflake III

Base ring: 6 ch, join with sl st.

1st round: 5 ch (count as 1 dtr, 1ch), *into ring work 1dtr, 2ch, 1dtr, 1ch; rep from * 4 more times, 1dtr, 2ch, join with sl st to 4th of first 5ch.

2nd round: 1ch, 1dc into 1-ch sp, *into next 2-ch sp work ([1dtr, 2ch] twice, 1dtr), 1dc into next 1-ch sp; rep from * 4 times more, into last 2-ch sp work ([1dtr, 2ch] twice, 1dtr), join with sl st to first dc.

3rd round: 4 ch (count as 1tr, 1ch), *[1dc into next 2ch sp, 1ch] twice, into next dc work [1dtr, 1ch, 1dtr, 5ch, 1dtr, 1ch, 1dtr] for corner, [1ch, 1dc into next 1ch sp] twice, 1ch, 1tr into next dc, 1ch; rep from * twice more omitting last tr, join with sl st to 3rd of first 4ch.

4th round: 3ch, 1tr into each of next 7 sts (including ch), *3 ch, 1tr into next dtr, 5tr into 5-ch sp, 1tr into next dtr, 3ch, 1tr into each of next 15 tr; rep from * twice more omitting 6 tr from last rep, join with sl st to 3rd of first 3ch.

5th round: 1ch, 1dc into each of next 7 tr, *into next 3-ch sp work [1dc, 4ch, 1dc], 1dc into each of next 7 tr, [1dc, 4ch, 1dc] into next 3-ch sp, 1dc into each of next 15 tr; rep from * twice more omitting 6 dc from last rep, join with sl st to first dc.

6th round: 1ch, 1dc into each of next 8 dc, *1ch, into next 4-ch sp work [2tr, 2ch, 3tr, 2ch, 3tr, 2ch, 2tr], 1ch for corner, 1dc into each of next 9 dc (short side), into next 4-ch sp work corner as above, 1dc into each of next 17 dc (long side); rep from * twice more omitting 8 dc from last long side, join with sl st to first dc.

7th round: 1ch, 1dc into each of next 4 dc, *sk 2dc, 1tr into next 1ch sp, 1tr into each of next 2 tr, [(1tr, 3ch, 1tr) into next 2-ch sp, 1tr into each of next 3 tr] twice, 1tr into next 2-ch sp, 3ch, 1tr into same sp, 1tr into each of next 2 tr, 1tr into 1-ch sp **, sk 2dc, 1dc into each of next 5 dc, work from * to ** for next corner, 1dc into each of next 13 dc; rep from * twice more omitting 4 dc from last rep, join with sl st to first dc.

Cast off.

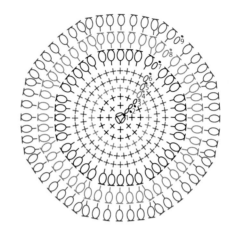

Loopy Wheel

Base ring: Using A, 3ch, join with sl st.

1st round: 1ch, 4dc into ring, sl st into first ch. (4dc)

2nd round: 1ch, 2dc into same place, 2dc into each dc to end, sl st to first ch.

3rd round: As 2nd round. Cast off A.

4th round: Join B, 1ch, dc in same st as 1ch, *2dc into next dc, 1dc into next dc; rep from * 7 more times, but miss last dc and work sl st into first dc. Cast off B.

5th round: Join C, 1ch, dc in same st as 1ch, *2dc into next dc, 1dc into each of next 2dc; rep from * 7 more times, but miss last dc and work sl st into first dc.

6th round: Using C, 1ch, dc in same st as 1ch, *2dc into next dc, 1dc into each of next 3dc; rep from * 7 more times, ending as before. Cast off C.

7th round: Turn work and join A with wrong side facing, 1ch, *yo, insert hook into next st, hold a pencil behind work and take the yarn around it to form a loop, yo, draw loop through, yo, draw through 3 loops on hook; rep from * to end, sl st to first ch. Cast off A.

8th round: Join B and work as 7th round, but inc 8 sts evenly in the round. Cast off B.

9th round: Join C and work as 8th round. Cast off.

Cartwheel

Base ring: 5ch, join with sl st.

1st round: 3ch (count as 1 tr), 2tr into ring, 1ch, [3tr into ring, 1ch] 5 times, join with sl st into top of 3ch.

2nd round: Sl st into each of next 2 tr, *1dc into next 1ch sp, 3ch; rep from * 5 more times, join with sl st to first dc.

3rd round: Sl st into first 3chsp, 3ch, [2tr, 1ch, 3tr] into same sp, *1ch, [3tr, 1ch, 3tr] into next sp; rep from * 4 more times, 1ch, sl st to first dc.

4th round: *3ch, 1dc into next sp; rep from * 10 more times, 3ch, sl st to first ch.

5th round: 3ch (count as 1tr), 2tr into first sp, 1ch, 3tr into same sp, 1ch, 3tr into next sp, 1ch, *[3tr, 1ch] twice into next sp (inc made), 3tr into next sp, 1ch; rep from * 4 more times, sl st to top of 3ch.

6th round: Rep 2nd round.

7th round: Sl st into first sp, work in 3tr group pattern with 1ch between patterns. Increase 6 group patterns around – be sure not to increase groups over previous increase groups – join with sl st.

8th round: Rep 2nd round.

9th round: Rep 7th round.

Cast off.

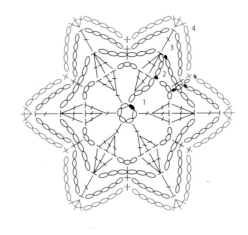

Little Gem

Special Abbreviation: Cluster = tr3tog.

Base ring: Using A, 5ch, join with sl st.

1st round: 4ch (count as 1dtr), 2tr into 4th ch from hook, *3ch, 1dtr into ring, 2tr into base of stem of dtr just made; rep from * 4 more times, 3ch, sl st to top of 4ch.

2nd round: 3ch, tr2tog over next 2tr (count as cluster), *6ch, miss 3ch, cluster over next 3 sts; rep from * 5 more times missing last cluster and ending sl st to top of first cluster. Cast off.

3rd round: Using B, join in to centre of 3ch sp of first round to enclose 6ch sp of 2nd round, 1ch, 1dc into same place as 1ch, *5ch, 1tr into top of next cluster; 5ch, 1dc into 3ch sp of first round at same time enclosing 6ch sp of 2nd round; rep from * 5 more times missing last dc and ending sl st to first dc. Cast off.

4th round: Using C join in to same place, 1ch, 1dc into same place as 1ch, *5ch, miss 5ch, 3dc into next tr, 5ch, miss 5ch, 1dc into next dc; rep from * 5 more times missing last dc and ending sl st to first dc.
Cast off.

Royal Square

Special Abbreviations: Quin tr (quintuple treble) = Yo 4 times, insert hook in next st, yo, draw through st, (yo, draw through 2 sps on hook) 5 times.

Sext tr (sextuple treble) = Yo 5 times, insert hook in next st, yo, draw through st, (yo, draw through 2 sps on hook) 6 times.

Cluster = tr3tog.

Base ring: 16ch, join with sl st.

1st round: 1ch, 24dc into ring, sl st to first dc. (24 sts)

2nd round: 1ch, 1dc into same place as 1ch, *4ch, trtr2tog over next 2 sts (count as cluster), into top of cluster just made work set of 3 leaves as follows: [8ch, 1 quin tr, 7ch, 1dc, 8ch, 1 sext tr, 8ch, 1dc, 7ch, 1 quin tr, 7ch, sl st], 4ch, 1dc into next st of first round, 7ch, miss 2 sts, 1dc into next st; rep from * 3 more times, missing dc at end of last rep, sl st to first dc. Cast off.

3rd round: Rejoin yarn at tip of 2nd Leaf of next set, 1ch,

1dc into top of 8ch before sext tr, *2ch, miss sext tr, 1dc into next ch, 5ch, into tip of 3rd Leaf of same set work 1dc just before and 1dc just after quin tr, 7ch, into tip of first Leaf of next set work 1dc just before and 1dc just after quin tr, 5ch, into tip of 2nd Leaf of same set work 1dc just before sext tr; rep from * 3 more times, missing dc at end of last rep, sl st to first dc.

4th round: 1ch, 1dc in same place as 1ch, *3dc into next 2ch sp, 1dc into next dc, 1dc into each of next 5ch, 1dc into each of next 2dc, 1dc into each of next 7ch, 1dc into each of next 2dc, 1dc into each of next 5ch, 1dc into next dc; rep from * 3 more times, missing dc at end of last rep, sl st to first dc.

5th round: Sl st into each of next 2dc to corner, 4ch (count as 1tr and 1ch), 1tr into same place as 4ch, *[1ch, miss 1 st, 1tr into next st] 13 times to next corner**, [1ch, 1tr] twice all into same place as last tr; rep from * twice more and from * to ** again, ending 1ch, sl st to 3rd of 4ch.

6th round: 4ch (count as 1tr and 1ch), 1tr into same place as 4ch, *[1ch, 1tr into next ch sp] 15 times, 1ch**, [1tr, 1ch, 1tr, 1ch, 1tr] all into next corner st; rep from * twice more and from * to ** again, ending 1tr into corner st, 1ch, sl st to 3rd of 4ch.

7th round: 3ch (count as 1tr), 1tr into same place as 3ch, *1ch, [1tr into next ch sp, 1tr into next tr, 1ch, miss 1ch, 1tr into next tr, 1tr into next ch sp, 1ch, miss 1tr] 5 times, 1tr into next ch sp, 1tr into next tr, 1ch, miss 1ch, 1tr into next tr, 1tr into next ch sp, 1ch**, 3tr into corner st; rep from * twice more and from * to ** again, ending 1tr into corner st, sl st to top of 3ch.

8th round: 4ch (count as 1tr and 1ch), 1tr into same place as 4ch, *1tr into next tr, [1ch, miss 1ch, 1tr into each of next 2 tr] 13 times to next corner, 1ch**, [1tr, 1ch, 1tr] into same place as last tr; rep from * twice more and from * to ** again, ending sl st to 3rd of 4ch.

9th round: 1ch, 2dc into same place as 1ch, 1dc into each ch sp and each tr all around, except 3dc into st at each of next 3 corners and ending 1dc into first corner, sl st to first dc.

10th round: 5ch, trtr2tog all into same place as 5ch (count as trtr3tog), 2ch, trtr3tog all into same place as last cluster, *5ch, miss 4 sts, trtr3tog all into next st, [5ch, miss 5 sts, trtr3tog all into next st] 6 times, 5ch, miss 4 sts**, [trtr3tog, 2ch, trtr3tog] all into next corner st; rep from * twice more and from * to ** again, ending sl st to top of first cluster.

11th round: Sl st to next 2ch sp, 8ch, 1dc into 5th ch from hook, 1tr into same 2ch sp, [5ch, 1dc into 5th ch from hook] (1 picot made), *1tr into next cluster, [picot, miss 2ch, 1tr into next ch, picot, miss 2ch, 1tr into next cluster] 8 times, picot**, [1tr, picot] twice into 2ch sp at corner; rep from * twice more and from * to ** again, ending sl st to 3rd of 8ch.
Cast off.

Magic Circle

Base ring: 16ch, join with sl st.

1st round: 2ch (count as 1htr), 35htr into ring, sl st into 2nd of 2ch at beg of round.

2nd round: 1ch, 1dc into same st as last sl st, [5ch, miss 2htr, 1dc into next htr] 11 times, 5ch, sl st to first dc. Cast off.

Green Leaf

Special Abbreviation: Picot = 3ch, sl st into first of these ch.

Base chain: 15ch, work in a spiral as follows:
1dc into 2nd ch from hook, working 1 st into each ch, 1htr, 3tr, 4dtr, 3tr, 1htr and 1dc, 3ch, then working 1 st into each ch on other side of base chain, 1dc, 1htr, 3tr, 4dtr, 3tr, 1htr, 1dc, 3ch, 1dc into first dc at beg of spiral, 1dc into next htr, 1 picot, [1dc into each of next 2 sts, 1 picot] 6 times, [1dc, 4ch, sl st into 3rd ch from hook, 1ch, 1dc] into 3ch sp at point of leaf, [1 picot, 1dc into each of next 2 sts] 7 times, sl st into 3ch sp.
Cast off.

Arcade Diamond

Base ring: 6ch, join with sl st.
1st round: 3ch (count as 1tr), 15tr into ring, sl st to 3rd of 3ch. (16 tr)
2nd round: 5ch (count as 1tr, 2ch), *1tr into next tr, 2ch; rep from * 14 more times, sl st to 3rd of 5ch.
3rd round: Sl st into first sp, 3ch (count as 1tr), [1tr, 3ch, 2tr] into same sp, *[2ch, 1dc into next sp] 3 times, 2ch, [2tr, 3ch, 2tr] into next sp; rep from * twice more, [2ch, 1dc into next sp] 3 times, 2ch, sl st to top of 3ch.
4th round: Sl st into next 3ch sp, 3ch (count as 1tr), [2tr, 3ch, 3tr] into same sp, *[2ch, 1dc into next 2ch sp] 4 times, 2ch, [3tr, 3ch, 3tr] into next 3ch sp; rep from * twice more, [2ch, 1dc into next 2ch sp] 4 times, 2ch, sl st to top of 3ch.
5th round: Sl st into next 3ch sp, 3ch (count as 1tr), [2tr, 2ch, 3tr] into same sp, *[1ch, 2tr into 2ch sp] 5 times, 1ch, [3tr, 2ch, 3tr] into next 3ch sp; rep from * twice more, [1ch, 2tr into 2ch sp] 5 times, 1ch, sl st to top of 3ch.

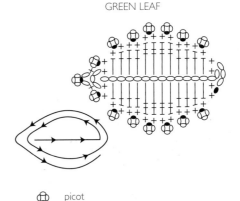

⊞ picot

ARCADE DIAMOND

Canterbury Bell

Special Abbreviation: Bobble = 5tr into next dc until 1 loop of each remains on hook, yo and draw through all 6 loops on hook.

Base ring: 6ch, join with sl st.

1st round: 1ch, 12dc into ring, sl st to first dc.

2nd round: 3ch, 4tr into same st as last sl st until 1 loop of each tr remains on hook, yo and draw through all 5 loops on hook (1 bobble made at beg of round), *5ch, miss 1dc, 1 bobble into next dc; rep from * 4 times more, 5ch, sl st to top of first bobble.

Cast off.

CANTERBURY BELL

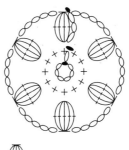

⊞ bobble

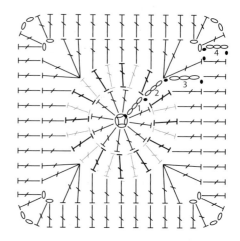

Graham Cracker

Base ring: 4ch, join with sl st.

1st round: 3ch (count as 1tr), 11tr into ring, sl st to top of 3ch. (12sts)

2nd round: 3ch (count as 1tr), 1tr into back loop of same st, *[1tr into front loop, 1tr into back loop] of next st; rep from * 10 more times, sl st to top of 3ch. (24sts)

3rd round: 3ch (count as 1tr), [1tr, 2ch, 2tr] into same place, *1tr into each of next 5 tr, [2tr, 2ch, 2tr] for a corner into next tr; rep from * twice more, 1tr into each of next 5tr; sl st to top of 3ch.

4th round: Sl st into next 2ch sp, 3ch (count as 1tr), [1tr, 2ch, 2tr] into same sp, *1tr into each of next 9tr, [2tr, 2ch, 2tr] into next 2ch sp; rep from * twice more, 1tr into each of next 9tr, sl st to top of 3ch.

Cast off.

When increasing and decreasing, make sure you note down the number of stitches at the end of each round. This can be especially helpful if the pattern provides a stitch count check for you to refer to.

Crystal Snowflake

Base ring: 12ch, join with sl st.

1st round: 1ch, 24dc into ring, sl st to first dc. (24 sts)

2nd round: 1ch, 1dc into same place as 1ch, *1dc into next st, [3ch, insert hook down through top of dc just made and work sl st] (one picot made)**, 1dc into next st; rep from * 10 more times and from * to ** again, sl st to first dc.

3rd round: 8ch (count as 1dtr and 4ch), miss picot, [1dtr into next dc between picots, 4ch] 11 times, sl st to 4th of 8ch.

4th round: 1ch, [5dc into next 4ch sp] 12 times, sl st to first dc.

5th round: 1ch, *1dc into back loop only of each of next 5dc, 15ch, miss next 5dc; rep from * 5 more times, sl st to first dc.

6th round: 1ch, *1dc into back loop only of each of next 5dc, 15dc into next 15ch sp; rep from * 5 more times, sl st to first dc.

7th round: Sl st into back loop only of next st, 1ch, 1dc into same place as 1ch, 1dc into back loop only of each of next 2dc, *miss 1dc, [1dc into each of next 3dc, picot] 4 times, 1dc into each of next 3dc, miss 1dc**, 1dc into back loop only of each of next 3dc; rep from * 4 more times and from * to ** again, sl st to first dc.
Cast off.

Elephant's Ear

Work as given for Flower Crystal (page 89), but working 1st and 2nd rounds in A and 3rd and 4th rounds in B.

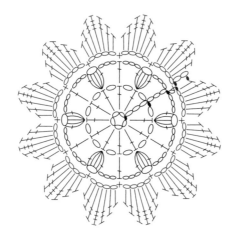

Rainbow Petal Motif

Centre

Base ring: Using A (Blue), 6ch, join with sl st.

1st round: 3ch (count as 1tr), 23tr into ring, sl st to top of 3ch. (24 sts)

2nd round: 1ch, 1dc into same place as 1ch, 1dc into front loop only of next and each st all around, sl st to first dc.

3rd round: 1ch, 1dc into same place as 1ch, *[1htr, 1tr, 1dtr] into next st, [1dtr, 1tr, 1htr] into next st, 1dc into next st; rep from * 7 more times, missing dc at end of last rep, sl st to first dc. Cast off.

Star Blocks

Make 6 Star Blocks alike, 2 each in Red, Green and Violet as follows:

1st Block

Join yarn to back loop of any st in first round of Centre, 10ch, turn.

1st row (RS): Miss 2ch (count as 1dc), 1dc into next and each ch to end, turn. (9dc)

2nd and every alt row: 1ch (counts as 1dc), miss first st, 1dc into next and each st to end, working last st into tch, turn.

3rd row: Work as 2nd row but make a 5tr popcorn (to stand out on right side of fabric) on 5th st.

5th row: As 2nd row but making 5tr popcorns on the 3rd and 7th sts.

7th row: As 3rd row.

Work 2 more rows as 2nd row (10 rows in all).

Cast off.

Remaining Blocks

Miss 3 sts of first round of Centre and join new yarn into back loop of next st, then work as for first Block.

Edging

Making sure all parts of fabric are right side facing, join A at left corner of first Block, 1ch, dc2tog over same place as 1ch and right corner of 2nd Block, *make 3 sps evenly spaced along edge of Block ending at top corner as follows: [3ch, 1dc into edge] 3 times, [5ch, 1dc, 7ch, 1dc, 5ch, 1dc] into same corner, work 3 sps evenly spaced as before along next edge of same Block as follows: [3ch, 1dc into edge] twice, 3ch**, dc2tog over left corner of same Block and right corner of next Block; rep from * 4 more times and from * to ** again, sl st to first dc.

Cast off.

 = popcorn

Ice Crystal

Special Abbreviation: Cluster = 1tr into each of next 5tr until 1 loop of each remains on hook, yo and draw through all 6 loops on hook.

Base ring: 6ch, join with sl st.

1st round: 1ch, 12dc into ring, sl st to first dc. (12 sts)

2nd round: 1ch, 1dc into same place as 1ch, [7ch, miss 1dc, 1dc into next dc] 5 times, 3ch, miss 1dc, 1dtr into top of first dc.

3rd round: 3ch (count as 1tr), 4tr into sp formed by dtr, [3ch, 5tr into next 7ch sp] 5 times, 3ch, sl st to top of 3ch.

4th round: 3ch (count as 1tr), 1tr into each of next 4tr, *3ch, 1dc into next 3ch sp, 3ch**, 1tr into each of next 5tr; rep from * 4 more times and from * to ** again, sl st to top of 3ch.

5th round: 3ch, tr4tog over next 4tr (count as cluster), *[5ch, 1dc into next 3ch sp] twice, 5ch**, cluster over next 5tr; rep from * 4 more times and from * to ** again, sl st to first cluster.

6th round: Sl st into each of next 3ch, 1ch, 1dc into same space, *5ch, 1dc into next 5ch sp; rep from * all around missing last dc and ending sl st to first dc.

7th round: Sl st into each of next 3ch, 1ch, 1dc into same space, *5ch, 1dc into next 5ch sp, 3ch, [5tr, 3ch, 5tr] into next sp, 3ch, 1dc into next sp; rep from * 5 more times missing last dc and ending sl st to first dc.

Cast off.

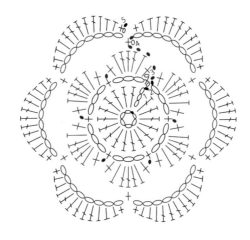

Scallop Flower

Base ring: Using A, 6ch, join with sl st.

1st round: 3ch (count as 1tr), 17tr into ring, sl st to top of 3ch (18 sts).

2nd round: 1ch, 1dc into same place as 1ch, *3ch, miss next 2 sts, 1dc into next st; rep from * 5 more times missing last dc and ending sl st to first dc. Cast off.

3rd round: Using B join in to next ch, 1ch, *work a Petal of [1dc, 1htr, 3tr, 1htr, 1dc] into net 3ch sp, sl st into next dc; rep from * 5 more times. (6 petals)

4th round: Sl st into each of next 4 sts to centre tr of next Petal, 1ch, 1dc into same place as 1ch, *8ch, 1dc into centre tr of next Petal; rep from * 5 more times missing last dc and ending sl st to first dc. Cast off.

5th round: Using A join in to next ch, 1ch, *[1dc, 3htr, 5tr, 3htr, 1dc] into next sp; rep from * 5 more times, ending sl st into first dc.
Cast off.

Very decorative stitches, such as loop and fur stitches, are usually more effective when used as trims rather than as all-over designs. Consider contrasting them with simple base fabrics like treble crochet and knitted moss stitch.

Plain Hexagon

Base ring: 4ch, join with sl st.

1st round: 1ch, 11dc into ring, sl st to first ch, turn.

2nd round: 2ch (count as 1htr), *3htr into next dc, 1htr into next dc; rep from * 4 times more, 3htr into next dc, sl st to top of 2ch, turn.

3rd round: 1ch, 1dc into same place as last sl st, *6ch, 1dc into 2nd ch from hook, 1htr into next ch, 1tr into next ch, 1dtr into next ch, 1trtr into next ch, miss 4 sts from 2nd round, 1dc into next st; rep from * 7 more times missing dc at end of last rep, sl st to first dc.

4th round: 2ch (count as 1htr), 1htr into each of next 2htr, *3htr into next htr, 1htr into each of next 5htr; rep from * 4 times more, 3htr into next htr, 1htr into each of next 2htr, sl st to top of 2ch, turn.

Cont in this way, working 2 more htr along each side in each round until hexagon is the required size.

Cast off.

Sun Fire

Base ring: 5ch, join with sl st.

1st round: 7ch (count as 1dtr and 3ch), [1dtr into ring, 3ch] 7 times, sl st to 4th of 7ch. (8 spaces)

2nd round: 3ch (count as 1tr), [4tr into next sp, 1tr into next dtr] 7 times, 4tr into next sp, sl st to top of 3ch. (40 sts)

3rd round: 1ch, 1dc into same place as last sl st, *6ch, 1dc into 2nd ch from hook, 1htr into next ch, 1tr into next ch, 1dtr into next ch, 1trtr into next ch, miss 4 sts, 1dc into next st; rep from * 7 more times missing dc at end of last rep, sl st to first dc.

Cast off.

PLAIN HEXAGON

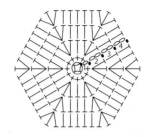

SUN FIRE

BRIAR ROSE

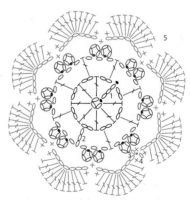

Briar Rose

Base ring: Using A, 3ch, join with sl st.

1st round: 5ch (count as 1tr and 2ch), [1tr into ring, 2ch] 7 times, sl st to 3rd of 5ch. Cast off. (8 spaces)

2nd round: Join B into a sp, 8ch, sl st into 4th ch from hook, work a picot of [5ch, sl st into 4th ch from hook], 1ch, *1tr into next sp, work a picot twice, 1ch; rep from * 6 more times, sl st to 3rd of 4ch at beg of round. Cast off.

3rd round: Join C into 1ch between 2 picots, 1ch, 1dc into same place as 1ch, *7ch, miss [1 picot, 1tr and 1 picot], 1dc into next ch between picots; rep from * 7 more times missing dc at end of last rep, sl st to first dc.

4th round: Sl st into next ch, 1ch, *[1dc, 1htr, 9tr, 1htr, 1dc] into next sp; rep from * 7 more times, sl st into first dc. Cast off.

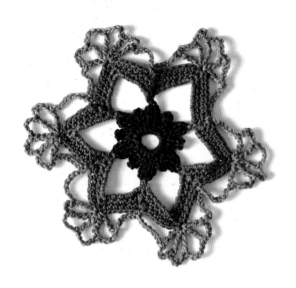

Crystal Motif

Special Abbreviation: Cluster = dc3tog.

Base ring: Using A, 12ch, join with sl st.

1st round: 1ch, 1dc into ring, *[7ch, 1dc, 4ch, 1trtr, 4ch, 1dc] into ring; rep from * 5 more times missing dc at end of last rep, sl st to first dc. Cast off.

2nd round: Join B into top of any trtr, 1ch, 1dc into same place as 1ch, *13ch, miss 7ch sp, 1dc into top of next trtr; rep from * 5 more times missing dc at end of last rep, sl st to first dc.

3rd round: 1ch, miss next ch, 1dc into each of next 5ch, *3dc into next ch, 1dc into each of next 5ch**, dc3tog over [next ch, next dc and next ch], 1dc into each of next 5ch; rep from * 4 more times and from * to ** again, sl st to first dc.

4th round: 1ch, miss first st, *1dc into each of next 5 sts, 3dc into next st, 1dc into each of next 5sts**, dc3tog over next 3 sts; rep from * 4 more times and from * to ** again, sl st to first dc.

5th round: As 4th round. Cast off.

6th round: Join C into same place, 1ch, 1dc into same place, *7ch, miss 6dc, (1trtr, [5ch, 1trtr] 4 times) into next dc at tip of star, 7ch, miss 6dc, 1dc into next dc cluster; rep from * 5 more times missing dc at end of last rep, sl st to first dc.

Cast off.

Mica Motif

Special Abbreviation: Cluster = tr4tog.

Base ring: 6ch, join with sl st.

1st round: 5ch (count as 1tr and 2ch), [1tr into ring, 2ch] 7 times, sl st to 3rd of 5ch. (8 spaces)

2nd round: 3ch (count as 1tr), [4tr into next sp, 1tr into next tr] 7 times, 4tr into next sp, sl st to top of 3ch.

3rd round: Sl st into next st, 3ch (count as 1tr), *1dc into each of next 2 sts, 1tr into next st, 5ch, miss 1 st**, 1tr into next st; rep from * 6 more times and from * to ** again, sl st to top of 3ch.

4th round: 3ch, tr3tog over next 3 sts (counts as tr4tog), *5ch, 1dc into next 5ch sp, 5ch**, tr4tog over next 4 sts; rep from * 6 more times and from * to ** again, sl st to top of first cluster.

5th round: 8ch (count as 1tr and 5ch), *1dc into next 5ch sp, 1dc into next dc, 1dc into next sp, 5ch**, 1tr into next cluster, 5ch; rep from * 6 more times and from * to ** again, sl st to 3rd of 8ch.

6th round: 10ch (count as 1tr and 7ch), miss 5ch, *1dc into 2nd of next 3dc, 7ch, miss 5ch**, 1tr into next tr, 7ch, miss 5ch; rep from * 6 more times and from * to ** again, sl st to 3rd of 10ch.

7th round: 6ch (count as 1tr and 3ch), 1tr into same place as 6ch, *[2ch, 1tr] 3 times into next 7ch sp, 1tr into next dc, [1tr, 2ch] 3 times into next 7-ch sp**, [1tr, 3ch, 1tr] into next tr; rep from * 6 more times and from * to ** again, sl st to 3rd of 6ch.

Cast off.

Astrolabe Motif

Base ring: 4ch, join with sl st.

1st round: 4ch (count as 1tr and 1ch), [1tr into ring, 1ch] 7 times, sl st to 3rd of 4ch. (8 spaces)

2nd round: 1ch, 1dc into same place as 1ch, [3ch, miss 1ch, 1dc into next tr] 8 times missing dc at end of last rep, sl st to first dc.

3rd round: Sl st into each of next 2ch, 1ch, 1dc into same space as 1ch, [6ch, 1dc into next 3ch sp] 8 times missing dc at end of last rep, sl st to first dc.

4th round: Sl st into each of next 3ch, 1ch, 1dc into same space as 1ch, [6ch, 1dc into next 6ch sp] 8 times missing dc at end of last rep, sl st to first dc.

5th round: 1ch, 1dc into same place as 1ch, *[2tr, 4ch, 2tr] into next sp, 1dc into next dc; rep from * 7 more times missing dc at end of last rep, sl st to first dc.

6th round: Sl st into each of next 2tr and next 2ch, 1ch, 1dc into same place as 1ch, [8ch, 1dc into next 4ch sp] 8 times missing dc at end of last rep, sl st to first dc.

7th round: 1ch, *work a Wave of [1dc, 1htr, 2tr, 1dtr, 2tr, 1htr, 1dc] into next 8ch sp; rep from * 7 more times, sl st to first dc.

8th round: Sl st into each of next 4 sts to dtr, 1ch, 1dc into same place as 1ch, [11ch, 1dc into dtr at centre of next Wave] 8 times missing dc at end of last rep, sl st to first dc.

9th round: 1ch, *[2dc, 2htr, 2tr, 4dtr, 2tr, 2htr, 2dc] into next 11ch sp; rep from * 7 more times, sl st to first dc. Cast off.

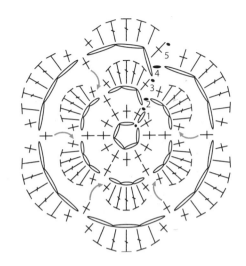

Buttercup

Base ring: Ch 5, join with sl st.

1st round: 1ch, 12dc into ring, sl st to first dc.

2nd round: [3ch, miss 1dc, 1dc into next dc] 5 times, 3ch, miss 1dc, sl st to first of 3ch.

3rd round: [1dc, 1htr, 3tr, 1htr, 1dc] into each 3ch sp, sl st to first dc. (6 petals)

4th round: *3ch, 1dc around bar of first dc of next petal; rep from * 4 more times, 3ch, sl st to first of first 3ch.

5th round: Rep 3rd round.

Cast off.

Keeping things simple is the key to success. Working in one colour will draw attention to the crochet stitches, show off their intricate detail and create a sophisticated and unique motif.

dc on 6th round, *[9ch, sl st into 6th ch from hook (1 picot made)] twice, 4ch, 1dc into next dc on 6th round, [13ch, sl st into 6th ch from hook (1 picot made)] twice, 8ch, 1dc into same dc as last dc, [9ch, sl st into 6th ch from hook] twice, 4ch, 1dc into next dc on 6th round; rep from * 3 more times missing 1dc at end of last rep, sl st to first dc.

9th round: Sl st into each of first 3ch, behind first picot and into next ch of sp between picots, 1ch, 1dc into same sp as sl st, **[10ch, sl st into 6th ch from hook] twice, 5ch, 1dc into corner loop between 2 picots, *[10ch, sl st into 6th ch from hook] twice, 5ch, 1dc into sp between 2 picots; rep from * once more; rep from ** 3 more times missing 1dc at end of last rep, sl st to first dc.

10th round: Sl st into each of first 4ch, behind first picot and into next 2ch of sp between 2 picots, 1ch, 1dc into same sp between 2 picots, **[10ch, sl st into 6th ch from hook] twice, 5ch, 1dc into next dc at top of loop, *[10ch, sl st into 6th ch from hook] twice, 5ch, 1dc into next sp between 2 picots; rep from * twice more; rep from ** 3 more times missing 1dc at end of last rep, sl st to first dc. Cast off.

Five Branches

Base ring: 7ch, join with sl st.

1st round: 1ch, 16dc into ring, sl st to first dc.

2nd round: 1ch, 1dc into first dc, [5ch, miss 1dc, 1dc into next dc] 7 times, 5ch, sl st to first dc.

3rd round: Sl st into first 5ch sp, 1ch, [1dc, 5htr, 1dc] into each 5ch sp to end, sl st into first dc. (8 petals)

4th round: 1ch, working behind each petal, 1dc into first dc on 2nd round, [6ch, 1dc into next dc on 2nd round] 7 times, 6ch, sl st to first dc.

5th round: Sl st into first 6ch sp, 1ch, [1dc, 6htr, 1dc] into each 6ch sp to end, sl st to first dc.

6th round: 1ch, working behind each petal, 1dc into first dc on 4th round, [7ch, 1dc into next dc on 4th round] 7 times, 7ch, sl st to first dc.

7th round: Sl st into first 7ch sp, 1ch, [1dc, 7htr, 1dc] into each 7ch sp to end, sl st to first dc.

8th round: 1ch, working behind each petal, 1dc into first

Wasp Medallion

Special Abbreviation: Popcorn = see page 26, make 4dtr popcorn.

Base ring: 7ch, join with sl st.

1st round: 3ch, 3dtr into ring, remove hook and insert through top of 3ch and into loop and draw through loop on hook (popcorn made), 3ch, [popcorn into ring, 3ch] 5 times, sl st to top of first popcorn.

2nd round: 3ch, (count as 1dtr) 2dtr into same place as sl st, *5dtr into next 3ch sp, 3dtr into top of next popcorn; rep from *4 more times, 5dtr into next 3ch sp, sl st to top of 3ch.

3rd round: 3ch (count as first leg of popcorn), make popcorn in same place as sl st, 3ch, *miss 1dtr, 1 popcorn in next dtr, 3ch; rep from * ending with sl st into top of first popcorn.

Cast off.

Use a large-dcale yarn in openwork patterns. The stitch or motif can then be embellished and elaborated with embroidery or freeform crochet.

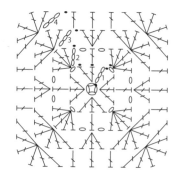

Granny Square

Base ring: 4ch, join with sl st.

1st round: 3ch (count as 1tr), 2tr into ring, *1ch, 3tr into ring; rep from * twice more, 1ch, sl st into top of 3ch.

2nd round: Sl st into each of next 2tr and next 1ch sp, 3ch, 4tr into same sp for a corner, *1tr into centre of next 3tr group, 5tr into next 1ch sp for a corner; rep from * twice more, 1tr into centre of next 3tr group, sl st to top of 3ch. Cast off.

3rd round: Join into centre of any corner group, 3ch, 5tr into same place for corner, *3tr into next tr, 6tr into centre of next corner group; rep from * twice, 3tr into next tr, sl st to top of 3ch. Cast off.

4th round: Join into centre space of any corner group, 3ch, 5tr into same place for corner, *1tr into last tr of same corner group, 1tr into centre of next 3tr group, 1tr into first tr of next corner group**, 6tr into centre space of same corner group; rep from * twice more, then from * to ** again, sl st to top of 3ch. Cast off.

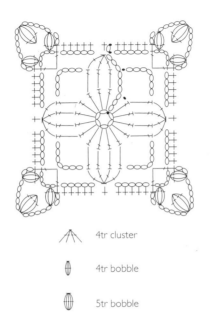

4tr cluster

4tr bobble

5tr bobble

Cross Panel

Special Abbreviations: 4tr cluster = 1tr into each of next 4tr until 1 loop of each remains on hook, yo and through all 5 loops on hook.

4tr bobble or 5tr bobble = 4tr (or 5tr) into next ch until 1 loop of each remains on hook, yo and through all 5 (or 6) loops on hook.

Base ring: 6ch, join with sl st.

1st round: 3ch (count as 1tr), 15tr into ring, sl st to top of 3ch.

2nd round: 3ch, 1tr into each of next 3tr; [7ch, 1tr into each of next 4tr] 3 times, 7ch, sl st to top of 3ch.

3rd round: 3ch, 1tr into each of next 3tr until 1 loop of each remains on hook, yo and through all 4 loops on hook (1 cluster made at beg of round), 5ch, miss 3ch, [1tr, 5ch, 1tr] into next ch, 5ch, *4tr cluster over next 4tr, 5ch, miss 3ch, [1tr, 5ch, 1tr] into next ch, 5ch; rep from * twice more, sl st into top of first cluster.

4th round: 1ch, *1dc into top of cluster, 1dc into each of next 5ch, 1dc into next tr, 2ch, 4tr bobble into next ch, 5ch, miss 1ch, 5tr bobble into next ch, 5ch, miss 1ch, 4tr bobble into next ch, 2ch, 1dc into next tr, 1dc into each of next 5ch; rep from * 3 times more, sl st to first dc. Cast off.

Spring Time

Base ring: 5ch, join with sl st.
1st round: 1ch, 10dc into ring, sl st into first dc.
2nd round: 1ch, 1dc into each dc, sl st to first dc.
3rd round: 2ch (count as 1htr), miss first dc, 2htr into each of next 9dc, 1htr into first dc, sl st into 2nd of 2ch.
4th round: *2ch, working into front loop only of each htr, 2tr into each of next 3htr, 2ch, sl st into next htr; rep from * 4 times more placing last sl into 2nd of 2ch at beg of previous round. (5 petals made)
5th round: Working behind each petal of previous round and into back loop of each htr on 3rd round, sl st into first 2htr, *4ch, 2trtr into each of next 3htr, 4ch, sl st into next htr; rep from * 3 times more, 4ch, 2trtr into next htr, 2trtr into 2nd of 2ch at beg of 3rd round, 2trtr into next htr, 4ch, sl st to next htr.
Cast off.

Gardenia Bloom

Base ring: 5ch, join with sl st.
1st round: 6ch (count as 1tr and 3ch), [1tr into ring, 3ch] 5 times, sl st to 3rd of 6ch.
2nd round: 1ch, 1dc into sl st, *[1tr, 1ch, 1tr, 1ch, 1tr] into next 3ch sp, 1dc into next tr; rep from * 5 more times missing dc at end of last rep, sl st to first dc.
3rd round: 1ch, 1dc into first dc, *1ch, miss 1tr, [1tr, 1ch] 5 times into next tr, miss 1tr, 1dc into next dc; rep from * 5 more times missing dc at end of last rep, sl st to first dc.
Cast off.

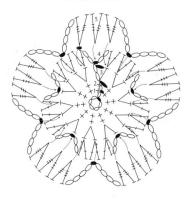

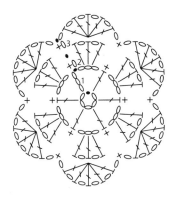

Wheelie

Base ring: 6ch, join with sl st.

1st round: 3ch (count as 1tr), 13tr into ring, sl st to top of 3ch.

2nd round: 3ch, 2tr into bottom of 3ch, 3tr into each of next 13tr, sl st to top of 3ch.

Cast off.

WHEELIE

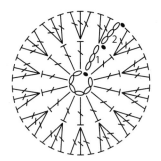

Granite Wheel

Special Abbreviation: Puff st = see page 27, work 3htr
leaving last loop on hook, yo and draw through all loops
on hook.

Base ring: 7ch, join with sl st.

1st round: 1ch, 12dc into ring, sl st to first dc. (12 sts)

2nd round: 3ch (count as 1tr), 1tr into next dc, *3ch, 1tr
into each of next 2 sts; rep from * 4 more times, 3ch, sl st
to top of 3ch.

3rd round: Sl st into next tr and next ch, 3ch, htr2tog into
same sp (counts as puff st), 4ch, puff st into same sp, *4ch,
[puff st, 4ch, puff st] into next sp; rep from * 4 more times,
4ch, sl st to top of first puff st. (12 puff sts)

4th round: 1ch, *[2dc, 3ch, 2dc] into next sp; rep from *
11 more times, sl st to first dc.

Cast off.

Galaxy Motif

Special Abbreviation: Puff st = see page 27, work 5htr
leaving last loop of each st on hook, yo and draw through all
1ps on hook.

Cluster = see page 25, work 3tr over sts indicated leaving
last 1p on hook, yo and draw through all 1ps on hook.

Base ring: 6ch, join with sl st.

1st round: 6ch (count as 1dtr and 2ch), [1dtr into ring, 2ch]
7 times, sl st to 4th of 6ch. (8 spaces)

2nd round: 2ch, htr4tog into next sp (counts as puff st),
[7ch, puff st into next sp] 7 times, 7ch, sl st to top of first
puff st.

3rd round: Sl st into each of next 3ch, 1ch, 3dc into same
sp, [9ch, 3dc into next sp] 7 times, 8ch, 1dc into first dc.

4th round: 3ch, tr2tog over next 1dc and next ch missing dc
between (counts as cluster), *2ch, miss 1ch, 1tr into next ch,
2ch, skip 1ch, [1tr, 3ch, 1tr] into next ch, 2ch, miss 1ch, 1tr
into next ch, 2ch, miss 1ch**, cluster over [next ch, 2nd of
next 3dc and next ch]; rep from * 6 more times and from *
to ** again, sl st to top of first cluster. Cast off.

Mayfair Square

Special Abbreviation: Bobble = see page 26, work 4tr into same sp leaving last loop of each tr on hook, yo and draw through all 5 loops on hook.

Base ring: 8ch, join with sl st.

1st round: 3ch, 3tr into ring (hold back last loop of each tr, yo and draw through all 4 loops on hook), *4ch, bobble into ring; rep from * twice more, 4ch, sl st to top of first bobble.

2nd round: Sl st into next 4ch sp, 3ch (count as 1tr), [2tr, 3ch, 3tr] into same sp, *1tr into top of next bobble, [3tr, 3ch, 3tr] into next 4ch sp; rep from * twice more, 1tr into top of next bobble, sl st to top of 3ch.

3rd round: 3ch, 1tr into each of next 2tr, [2tr, 3ch, 2tr] into next 3ch sp, *1tr into each of next 7tr, [2tr, 3ch, 2tr] into next 3ch sp; rep from * twice more, 1tr into each of next 4tr, sl st to top of 3ch.

MAYFAIR SQUARE

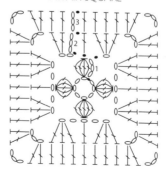

Sylvan Circles

Base ring: 8ch, join with sl st.

1st round: 3ch (count as 1tr), 31tr into ring, sl st to top of 3ch. (32 sts)

2nd round: 3ch, 1tr into same place as 3ch (count as tr2tog), 3ch, tr2tog into same place as last tr2tog, *7ch, miss 3 sts, [tr2tog, 3ch, tr2tog] into next st; rep from * 6 more times, 7ch, miss 3 sts, sl st to top of first tr2tog.

3rd round: Sl st into next 3ch sp, 3ch, 1tr into same place as 3ch (count as tr2tog), 3ch, tr2tog into same 3ch sp, *7ch, miss 7ch, [tr2tog, 3ch, tr2tog] into next 3ch sp; rep from * 6 more times, 7ch, miss 7ch, sl st to top of first tr2tog.

4th round: Sl st into next 3ch sp, 3ch, 1tr into same place as 3ch (count as tr2tog), 3ch, tr2tog into same 3ch sp, *4ch, 1dc under 7ch sp of 2nd round to enclose 7ch sp of 3rd round, 4ch**, [tr2tog, 3ch, tr2tog] into next 3ch sp; rep from * 6 more times and from * to ** again, sl st to top of first tr2tog.

5th round: Sl st into next 3ch sp, 3ch, 1tr into same place as 3ch (count as tr2tog), 3ch, tr2tog into same 3ch sp, *15ch, sl st into 12th ch from hook, 3ch, sl st to top of previous tr2tog, 6tr into 12ch ring, miss 4ch, sl st to next dc, 8tr into ring, miss 4ch, (inner half of Sylvan Circle completed)**, [tr2tog, 3ch, tr2tog] into next 3ch sp; rep from * 6 more times and from * to ** again, sl st to top of first tr2tog.

6th round: *1ch, [tr2tog, 6ch, sl st to 5th ch from hook, 1ch, tr2tog] into next 3ch sp, 1ch, sl st to top of next tr2tog, 16tr into 12ch ring (outer half of Sylvan Circle completed), sl st to top of next tr2tog; rep from * 7 more times.

Cast off.

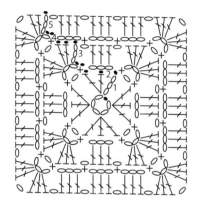

Spring Mosaic

Base ring: 5ch, join with sl st.

1st round: 3ch (count as 1 tr), 2tr into ring, [1ch, 3tr into ring] 3 times, 1ch, sl st to top of 3ch.

2nd round: Sl st into each of next 2 tr, *[1dc, 3ch, 1dc] into next sp for a corner, 3ch; rep from * 3 more times, sl st to first dc.

3rd round: Sl st into next sp, 3ch, [2tr, 1ch, 3tr] into same sp for a corner, *1ch, 3tr into next sp, 1ch, [3tr, 1ch, 3tr] into next sp for a corner; rep from * twice more, 1ch, 3tr into next sp, 1ch, sl st to top of 3ch.

4th round: Sl st into next corner sp, *[1dc, 3ch, 1dc] into next corner sp, [3ch, 1dc into next sp] twice, 3ch; rep from * 3 times more, sl st to first dc.

5th round: Sl st into next corner sp, 3ch, [2tr, 1ch, 3tr into same corner sp, *[1ch, 3tr into next sp] 3 times, 1ch, [3tr, 1ch, 3tr] into next corner sp; rep from * twice more, [1ch, 3tr into next sp] 3 times, 1ch, sl st to top of 3ch.

Rep 4th and 5th rounds for patt st, inc each row in corner spaces.

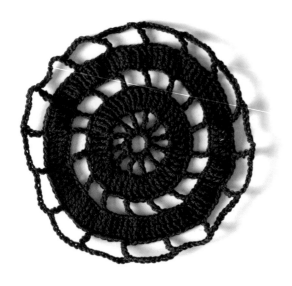

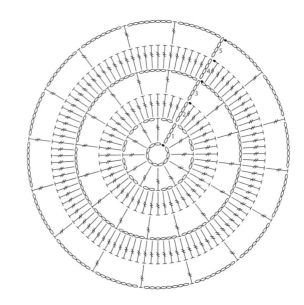

Ring Web

Base ring: 10ch, join with sl st.

1st round: 6ch (count as 1dtr and 2ch), [1dtr into ring, 2ch] 11 times, sl st to 4th of 6ch.

2nd round: 4ch, 3dtr into next sp, [1dtr into next dtr, 3dtr into next sp] 11 times, sl st to top of 4ch.

3rd round: 9ch, miss next 2dtr, [1dtr into next dtr, 5ch, miss next 2dtr] 15 times, sl st to 4th of 9ch.

4th round: 4ch, 1dtr into each of next 5ch, [1dtr into next dtr, 1dtr into each of next 5ch] 15 times, sl st to top of 4ch.

5th round: 12ch (count as 1dtr and 8ch), [miss next 5dtr, 1dtr into next dtr, 8ch] 15 times, miss next 5dtr, sl st to 4th of 12ch.

Cast off.

Before linking your new collection of motifs together, lay them out carefully and pin them to a sheet of paper. When you come to joining them, you will find it much easier work.

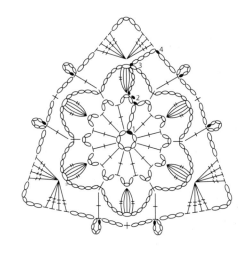

Floral Pyramid

Special Abbreviations: Popcorn = 5dtr into next ch, drop loop from hook, insert hook from the front into first of these dtr, pick up dropped loop and draw through, 1ch to secure.

Picot = 5ch, sl st into top of tr just worked.

Base ring: 6ch, join with sl st.

1st round: 6ch (count as 1tr, 3ch), [1tr, 3ch] 11 times into ring, sl st to 3rd of 6ch.

2nd round: Sl st into each of first 2ch of first sp, 4ch (count as 1dtr), 4dtr into same ch as last sl st, drop loop from hook, insert hook from the front into 4th of 4ch, pick up dropped loop and draw through, 1ch to secure

(popcorn made at beg of round), 5ch, 1dc into next 3ch sp, [5ch, miss 1ch of next 3ch sp, 1 popcorn into next ch, 5ch, 1dc into next 3ch sp] 5 times, 5ch, sl st into top of first popcorn.

3rd round: 4ch, [3dtr, 5ch, 4dtr] into top of first popcorn, 3ch, 1tr into next dc, 1 picot, 3ch, 1dc into top of next popcorn, 3ch, 1tr into next dc, 1 picot, 3ch, *[4dtr, 5ch, 4dtr] into top of next popcorn, 3ch, 1tr into next dc, 1 picot, 3ch, 1dc into top of next popcorn, 3ch, 1tr into next dc, 1 picot, 3ch; rep from * once more, sl st into top of 4ch. Cast off.

Barnacle Motif

Base ring: 8ch, join with sl st.

1st round: 1ch, [1dc into ring, 3ch, 1dtr into ring, 3ch] 8 times, sl st to first dc.

2nd round: Sl st into each of next 3ch and into dtr, [12ch, 1tr into 9th ch from hook, 3ch, sl st to top of next dtr] 8 times.

3rd round: Sl st into each of next 4ch, 3ch (count as 1tr), *[1htr, 7dc, 1htr] into next 8ch sp, 1tr into next tr, miss last 3ch of same segment and first 3ch of next segment**, 1tr into next ch, (i.e. opposite side of same ch as tr of 2nd round); rep from * 6 more times and from * to ** again, sl st to top of 3ch.

4th round: 1ch, 1dc inserting hook under sl st which joined 3rd round, *3ch, miss [1htr and 1dc], 1dc into next dc, 3ch, miss 1dc, [1dc, 4ch, 1dc] into next dc, 3ch, miss 1dc, 1dc into next dc, 3ch, miss [1dc, 1htr and 1tr]**, 1dc between 2tr, miss 1tr; rep from * 6 more times and from * to ** again, sl st to first dc.

Cast off.

Amanda Whorl

1st Segment

Base ring: Using A, 12ch, join with sl st.

1st row (right side): 4ch (count as 1dtr), [1dtr into ring, 6ch, 1tr into top of dtr just made, 1dtr into ring] 3 times, 1dtr into ring, 2ch, 10dtr into ring, turn.

2nd row: Work a picot of [5ch, sl st to 5th ch from hook], *miss first dtr, 1dc into each of next 9dtr, change to next colour, turn.

2nd Segment

1ch, 1dc into same place as 1ch, 3ch, miss 3dc, 1dc into next dc, 9ch, sl st to first dc to complete joined base ring.

1st row: As given for 1st Segment.

2nd row: 2ch, 1dc into picot of previous Segment, 3ch, sl st to first ch of row to complete picot, continue as for 1st Segment from *.

Work 5 more Segments as 2nd Segment using C, D, A, B and C.

8th Segment

Using D, work as for previous Segments, except also join to 1st Segment during 2nd row as follows: 2ch, 1dc into picot of 7th Segment, 1ch, 1dc into picot of 1st Segment, 2ch, sl st to first ch of row to complete picot, miss first dtr, 1dc into each of next 5dtr, sl st to 1st Segment, 1dc into each of next 4dtr, sl st to 1st Segment. Cast off.

Centre Ring

Using A, work inward round centre to make edging as follows: join into any dc, 1ch, 1dc into same place as 1ch, [1dc into next picot, 1dc into side of next dc] 7 times, 1dc into next picot, sl st to first dc.

Cast off.

Celtic Motif

Base ring: Using A, 6ch, join with sl st.
1st round: Work a Leaf of [3ch, 2tr into ring, 3ch, sl st into ring] 4 times. Cast off.
2nd round: Join B into same place, 6ch (count as 1tr and 3ch), miss next Leaf, *[1tr, 3ch, 1tr] into sl st, 3ch, miss next Leaf; rep from * twice more, 1tr into next sl st, 3ch, sl st to 3rd of 6ch.
3rd round: 1ch, 1dc into same place as 1ch, *work a Leaf of [3ch, 3tr into next 3ch sp, 3ch, 1dc into next tr]; rep from * 7 more times missing dc at end of last rep, sl st to first dc. Cast off.
4th round: Join C into same place, 1ch, 1dc into same place as 1ch, *4ch, miss next Leaf, 1dc into next dc; rep from * 7 more times missing dc at end of last rep, sl st to first dc.

5th round: 3ch (count as 1tr), 4tr into next 4ch sp, [2ch, 5tr into next sp] 7 times, 2ch, sl st to top of 3ch.
6th round: 1ch, 1dc into same place as 1ch, 1dc into each of next 4tr, *[1dc, 3ch, insert hook down through top of dc just made and work sl st to close, 1dc] into next 2ch sp**, 1dc into each of next 5tr; rep from * 6 more times and from * to ** again, sl st to first dc.
Cast off.

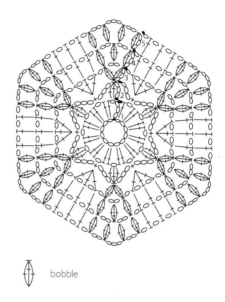

bobble

Baby Bud

Special Abbreviation: Bobble = 3tr into next dc until 1 loop of each remains on hook, yo and draw through all 4 loops on hook.

Base ring: 12ch, sl st into first ch to form a ring.

1st round: 4ch (count as 1tr, 1ch), [2tr, 1ch] 11 times into ring, 1tr into ring, sl st to 3rd of 4ch.

2nd round: Sl st into first ch sp, 3ch, 2tr into same sp until 1 loop of each remains on hook, yo and through all 3 loops on hook (1 bobble made at beg of round), 3ch, 1dc into next ch sp, 3ch, [1 bobble into next ch sp, 3ch, 1dc into next ch sp, 3ch] 5 times, sl st into top of first bobble.

3rd round: 3ch, [first bobble as at beg of previous round, 2ch, 1 bobble] into top of first bobble, [1ch, 1tr] 3 times into next dc, 1ch, *[1 bobble, 2ch, 1 bobble] into top of next bobble, [1ch, 1tr] 3 times into next dc, 1ch; rep from * 4 times more, sl st to top of first bobble.

4th round: 3ch, 1 bobble into first bobble as at beg of 2nd round, 2ch, 1 bobble into next 2ch sp, 2ch, 1 bobble into top of next bobble, 1ch, [1tr into next tr, 1ch] 3 times, *1 bobble into next bobble, 2ch, 1 bobble into next 2ch sp, 2ch, 1 bobble into next bobble, 1ch, [1tr into next tr, 1ch] 3 times; rep from * 4 times more, sl st to top of first bobble.

5th round: 3ch, 1 bobble into first bobble as at beg of 2nd round, 2ch, 1 bobble into next 2ch sp, 3ch, 1 bobble into next 2ch sp, 2ch, 1 bobble into next bobble, 1ch, [1tr into next tr, 1ch] 3 times, *1 bobble into next bobble, 2ch, 1 bobble into next 2ch sp, 3ch, 1 bobble into next 2ch sp, 2ch, 1 bobble into next bobble, 1ch, [1tr into next tr, 1ch] 3 times; rep from * 4 times more, sl st to first bobble. Cast off.

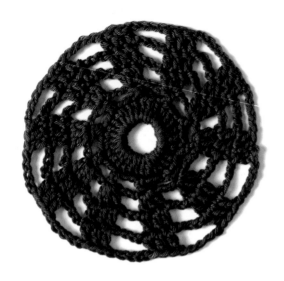

Geometric Circle

Base ring: 10ch, join with sl st.
1st round: 3ch (count as 1tr), 29tr into ring, sl st to top of 3ch. (30 tr)
2nd round: 6ch (count as 1tr and 3ch), miss next 2tr, [1tr into next tr, 3ch, miss next 2tr] 9 times, sl st to 3rd of 5ch.
3rd round: 3ch (count as 1tr), 2tr into same place as last sl st, 3ch, [3tr into next tr, 3ch] 9 times, sl st to top of 3ch.
4th round: 3ch (count as 1tr), 1tr into each of next 2tr, 4ch, [1tr into each of next 3tr, 4ch] 9 times, sl st to top of 3ch.
5th round: 3ch (count as 1tr), 1tr into each of next 2tr, 5ch, [1tr into each of next 3tr, 5ch] 9 times, sl st to top of 3ch.
Cast off.

Spiral Hexagon

Base ring: 5ch, join with sl st.
1st round: [6ch, 1dc into ring] 6 times, sl st into first 3ch of first sp.
2nd round: [4ch, 1dc into next 6ch sp] 6 times, working last dc into sl st before the first 4ch sp.
3rd round: [4ch, 2dc into next 4ch sp, 1dc into next dc] 6 times,, working last dc into last dc at end of last round.
4th round: * 4ch, 2dc into next 4ch sp, 1dc into each of next 2dc; rep from * to end.
5th round: *4ch, 2dc into next 4ch sp, 1dc into each of next 3dc; rep from * to end.
Cont in this way, working 1 more dc in each group on each round until motif is the required size, ending with a sl st into next dc.
Cast off.

Popcorn Wheel Square

Special Abbreviation: Popcorn = see page 26.

1st round: 3ch, 4tr popcorn into ring (counts as 5tr popcorn), [3ch, 5tr popcorn into ring] 7 times, 3ch, sl st to first popcorn.

2nd round: 3ch (count as 1tr), 2tr into next 3ch sp, [9tr into next sp, 2tr into next sp] 3 times, 8tr into last sp, sl st to top of 3ch.

3rd round: 1ch, 1dc into same place as 1ch, 1dc into each of next 2 sts, *into next 9tr group work 1dc into each of first 3tr, miss 1tr, [1htr, 4tr, 1htr] into next tr, miss 1tr, **1dc into each of last 3tr, 1dc into each of next 2 sts; rep from * twice more and from * to ** again, 1dc into each of last 2tr, sl st to first dc.

Cast off.

SPIRAL HEXAGON

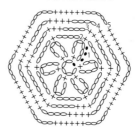

POPCORN WHEEL SQUARE

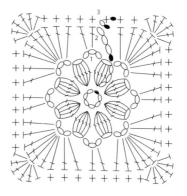

popcorn

Crystal Hexagon

Base ring: 6ch, join with sl st.

1st round: 5ch (count as 1tr and 2ch), [1tr into ring, 2ch] 5 times, sl st to 3rd of 5ch.

2nd round: 4ch, 2dtr in same place as sl st, *2ch, 1dtr into next sp, 3ch, sl st into last dtr, 2ch**, 3dtr into next dtr; rep from * 4 more times, then from * to ** again, sl st to top of 4ch.

Work in back loop only of each dtr from now on.

3rd round: 4ch, 1dtr into same place as sl st, *1dtr into next dtr, 2dtr in next dtr, 7ch**, 2dtr in first dtr of next 3dtr group; rep from * 4 more times, then from * to ** again, sl st to top of 4ch.

4th round: 4ch, 1dtr into same place as sl st, *1dtr into each of next 3 dtr, 2dtr into next dtr, 4ch, miss first 3ch of next 7ch, 1dc into next ch, 3ch, 1dc into same sp, 4ch**, 2dtr into next dtr; rep from * 4 more times, then from * to ** again, sl st to top of 4ch. Cast off.

Flemish Motif

Base ring: 8ch, join with sl st.

1st round: 1ch, 16dc into ring, sl st to first dc. (16 sts).

2nd round: 12ch (count as 1dtr and 8ch), miss first 2dc, [1dtr into next dc, 8ch, miss 1dc] 7 times, sl st to 4th of 12ch.

3rd round: 1ch, *[1dc, 1htr, 1tr, 3dtr, 4ch, insert hook down through top of dtr just made and work a sl st to close, 2dtr, 1tr, 1htr, 1dc] into next 8ch sp; rep from * 7 more times, sl st to first dc.

Cast off.

FLEMISH MOTIF

Boat Steer

Base ring: 4ch, join with sl st.

1st round: 1ch, 10dc into ring, sl st to first dc.

2nd round: 1ch, 1dc into same place as last sl st, [4ch, miss 1dc, 1dc into next dc] 4 times, 4ch, miss 1dc, sl st to first dc.

3rd round: [Sl st into next 4ch sp, 5dc into same loop] 5 times, sl st to first sl st.

Cast off.

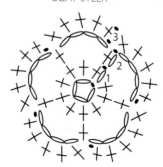

BOAT STEER

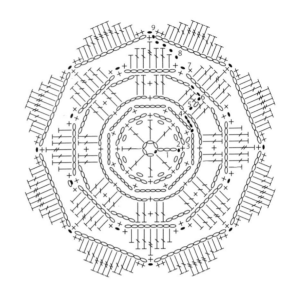

Astro Waves

Base ring: 5ch, join with sl st.

1st round: 4ch, [1tr into ring, 1ch] 7 times, sl st to 3rd of 4ch.

2nd round: [3ch, 1dc into next tr] 8 times, working last dc into first of first 3ch. (8 3ch loops).

3rd round: 1ch, [1dc into next 3ch sp, 6ch] 8 times, sl st to first dc. (8 6ch sps)

4th round: Sl st into each of first 3ch of next 6ch sp, 1dc into same 6ch sp, 6ch, [1dc into next 6ch sp] 7 times, sl st to first dc.

5th round: 1ch, 1dc into same place, *[2tr, 4ch, 2tr] into next 6ch sp, 1dc into next dc; rep from * 6 more times, [2tr, 4ch, 2tr] into next 6ch sp, sl st to first dc.

6th round: Sl st into each of first 2 tr, [1dc into next 4ch sp, 8ch] 8 times, sl st to first dc.

7th round: *[1dc, 1htr, 2tr, 1dtr, 2tr, 1htr, 1dc] into next 8ch sp, sl st into next dc; rep from * 7 more times, working last sl st into first dc.

8th round: Sl st into each of first dc, htr, 2tr and dtr, 1dc in same dtr, 11ch, [1dc in next dtr, 11ch] 7 times, sl st to first dc.

9th round: *[2dc, 2htr, 2tr, 4dtr, 2tr, 2htr, 2dc] into next 11ch loop, sl st into next dc; rep from * 7 more times, working last sl st into first dc.

Cast off.

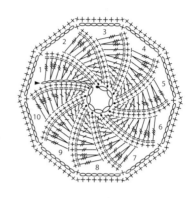

Lazy Wheel

Special Abbreviation: Corded dc = working from left to right, insert hook into each stitch and complete as for dc.

1st Segment

17ch, sl st into 8th ch from hook.

1st row: 1dc into next ch, 1htr into next ch, 1tr into next ch, 2tr into next ch, 1tr into next ch, 2dtr into next ch, 1dtr into next ch, 2trtr into next ch, 1trtr into last ch, 1ch. Do not turn.

2nd row: Work corded dc back from left to right inserting hook under front loop only of each st, ending sl st into ring.

2nd Segment

1st row: Working behind corded dc row into back loop only of 1st row of previous Segment, 1dc into first st, 1htr into next st, 1tr into next st, 2tr into next st, 1tr into next st, 2dtr into next st, 1dtr into next st, 2trtr into next st, 1trtr into next st, 1ch. Do not turn.

2nd row: Complete as for 1st segment.

3rd to 10th Segments

Work as given for 2nd Segment.

Cast off leaving enough yarn to sew 10th Segment to 1st Segment on wrong side.

Edging

1st row (RS): Rejoin yarn at tip of any Segment in corded edge row, 1ch, 1dc into same place as 1ch, [7ch, 1dc into tip of next Segment] 9 times, 7ch, sl st to first dc.

2nd row: 1ch, 2dc into same place as 1ch, *7dc into next sp**, 2dc into next dc; rep from * 8 more times and from * to ** again, sl st to first dc.

Cast off.

Tea Rose I

Base ring: 8ch, join with sl st.

1st round: 1ch, 16dc into ring, sl st into first dc.

2nd round: 5ch (count as 1tr, 2ch), miss next dc, [1tr into next dc, 2ch, miss 1dc] 7 times, sl st into 3rd of 5ch.

3rd round: Sl st into next 2ch sp, 1ch, [1dc, 1htr, 1tr, 1htr, 1dc] into each of the 8 2ch sps, sl st to first dc. (8 petals)

4th round: Working behind each petal, sl st into base of each of next 2 sts, 1ch, 1dc into base of same tr as last sl st, [3ch, miss 4 sts, 1dc into base of next tr] 7 times, 3ch, sl st into first dc.

5th round: Sl st into next 3ch sp, 1ch, [1dc, 1htr, 3tr, 1htr, 1dc] into each of the 8 3ch sps, sl st to first dc.

6th round: Working behind each petal, sl st into base of each of next 3 sts, 1ch, 1dc into base of same tr as last sl st, [5ch, miss 6 sts, 1dc into base of next tr] 7 times, 5ch, sl st to first dc.

7th round: Sl st into next 5ch sp, 1ch, [1dc, 1htr, 5tr, 1htr, 1dc] into each of the 8 5ch sps, sl st to first dc.

8th round: Working behind each petal, sl st into base of each of next 4 sts, 1ch, 1dc into base of same tr as last sl st, [7ch, miss 8 sts, 1dc into base of next tr] 7 times, 7ch, sl st to first dc.

9th round: Sl st into next 7ch sp, 1ch, [1dc, 1htr, 7tr, 1htr, 1dc] into each of the 8 7ch sps, sl st to first dc.

10th round: Working behind each petal, sl st into base of each of next 5 sts, 1ch, 1dc into base of same tr as last sl st, [9ch, miss 10 sts, 1dc into base of next tr] 7 times, 9ch, sl st to first dc.

11th round: Sl st into next 9ch sp, 1ch, [1dc, 1htr, 9tr, 1htr, 1dc] into each of the 8 9ch sps, sl st to first dc. Cast off.

Tea Rose II

Work as given for 1st to 7th round of Tea Rose I.
Cast off.

There is no shortage of inspiration in the everyday
environment. The colours from your favorite dress,
wallpaper and painting have been carefully selected by
the artist so why not use them as inspiration for your own
colour selection? Ensure that you make the most of a
colour palette that has been carefully chosen by an expert.

Celestial Cluster

Base ring: 3ch, join with sl st.

1st round: 10dc into ring, join with a sl st to first dc.

2nd round: [3ch, miss 1dc, 1dc into next dc] 5 times, working last dc into base of first 3ch.

3rd round: *[1dc, 1htr, 1tr, 2ch, 1tr, 1htr, 1dc, 1ch] into each 3ch sp around sl st to first dc.

4th round: Sl st into last 1ch sp, 4ch (count as 1tr and 1ch), *[3tr, 2ch, 3tr] into next 2ch sp, 1ch**, 1tr into next 1ch sp, 1ch; rep from * 3 more times, then from * to ** again, sl st to 3rd of 4ch.

5th round: 4ch (count as 1tr and 1ch), 1tr into same place, 3ch, *[1dc, 3ch, 1dc] into next 2ch sp, 3ch, miss next 3tr and 1ch sp**, [1tr, 1ch, 1tr] into next tr, 3ch; rep from * 3 more times, then from * to ** again, sl st to 3rd of 4ch.

Cast off.

Buckle

1st round: 18ch, sl st to first ch, turn and 7ch, sl st to opposite side of circle.

2nd round: Sl st into next ch, 1dc into each ch around, sl st to first dc.

Cast off.

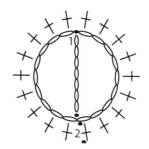

Hydrangea

Special Abbreviation: Bobble = dtr4tog.

Base ring: 7ch, join with sl st.

1st round: 3ch (count as 1tr), 13tr into ring, sl st to top of 3ch. (14tr)

2nd round: 9ch (count as 1dtr and 5ch), 1dtr into next tr, [5ch, 1dtr into next tr] 12 times, 5ch, sl st to 4th of 9ch.

3rd round: 4ch, hold back last loop of each dtr, 3dtr into first sp, yo and draw through all 4 sps on hook (count as first bobble), [5ch, bobble into next 5ch sp] 13 times, 5ch, sl st to top of first bobble.

4th round: Sl st into next 5ch sp, 3ch (count as 1tr), 2tr into same sp, [5ch, 3tr into next 5ch sp] 13 times, sl st to top of 3ch.

Cast off.

HYDRANGEA

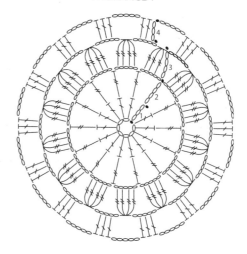

 popcorn

 picot

Stained Glass

Special Abbreviations: Popcorn = 5htr into next dc, drop loop from hook, insert hook from the front into top of first of these htr, pick up dropped loop and draw through, 1ch to secure popcorn.

Picot = 3ch, 1dc into first of these ch.

Base ring: 10ch, join with sl st.

1st round: 1ch, 16dc into ring, sl st into first dc.

2nd round: 2ch, 4htr into first dc, drop loop from hook, insert hook from the front into 2nd of 2ch, pick up dropped loop and draw through, 1ch to secure (1 popcorn made at beg of round), 2ch, 1 picot, 2ch, [miss 1dc, 1 popcorn into next dc, 2ch, 1 picot, 2ch] 7 times, sl st to top of first popcorn.

3rd round: 1ch, 1dc into same st as last sl st, [9ch, 1dc into top of next popcorn] 7 times, 4ch, 1trtr into first dc.

4th round: Sl st into sp just formed, 3ch (count as 1tr), 4tr into same sp as last sl st, 4ch, 1dc into next 9ch sp, 4ch, *[5tr, 5ch, 5tr] into next 9ch sp, 4ch, 1dc into next 9ch sp, 4ch; rep from * twice more, 5tr into same sp as first 5tr, 5ch, sl st to top of 3ch.

5th round: 7ch (count as 1tr, 4ch), *1dc into next 4ch sp, 6ch, 1dc into next 4ch sp, 4ch, [5tr, 3ch, 5tr] into next 5ch sp, 4ch; rep from * 3 more times missing 1tr and 4ch at end of last rep, sl st to 3rd of 7ch.

Cast off.

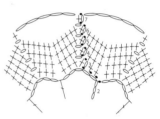

Windmills

Base ring: 6ch, join with sl st.

1st round: 3ch (count as 1tr), 17tr into ring, sl st to top of 3ch.

2nd round: 8ch (count as 1tr, 5ch), [1tr into next tr, 5ch] 17 times, sl st to 3rd of 8ch.

3rd round: Sl st into each of next 3ch of first sp, 1ch, [1dc, 1ch, 1dc] into same ch as last sl st, *2dc into 2nd part of sp and 2dc into first part of next sp, [1dc, 1ch, 1dc] into centre ch of same sp; rep from * 16 more times, 2dc into 2nd part of last sp, 2dc into first part of first sp, sl st to first dc.

4th round: Sl st into first ch sp, 1ch, [1dc, 1ch, 1dc] into same sp as last sl st, 1dc into each of next 6dc, *[1dc, 1ch, 1dc] into next ch sp, 1dc into each of next 6dc; rep from * 16 more times, sl st to first dc.

5th round: Sl st into first ch sp, 1ch, [1dc, 1ch, 1dc] into same sp as last sl st, 1dc into each of next 8dc, *[1dc, 1ch, 1dc] into next ch sp, 1dc into each of next 8dc; rep from * 16 more times, sl st to first dc.

6th round: Sl st into first ch sp, 1ch, [1dc, 1ch, 1dc] into same sp as last sl st, 1dc into each of next 10dc, *[1dc, 1ch, 1dc] into next ch sp, 1dc into each of next 10dc; rep from * 16 more times, sl st to first dc.

7th round: Sl st into first ch sp, 1ch, 1dc into same sp as last sl st, 5ch, [1dc into next ch sp, 5ch] 17 times, sl st to first dc.

8th round: 1ch, 1dc into first dc of previous round, 3ch, 1dc into next 5ch sp, [3ch, 1dc into next dc, 3ch, 1dc into next 5ch sp] 17 times, 3ch, sl st to first dc.

9th round: Sl st into first ch of first 3ch sp, 1ch, 1dc into same sp as last sl st, *4ch, 1dc into next 3ch sp; rep from * to end, 4ch, sl st to first dc.

10th round: Sl st into each of first 2ch of first 4ch sp, 1ch, 1dc into same sp as last sl sts, *5ch, 1dc into next 4ch sp; rep from * to end, 5ch, sl st to first dc.

Cast off.

Window Pane

Base chain: 8ch, join with sl st.

1st round: 1ch, 12sc into ring, sl st to first sc.

2nd round: 7ch (count as 1tr), 1tr into same sc as sl st, *10ch, miss 2 sc, [1tr, 3ch, 1tr] into next sc; rep from * twice more, 5ch, 1tr into 4th of 7ch.

3rd round: *3tr into next 3ch sp, 4ch, sl st into last tr (picot) [4tr, picot, 4tr, picot, 3tr] into same 3ch sp, 1sc into next 10ch sp; rep from * 3 times more working last sc into sp formed by last tr of previous round, sl st to first tr of round.

Cast off.

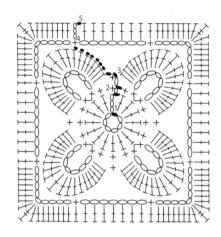

Appliqué Square

Base ring: 6ch, join with sl st.

1st round: 3ch (count as 1dc), 15dc into ring, sl st to top of 3ch.

2nd round: 1ch, 1sc into same st as last sl st, 1sc into next dc, *[1sc, 7ch, 1sc] into next dc, 1sc into each of next 3dc; rep from * 3 more times missing 2sc at end of last rep, sl st to first sc.

3rd round: 1ch, 1sc into same st as last sl st, *[2hdc, 17dc, 2hdc] into next 7ch sp (1 shell made), miss 2sc, 1sc into next sc; rep from * 3 more times missing 1sc at end of last rep, sl st to first sc.

4th round: Sl st into each of first 2hdc and 6dc of first shell, 1ch, 1sc into same st as last sl st, 9ch, miss 5dc, 1sc into next dc, *7ch, miss first 2hdc and 5dc on next shell, 1sc into next dc, 9ch, miss 5dc, 1sc into next dc; rep from * twice more, 7ch, sl st to first sc.

5th round: 3ch, *[8dc, 1tr, 8dc] into next 9ch sp, 1dc into next sc, 7dc into next 7ch sp, 1dc into next sc; rep from * 3 more times missing 1dc at end of last rep, sl st to top of 3ch.

Cast off.

Ridged Hexagon I

Special Abbreviations: Dc/rb = treble crochet around the back. Yo, insert the hook from the back and from right to left around the stem of the appropriate stitch and complete the treble crochet stitch as usual.

V st = [1dc, 1ch, 1dc]

Base ring: 4ch, join with sl st.

1st round: 3ch (count as 1dc), 1dc into ring, [1ch, 2dc into ring] 5 times, 1ch, sl st to top of 3ch. (6 spaces)

2nd round: Sl st into next dc and into next ch, 3ch (count as 1dc), *1dc/rb around each of next 2dc**, work a V st into next sp; rep from * 4 more times and from * to ** again, 1dc into last sp, 1ch, sl st to top of 3ch.

3rd round: 3ch (count as 1dc), 1dc/rb around each dc and 1 V st into each sp all around, ending with a sl st to top of 3ch. (6 groups of 6dc)

4th round: As 3rd round. (6 groups of 8 dc)

5th round: As 3rd round. (6 groups of 10 dc)

Cast off.

Ridged Hexagon II

Worked as Ridged Hexagon I.
Work 1 round each in colours A, B, C, D and E.

Working in rounds won't give you a headache – you never have to turn the fabric as the correct side always faces you.

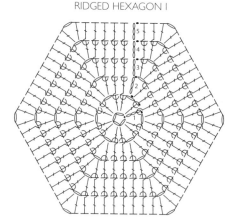
RIDGED HEXAGON I

RIDGED HEXAGON II

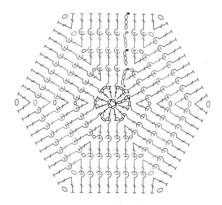

SAMOSA MOTIF

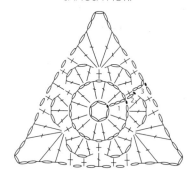

Samosa Motif

Note: On the 1st and 2nd rounds, draw dc loops up to 1.3 cm (½ in.).

Base ring: 6ch, join with sl st to form a ring.

1st round: 4ch (count as 1dc, 1ch), 1dc into ring, *[2ch, 1dc, 1ch, 1dc] 5 times, 2ch, sl st to 3rd of 4ch.

2nd round: *1sc into next sp, [1dc, 1ch] twice into next sp, 1dc into same sp; rep from * 5 more times, sl st to first sc.

3rd round: 4ch (count as 1dc, 1ch), *[1sc into next 1ch sp, 1ch] twice, (1 long dc drawing loop up to 1 inch, 1ch, 1 long dc, 5ch, 1 long dc, 1ch, 1 long dc) into next sc for a corner group, [1ch, 1sc into next 1ch sp] twice, 1ch**, 1dc into next sc, 1ch; rep from * once more, then from * to ** again, sl st to 3rd of 4ch.

Cast off.

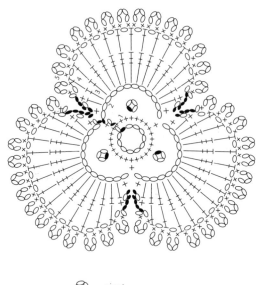

Solar System

Special Abbreviation: Picot = 3ch, sl st to first of these ch.
Base ring: 10ch, join with sl st.
1st round: 1ch, 5sc into ring, 1 picot, [8sc into ring, 1 picot] twice, 3sc into ring, sl st into first sc.
2nd round: 1ch, 1sc into same st as last sl st, *12ch, miss [4sc, 1 picot, 3sc], 1sc into next sc; rep from * once more, 12ch, sl st to first sc.
3rd round: Sl st into first 12ch sp, 1ch, [1sc, 1hdc, 2dc, 9tr, 2dc, 1hdc, 1sc] into each of the 3 spaces, sl st to first sc.
4th round: *1ch, 1sc into next hdc, 1ch, [1dc into next st, 1ch] 13 times, 1sc into next hdc, 1ch, sl st into each of next 2sc; rep from * twice more missing 1 sl st at end of last rep.

5th round: Sl st into each of first [sl st, ch sp, sc and ch sp], 1ch, [1sc, 4ch, 1sc] into same ch sp as last sl st, [1sc, 4ch, 1sc] into each of next 13 ch sps, *1ch, sl st into each of next [sc, ch sp, 2 sl sts, ch sp, sc and ch sp], 1ch, [1sc, 4ch, 1sc] into same sp as last sl st, [1sc, 4ch, 1sc] into each of next 13 ch sps; rep from * once more, 1ch, sl st into each of last [sc, ch sp and sl st].
Cast off.

Tribal Star

Base ring: 9ch, join with sl st.

1st round: 3ch (count as 1dc), 23dc into ring, sl st to top of 3ch.

2nd round: 10ch (count as 1dc, 8ch), 1sc into 4th ch from hook, 1dc into each of next 4ch, miss 1 dc into ring, 1dc into next dc, *8ch, 1sc in 4th ch from hook, 1dc into each of next 4 ch, miss 1 dc, 1dc into next dc; rep from * 9 more times, 8ch, 1sc into 4th ch from hook, 1dc into each of next 4 ch, sl st to 3rd of 10ch.

Cast off.

Gemini

Base ring: 8ch, join with sl st.
1st round: 4ch (count as 1dc and 1ch), [1dc, 1ch] 11 times into ring, sl st to 3rd of 4ch. (12 dc)
2nd round: 1ch, 1sc into first 1ch sp, 4ch, [miss 2 dc, 1sc into next 1ch sp, 4ch] 5 times, sl st to first sc. (6 4ch sps).
3rd round: 1ch, 1sc into same sc as last sl st, *1ch, [1 long dc drawing loop up to 1 inch, 1ch] 4 times into next 4ch sp, 1sc into next sc; rep from * 4 more times, 1ch [1 long dc, 1ch] 4 times into next 4ch sp, sl st to first sc.
4th round: 5ch (count as 1tr, 1ch), 1tr into same place as last sl st, 1ch, *miss 2 long dc, 1sc into next 1ch sp, 1ch, [1tr, 1ch] 4 times into next sc; rep from * 5 more times, ending [1tr, 1ch] twice into same place as last sl st of previous round, sl st to 4th of 5ch.
Cast off.

Bean Cluster

Special abbreviation: Puff = [yo, insert hook in sp indicated and pull up loop] twice, yo and draw through all 5 loops on hook.
Base ring: 5ch, join with sl st.
1st round: 1ch, [puff into ring, 1ch] 8 times, sl st to top of first puff.
2nd round: 1ch, *[puff, 1ch] twice into next ch sp; rep from * 7 more times, sl st to top of first puff.
3rd round: Sl st into ch sp between first 2 puffs, 3ch (count as 1dc), 4dc into same ch sp, [miss next ch sp, 5dc into next ch sp] 7 times, sl st to top of 3ch.
Cast off.

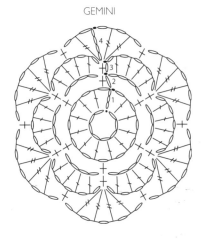

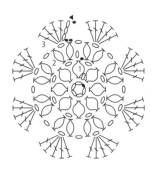

Chrysanthemum

Special Abbreviation: Dtr2tog = 2dtr into next sp until 1 loop of each remains on hook, yo and draw through all 3 loops on hook.

1st round: 5ch (count as 1tr), 19tr into first ch, sl st to 5th ch of 5ch. (20tr)

2nd round: 8ch (count as 1dtr, 3ch), [1dtr into next tr, 3ch] 19 times, sl st to 5th of 8ch. (20 sps)

3rd round: Sl st into first sp, 5ch (count as 1dtr), 1dtr into same sp as sl st, 6ch, [1 dtr2tog into next sp, 6ch] 19 times, sl st to top of first dtr.

4th round: Sl st into each of first 3ch of first sp, 1ch, 1sc into same sp as sl sts, [8ch, 1sc into next 6ch sp] 19 times, 4ch, 1tr to first sc.

5th round: 1ch, 1sc into sp just formed, 9ch, [1sc into next 8ch sp, 9ch] 19 times, sl st into first sc.

off.

CHRYSANTHEMUM

 cluster

Showtime

Base ring: 8ch, join with sl st.

1st round: 1ch, 15sc into ring, sl st to first sc.

2nd round: 5ch, miss first 3sc, [sl st into next sc, 5ch, miss 2sc] 4 times, sl st into sl st at end of previous round.

3rd round: Sl st into first 5ch sp, 1ch, [1sc, 1hdc, 5dc, 1hdc, 1sc] into same sp and each of next 4 sps, sl st to first sc. (5 petals)

4th round: 1ch, working behind each petal of previous round, 1 sl st into last sl st on 2nd round, 8ch, [1 sl st into next sl st on 2nd round, 8ch] 4 times, sl st to same st as first sl st at beg of round.

5th round: Sl st into first 8ch sp, 1ch, [1sc, 1hdc, 8dc, 1hdc, 1sc] into same sp and each of next 4 sps, sl st to first sc.

6th round: 2ch, working behind each petal of previous round 1sl st into last sl st on 2nd round, 10ch, [1sl st into

next sl st on 2nd round, 10ch] 4 times, sl st to same st as first sl st at beg of round.

7th round: Sl st into first 10ch sp, 1ch, 15sc into same sp and into each of next 4 sps, sl st to first sc.

8th round: Sl st into next sc, *[4ch, miss 1sc, sl st into next sc] 6 times, turn, 2 sl sts into first 4ch sp, [4ch, sl st into next 4ch sp] 5 times, turn, 2 sl sts into first 4ch sp, [4ch, sl st into next 4ch sp] 4 times, turn, 2 sl sts into first 4ch sp, [4ch, sl st into next 4ch sp] 3 times, turn, 2 sl sts into first 4ch sp, [4ch, sl st into next 4ch sp] twice, turn, 2 sl sts into first 4ch sp, 4ch sl st into next sp and Cast off*. [With right side facing, miss next 2sc on 7th round, rejoin yarn to next sc and rep from * to *] 4 more times.

Bird Of Paradise

Flower petals: *20ch, miss 2 ch, 1sc into each of next 2 ch, 1hdc into next ch, 1dc into each of next 2 ch, 1tr into each of next 2 ch, holding back last loop of each tr, 1tr into each of next 2 ch, yo and draw through all 3 loops on hook, 1dc into each of next 3 ch, 1hdc into next ch, sl st into each of last 5 ch; rep from * 5 more times. (6 petals made)

Flower base: 1ch, 1sc in base of each of 6 petals, 5ch, turn. Holding back last loop of each tr, 1tr into each of first 5 sc, 2tr into last sc, yo and through all 8 loops on hook.

Stem: 30ch, miss 2ch, 1hdc into each ch to base of flower, sl st to base of flower.

Cast off.

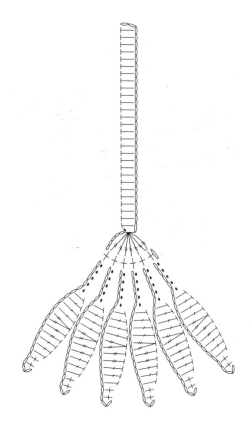

Keep your work clean and protected by wrapping it in a soft fabric or case. This will keep it safe and fresh wherever it goes.

Pulsar Motif

Special Abbreviations: Picot = 5ch, insert hook through top of last dc made, sl st to close.

V st = [2dc, 2ch, 2dc]

Base ring: 8ch, join with sl st.

1st round: 8ch, sl st into 6th ch from hook (counts as 1dc and picot), *4dc into ring, picot; rep from * 6 more times, 3dc into ring, sl st to 3rd of 8ch. (8 picots)

2nd round: Sl st into each of next 2ch, 3ch (count as 1dc), [1dc, 2ch, 2dc] into same picot, *4ch, V st into next picot; rep from * 6 more times, 4ch, sl st to top of 3ch.

3rd round: Sl st into next dc and next ch sp, 3ch (count as 1dc), [1dc, 2ch, 2dc] into same sp, *6ch, V st into next V st

ch sp; rep from * 6 more times, 6ch, sl st to top of 3ch.

4th round: Sl st into next dc and next ch sp, 3ch (count as 1dc), [1dc, 2ch, 2dc] into same sp, *8ch, V st into next V st ch sp; rep from * 6 more times, 8ch, sl st to top of 3ch.

5th round: Sl st into next dc and 2ch sp, 3ch (count as 1dc), 4dc into same ch sp, *1sc into each of next 8ch, 5dc into next 2ch sp; rep from * 6 more times, 1sc into each of next 8ch, sl st to top of 3ch.

Cast off.

picot

bobble

Six-Point Motif

Special Abbreviations: Bobble = 3dc into next st until I loop of each remains on hook, yo and draw through all 4 loops on hook.

Picot = 3ch, sl st into first of these ch.

1st round: 2ch, 12sc into 2nd ch from hook, sl st to first sc.

2nd round: 3ch (count as 1dc), miss first sc, 1dc into next sc, 3ch, [1dc into each of next 2sc, 3ch] 5 times, sl st to top of 3ch.

3rd round: Sl st into next next dc and 3ch sp, 3ch (count as 1dc), [2dc until 1 loop of each remains on hook, yo and

through all 3 loops on hook (bobble made at beg of round), 3ch, 1 bobble] into same 3ch sp, 7ch, *[1 bobble, 3ch, 1 bobble] into next 3ch sp, 7ch; rep from * 4 more times, sl st to top of first bobble.

4th round: 2sl sts into first 3ch sp, 1ch, 1sc into same sp, *[6dc, 1 picot, 6dc] into next 7ch sp, 1sc into next 3ch sp; rep from * 5 more times, missing sc at end of last rep, sl st to first sc.

Cast off.

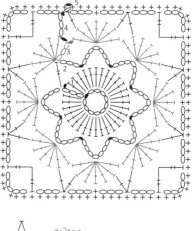

 dc2tog

Celestial Square

Work as given for Floral Lace (page 200), but working 1
round in each of colours A, B and C, then work 4th and
5th rounds in A.

Stay organised and ensure accuracy by clearing a large
space and laying your work out flat when you are
measuring or arranging. Don't try and make do with a
cramped space or working on your lap – it will show in the
quality of your work.

Traffic Lights

Base ring: 6ch, join with sl st.

1st round: 1ch, 2sc into ring, *13ch, sl st into 6th ch from hook, 3ch, miss 3ch, sl st into next ch, 3ch, sl st into side of last sc worked, 4sc into ring; rep from * 3 more times missing 2sc at end of last rep, sl st to first sc. (4 points made)

2nd round: *[1sc, 3dc, 1sc] into each of first 2 sps on next point, 1sc into top sp of same point, [3dc, 1sc] twice into same top sp, then working on other side of loop [1sc, 3dc, 1sc] into each of next 2 sps, 1sl st into each of next 3 sc on first round; rep from * 3 more times missing 1sl st at end of last rep.

3rd round: 1ch, 1sc into same sc as last sl st, *16ch, 1sc into centre sc at top of point, 16ch, 1sc into centre sl st between 2 points on first round; rep from * 3 more times missing 1sc at end of last rep, sl st to first sc.

4th round: 1ch, *1sc into each of next 16ch, 1sc into next sc, 1sc into each of next 16ch, miss 1sc; rep from * 3 more times, sl st to first sc.

Cast off.

4th round: 11ch, miss [first 3sc, 1Sc-Clones Knot, 2sc], sl st into next sc, *11ch, miss [2sc, 1Sc-Clones Knot, 2sc], sl st into next sc; rep from * 4 more times placing last sl st into first sc of previous round.

5th round: 1ch, 15sc into each of the 6 ch sps, sl st to first sc.

6th round: 1ch, 1sc into next sc, 2ch, 1dc into next sc, [1ch, miss 1sc, 1dc into next sc] 5 times, 2ch, 1sc into next sc, *miss 2sc, 1sc into next sc, 2ch, 1dc into next sc, [1ch, miss 1sc, 1dc into next sc] 5 times, 2ch, 1sc into next sc; rep from * 4 more times, sl st to first sc.

7th round: Sl st into first ch, 1ch, 1sc into 2ch sp, *4ch, 1 Clones Knot, 4ch, miss 3dc, 1sc into next ch sp, [4ch, 1 Clones Knot, 4ch, 1sc into next 2ch sp] twice; rep from * 5 more times missing 1sc at end of last rep, sl st to first sc.

8th round: Sl st into each ch to first Clones Knot, 1ch, [working behind Clones Knot 1sc into sc securing Clones Knot, 4ch, 1 Clones Knot, 4ch] 18 times, sl st to first sc. Cast off.

Irish Eyes

Special Abbreviations: Clones Knot = *draw up a chain to required length and hold in place, *yo, twist hook over then under the loop, then pull the yarn back under the loop with the hook; rep from * until the loop is completely covered. Yo, draw hook through all loops on hook**. To secure knot work 1sc into last ch before Clones Knot.

Sc-Clones Knot = work as given for Clones Knot from * to **.

To secure knot work 1sc into last sc before Clones Knot.

Base ring: 18ch, sl st into first ch to form a ring.

1st round: 1ch, 36sc into ring, sl st to first sc.

2nd round: 1ch, 1sc into same st as last sl st, 1sc into each of next 35sc, sl st to first sc.

3rd round: 1ch, 1sc into same st as last sl st, 1sc into each of next 2sc, *[1sc, 1Sc-Clones Knot] into next sc, 1sc into each of next 5sc; rep from * 5 more times missing 3sc at end of last rep, sl st to first sc.

ⓐ   key words

ⓐ   key words

—   key words

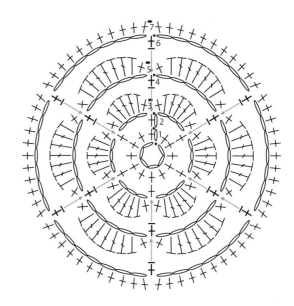

Blossom

Base ring: 6ch, join with sl st.

1st round: 12sc into ring, sl st to first sc.

2nd round: 1ch, 1sc into same sc, [3ch, miss 1sc, 1sc into next sc] 5 times, 3ch, miss 1sc, sl st to first sc.

3rd round: *[1sc, 1hdc, 3dc, 1hdc, 1sc] into next 3ch sp; rep from * 5 more times, sl st to first sc.
Cast off.

4th round: Working in back of petals, join yarn in back loop of sc on 2nd round below last and first petals, [5ch, 1sc in back loop of next sc on 2nd round below next 2 petals] 5 times, 5ch, 1sc into joining st.

5th round: *[1sc, 1hdc, 5dc, 1hdc, 1sc] into next 5ch sp; rep from * 5 more times, sl st to first sc.
Cast off.

6th round: Rep 4th round with 7ch instead of 5ch for each ch sp.

7th round: 11sc into each 7ch sp, sl st to first sc.
Cast off.

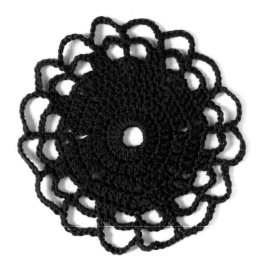

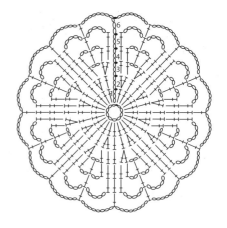

La Fleur De Vie

Base ring: 10ch, join with sl st.

1st round: 3ch (count as 1dc), 23dc into ring, sl st to top of 3ch.

2nd round: 3ch (count as 1dc), 1dc into next dc, 2dc into next dc, [1dc into each of next 2dc, 2dc into next dc] 7 times, sl st to top of 3ch.

3rd round: 3ch, 2dc into next dc, 2ch, [1dc into each of next 3dc, 2dc into next dc, 2ch] 7 times, 1dc into each of last 2dc, sl st to top of 3ch.

4th round: 3ch, 1dc into each of next 2dc, 2ch, 1dc into next 2ch sp, 2ch, [1dc into each of next 5dc, 2ch, 1dc into next 2ch sp, 2ch] 7 times, 1dc into each of last 2dc, sl st to top of 3ch.

5th round: 3ch, 1dc into next dc, 5ch, miss 1dc, 1dc into next dc, [5ch, miss 1dc, 1dc into each of next 3dc, 5ch, miss 1dc, 1dc into next dc] 7 times, 5ch, miss 1dc, 1dc into last dc, sl st to top of 3ch.

6th round: 11ch (count as 1dc and 8ch), miss next dc, 1dc into next dc, [8ch, miss 1dc, 1dc into next dc] 14 times, 8ch, sl st to 3rd of 11ch.

Cast off.

Shamrock

Base ring: 9ch, join with sl st.

1st round: 1ch, 16sc into ring, sl st to first sc.

2nd round: 5ch (count as 1tr), 2tr into same st as last sl st, 3tr into next sc, [7ch, miss 2sc, 3tr into each of next 2sc] 3 times, 7ch, sl st to top of 5ch.

3rd round: 1ch, 1sc into same st as last sl st, *1dc into next tr, 2dc into next tr, 4ch, sl st through top of last dc (picot), 2dc into next tr, 1dc into next tr, 1sc into next tr, 7sc into next 7ch sp, 1sc into next tr; rep from * 3 times more, missing 1sc at end of last rep, sl st to first sc.

Cast off.

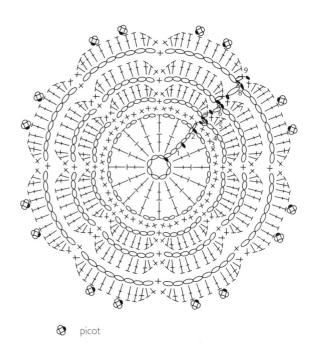

 picot

Anemone

Special Abbreviation: Picot = 3ch, sl st into first of these ch.

Base ring: 8ch, join with sl st.

1st round: 3ch (count as 1dc), 15dc into ring, sl st into top of 3ch.

2nd round: 5ch (count as 1dc, 2ch), [1dc into next dc, 2ch] 15 times, sl st to 3rd of 5ch.

3rd round: 1ch, 3sc into each of the 16 2ch sps, sl st to first sc.

4th round: 1ch, 1sc into same sc as last sl st, *6ch, miss 5 sc, 1sc into next sc; rep from * 6 more times, 6ch, sl st to first sc.

5th round: Sl st into first 6ch sp, 1ch, [1sc, 1hdc, 6dc, 1hdc, 1sc] into each of the 8 6ch sps, sl st to first sc. (8 petals worked)

6th round: 1ch, working behind each petal of previous round, 1sc into first sc on 4th round, *7ch, 1sc into next sc on 4th round; rep from * 6 more times, 7ch, sl st to first sc.

7th round: Sl st into first 7ch sp, 1ch, [1sc, 1hdc, 7dc, 1hdc, 1sc] into each of the 8 7ch sps, sl st to first sc.

8th round: 1ch, working behind each petal of previous round, 1sc into first sc on 6th round, *8ch, 1sc into next sc on 6th round; rep from * 6 more times, 8ch, sl st to first sc.

9th round: Sl st into first 8ch sp, 1ch, [1sc, 1hdc, 3dc, 1 picot, 3dc, 1 picot, 3dc, 1hdc, 1sc] into each of the 8 8ch sps, sl st to first sc.

Cast off.

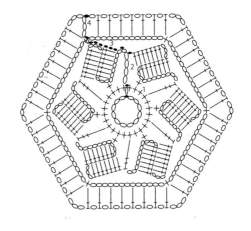

Hamster Wheel

Base ring: 12ch, join with sl st.

1st round: 1ch, 24sc into ring, sl st to first sc.

2nd round: 12ch, miss next sc, 1sc into next sc, turn, *3ch (count as 1dc), 1dc into each of first 7ch of 12ch sp, turn, 3ch, miss first dc, 1dc into each of next 6dc, 1dc into top of 3ch, (one block made)**, miss next sc on ring, 1tr into next sc, 8ch, miss 1sc, 1sc into next sc, turn; rep from * 4 more times, then from * to ** again, sl st to 4th of 12ch.

3rd round: Sl st to 3rd of 3ch at top corner of first block, 1ch, 1sc into top of 3ch, 13ch, [1sc into 3rd of 3ch at top of next block, 13ch] 5 times, sl st to first sc.

4th round: 6ch (count as 1dc and 3ch), 1dc into same place as last sl st, [1ch, miss 1ch, 1dc into next ch] 6 times, 1ch *[1dc, 3ch, 1dc] into next sc, [1ch, miss 1ch, 1dc into next ch] 6 times, 1ch; rep from * 4 more times, sl st to 3rd of 6ch.

Cast off.

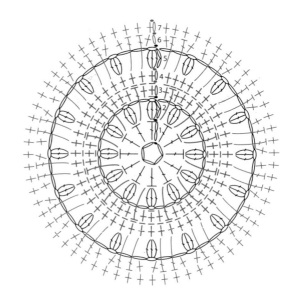

Snail Shell

Special Abbreviations: Popcorn = work 3dc into st, drop loop from hook and insert hook into the first of these 3dc and pick up dropped loop, tighten and draw loop through, 1ch.

Long dc (long double crochet) = yo, insert hook in designated st or row, pull up long lp on hook, (yo, pull through 2 loops on hook) 2 times.

Base ring: Using A, 5ch, join with sl st.

1st round: 2ch, 12dc into ring, sl st to first dc (not in 2ch).

2nd round: 2ch, popcorn into same place as sl st, [2ch, popcorn into next dc] 11 times, 2ch (12 popcorns), draw B through, sl st to back loop of first popcorn.

3rd round: 1ch, 1sc into same place as last sl st, [1sc into next 2ch sp, 1 long dc into base of next popcorn, 1sc into same 2ch sp, 1sc into back loop of top of same popcorn as last long dc] 12 times, missing 1sc at end of last rep, sl st to back loop of first sc.

4th round: 1ch, 1sc into back loop of each st around, sl st to first sc, drop B, draw A through loop.

5th round: 2ch, 1 popcorn into same place as last sl st, [2ch, miss 2sc, 1 popcorn into next sc] 15 times, 2ch (16 popcorns), sl st to back loop of first popcorn, draw B through loop, Cast off A.

6th round: 1ch, 1sc into same place as last sl st, [1sc in next 2ch sp, 1 long dc into each of 2sc between popcorns, 1sc into same 2ch sp] 16 times, sl st to first sc.

7th round: 1ch, 1sc into each st around, sl st to first sc. Cast off.

Spanish Square

Base ring: 8ch, join with sl st.

1st round: 1ch, 16sc into ring, sl st to first sc. (16 sts)

2nd round: 1ch, 1sc into same place as 1ch, [7ch, miss 3 sts, 1sc into next st] 3 times, 7ch, miss 3 sts, sl st to first sc.

3rd round: Sl st across to 3rd ch of next 7ch sp, 3ch (count as 1dc), 1dc into same sp, *[3ch, 2dc] into same sp, 3ch, dc2tog inserting hook into same sp for first leg and into next sp for 2nd leg, 3ch, 2dc into same sp; rep from * 3 more times, missing 2dc at end of last rep, sl st to top of 3ch.

4th round: Sl st into next dc and next ch sp, 3ch (count as 1dc), 1dc into same sp, *[3ch, 2dc] into same sp, 3ch, miss 2dc, 1dc into each of next 3ch, 1dc into next dc2tog, 1dc into each of next 3ch, 3ch, miss 2dc, 2dc into next sp; rep from * 3 more times, missing 2dc at end of last rep, sl st to top of 3ch.

5th round: Sl st into next dc and next ch sp, 3ch, 2dc into same sp, *[3ch, 3dc] into same sp, 6ch, miss [2dc, 3ch, 1dc], 1dc into each of next 5dc, 6ch, miss [1dc, 3ch, 2dc], 3dc into next 3ch sp; rep from * 3 more times, missing 3dc at end of last rep, sl st to top of 3ch.

6th round: 3ch (count as 1dc), 1dc into each of next 2dc, *[3dc, 5ch, 3dc] into next 3ch sp, 1dc into each of next 3dc, 6ch, miss [6ch and 1dc], 1dc into each of next 3dc, 6ch, miss [1dc and 6ch], 1dc into each of next 3dc; rep from * 3 more times, missing 3dc at end of last rep, sl st to top of 3ch.

Cast off.

Crystal Square

Base ring: 10ch, join with sl st.

1st round: 14ch (count as 1dc, 11ch), [5dc into ring, 11ch] 3 times, 4dc into ring, sl st to 3rd of 14ch.

2nd round: Sl st into each of next 5ch, 3ch (count as 1dc), [2dc, 3ch, 3dc] into same ch sp, *9ch, [3dc, 3ch, 3dc] into next sp; rep from * twice more, 9ch, sl st to top of 3ch.

3rd round: 3ch (count as 1dc), 1dc into each of next 2dc, *[3dc, 3ch, 3dc] into next 3ch sp, 1dc into each of next 3dc, 4ch, miss 4ch, 1sc into next ch, make a picot of [3ch, sl st down through top of last st], 4ch, miss 4ch**, 1dc into each of next 3dc; rep from * twice more and from * to ** again, sl st to top of 3ch.

4th round: 3ch (count as 1dc), 1dc into each of next 5dc, *[3dc, 3ch, 3dc] into next 3ch sp, 1dc into each of next 6dc, 9ch**, 1dc into each of next 6dc; rep from * twice more and from * to ** again, sl st to top of 3ch.

5th round: 6ch, sl st to 4th ch from hook (counts as 1dc and picot), *[1dc into each of next 4dc, picot] twice, [3dc, 5ch, sl st to 4th ch from hook, 1ch, 3dc] into next 3ch sp, 1dc into next dc, picot, [1dc into each of next 4dc, picot] twice, 4ch, miss 4ch, 1sc into next ch, picot, 4ch, miss 4ch**, 1dc into next dc, picot; rep from * twice more and from * to ** again, sl st to top of 3ch.

Cast off.

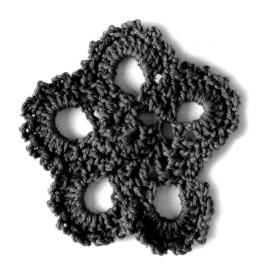

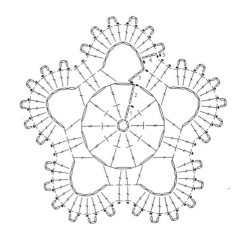

Star Bright

Base ring: 5ch, join with sl st.

1st round: 3ch (count as 1dc), 9dc into ring, sl st to top of 3ch.

2nd round: 5ch (count as 1tr and 1ch), [1tr into next dc, 1ch] 9 times, sl st to 4th of 5ch.

3rd round: Sl st into first sp, 11ch (count as 1dc and 8ch), [1dc into same sp, 2dc into next sp, 1dc into next sp, 8ch] 4 times, 1dc into same sp, 2dc into next sp, sl st to 3rd of 11ch.

4th round: Sl st into first 8ch sp, 3ch, 11dc into same sp, [miss 1dc, 1dc into each of next 2dc, miss 1dc, 12dc into next sp] 4 times, miss 1dc, 1dc into each of next 2dc, sl st to top of 3ch.

5th round: *[3ch, sl st into each of next 2dc] 5 times, 3ch, sl st into each of next 4dc; rep from * 4 times more missing 1dc at end of last rep, sl st to first of first 3ch. Cast off.

Invest in a good-quality tape measure and replace it as soon as it starts to tire. Over the years they can become stretched and worn–an elastic measure will certainly do you no favours.

Eyelet Square

Base ring: 8ch, join with sl st.

1st round: 1ch, 16dc into ring, sl st to first dc.

2nd round: 1ch, 1dc into same place as last sl st, [10ch, miss 3dc, 1dc into next dc] 3 times, 10ch, miss 3dc, sl st to first dc.

3rd round: 1ch, 1dc into same place as last sl st, [11dc into next 10ch sp, 1dc into next dc] 3 times, 11dc into next 10ch sp, sl st to first dc.

4th round: 1ch, 1dc into same place as last sl st, 1dc into each of next 5dc, [2dc into next dc to form corner, 1dc into each of next 11sts] 3 times, 2dc into next dc, 1dc into each of next 5dc, sl st to first dc.

5th round: 1ch, 1dc into each dc and 2dc in first dc of increase at each corner, sl st to first dc.

Rep 5th round for desired size.

Cast off.

Magdalene Motif

Base ring: 5ch, join with sl st.

1st round: 6ch (count as 1dtr, 2ch), *dtr in ring, 2ch; rep from * around 6 times more, join with sl st in 4th of 6ch.

2nd round: Sl st in next sp, 4ch (count as 1dtr), 4dtr in same sp, *2ch, 5dtr in next sp; rep from * around, 2ch, sl st to top of 4ch.

3rd round: 4ch (count as 1dtr), 1dtr in same place as sl st, 1dtr in next 4dtr, *1dtr in first ch of 2ch, 3ch, 1dtr in next ch of same 2ch, 1dtr in next 5 dtr; rep from * around to last 2ch sp, 1dtr in first ch of 2ch, 3ch, sl st to top of 4ch.

Cast off.

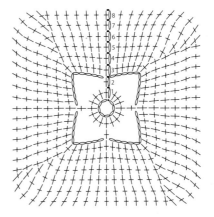

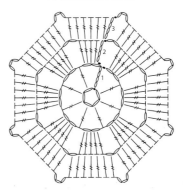

MAGDELENE MOTIF

Begonia Square

Special Abbreviation: Bobble = work 5dtr until 1 loop of each remains on hook, yo and draw through all 6 loops on hook.

Base ring: Using A, 4ch, join with sl st.

1st round: Using A, 4ch, work 4dtr until loop of each remains on hook, yo and draw through all 5 loops on hook (count as 1st bobble), 4ch, *[bobble, 4ch into ring] 7 times, sl st to top of first bobble. Cast off A.

2nd round: Join B to a 4ch sp, 3ch (count as 1tr), 3tr into same sp, *4tr into next sp, 6ch, 4tr into next sp; rep from * twice more, 4tr into next sp, 6ch, sl st to top of 3ch (count as 1tr).

Cast off.

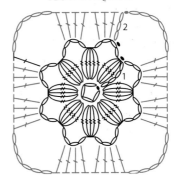

BEGONIA SQUARE

Prairie Motif

Special Abbreviation: Popcorn = 4tr into next ch sp, drop loop from hook, insert hook under 2 loops at top of first of the 4tr and through dropped loop, draw loop through tr.

Base ring: Using A, 12ch, join with sl st.

1st round: 5ch (count as 1dtr, 1ch), [1dtr in ring, 1ch] 15 times, sl st to 4th of 5ch. (16ch sps)

2nd round: 4ch, 3tr into first ch sp, drop loop from hook, insert hook in 4th of 4ch and through dropped loop, draw loop through ch (count as 1st popcorn), 2ch, [popcorn, 2ch] 15 times, sl st to top of 4ch. Cast off A.

3rd round: Join B in any 2ch sp, 3ch (count as 1tr), 3tr into same sp, 2ch, 4tr into same sp (corner), *[3ch, 1dc into next 2ch sp] 3 times, 3ch, [4tr, 2ch, 4tr] into next 2ch sp for corner; rep from * twice more, [3ch, 1dc into next 2ch sp] 3 times, 3ch, sl st to top of 3ch.

4th round: Sl st to first 2ch sp, 3ch (count as 1tr), [3tr, 2ch, 4tr] into same sp, *1ch, miss next 3ch sp, [4tr into next 3ch sp, 1ch] twice, [4tr, 2ch, 4tr] into corner sp; rep from * twice more, 1ch, miss next 3ch sp, [4tr into next 3ch sp, 1ch] twice, sl st to top of 3ch. Cast off B.

5th round: Join A in a corner 2ch sp, 3ch (count as 1tr), [3tr, 2ch, 4tr] into same sp, *[4tr into next 1ch sp] 3 times, [4tr, 2ch, 4tr] into corner sp; rep from * twice more, [4tr into next 1ch sp] 3 times, sl st to top of 3ch. Cast off.

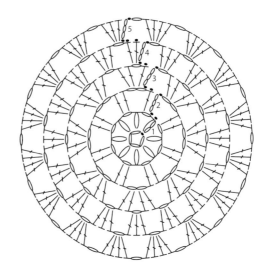

Wagon Wheel

Special Abbreviation: Puff st = [yo, insert hook into ring, draw up a loop] twice, yo and through all 5 loops on hook.

Base ring: 4ch, join with sl st.

1st round: 3ch, htr into ring (counts as 1st puff st), 1ch [puff st, 1ch], 7 times into ring, sl st to top of first puff st (8 petals).

2nd round: Sl st into next ch sp, 3ch, 1tr into first ch sp, 2ch, [2tr, 2ch] into each of next 7ch sps, sl st into top of 3ch.

3rd round: Sl st into next ch sp, 3ch, [1tr, 1ch, 2tr, 1ch] into same ch sp, [2tr, 1ch] twice into each of next 7 ch sps, sl st to top of 3ch.

4th round: Sl st into next ch sp, 3ch, 2tr into same ch sp, 1ch, [3tr, 1ch] into each of next 15 ch sps, sl st to top of 3ch.

5th round: Sl st into next ch sp, 3ch, 3tr into same ch sp, 1ch, [4tr, 1ch] into each of next 15 ch sps, sl st to top of 3ch.

Rep 4th 5th round as many times as desired for size but after 5th round, 2ch between tr groups.

Cast off.

Summer Spiral

Base ring: 6ch, join with sl st.
1st round: 6ch (count as 1dtr and 2ch), [1dtr into ring, 2ch] 7 times, sl st to 4th of 6ch.
2nd round: Sl st into next sp, 4ch (count as 1dtr), 4dtr into same sp, [2ch, 5dtr into next sp] 7 times, 2ch, sl st to top of 4ch.
3rd round: 4ch, 1dtr into each of next 4dtr, [1dtr into first ch of next 2ch, 3ch, 1dtr into next ch of same 2ch, 1dtr into each of next 5dtr] 7 times, 1dtr into first ch of next 2ch, 3ch, 1dtr into next ch of same 2ch, sl st to top of 4ch.
Cast off.

Starfish

Base ring: 9ch, join with sl st.
1st round: 1ch, 18dc into ring, sl st to first dc.
2nd round: 9ch, 1dc into 4th ch from hook, 1htr into each of next 2ch, 1tr into each of next 3ch, miss first 3dc on ring, sl st into next dc, *9ch, 1dc into 4th ch from hook, 1htr into each of next 2ch, 1tr into each of next 3ch, miss next 2 dc on ring, sl st into next dc; rep from * 4 times more placing last sl st into same st as sl st of previous round.
Cast off.

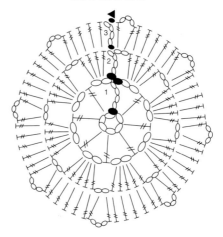

STARFISH

Petit Point

Base ring: 6ch, join with sl st.

1st round: 1ch, 12dc into ring, sl st to first dc.

2nd round: 1ch, [1dc into next dc, 2dc into next dc] 6 times, sl st to first dc.

3rd round: 1ch, [1dc into next dc, 3ch, miss 2dc] 6 times, sl st to first dc.

4th round: [1dc, 1htr, 1tr, 1dtr, 1tr, 1htr, 1dc] into next 3ch sp] 6 times, sl st to first dc.

Cast off.

PETIT POINT

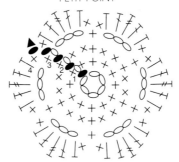

Dutch Medallion

Special Abbreviations: 2dtr bobble = leaving last loop of each on hook, work 2dtr into ring, yo, draw through all 3 loops on hook.

3dtr bobble = leaving last loop of each st on hook, work 3dtr into ring, yo and draw through all 4 loops on hook.

Base ring: 10ch, join with sl st.

1st round: 4ch, 2dtr bobble into ring, *6ch, 3dtr bobble into ring; rep from * 6 more times, 6ch, sl st to top of first bobble.

2nd round: Sl st into each of next 3ch, 4ch, [2dtr bobble, 5ch, 3dtr bobble] into same sp, *5ch, [3dtr bobble, 7ch, 1tr] into next sp, 7ch**, [3dtr bobble, 5ch, 3dtr bobble] into next sp; rep from * twice more, then from * to ** again, sl st to top of first bobble.

Cast off.

Using a smaller sized hook when working on trims will help to create a sharper, tidier and more stylish finish.

French Truffle

Special Abbreviations: 3tr Popcorn = 3tr into ring, drop loop from hook, insert hook in top of 3ch, pick up loop and pull through, 1ch to tighten.

4tr Popcorn = 4tr into ring, drop loop from hook, insert hook in first of the 4tr, pick up loop and pull through, 1ch to tighten.

5tr Popcorn = 5tr into ring, drop loop from hook, insert hook in first of the 5tr, pick up loop and pull through, 1ch to tighten.

Base ring: Using A, 4ch, join with sl st.

1st round: 3ch, 3tr popcorn into ring, *1ch, 4tr popcorn into ring; rep from * twice more, 1ch, sl st to top of first popcorn.
Cast off.

2nd round: Attach B in any ch sp, 3ch, [4tr popcorn, 1ch, 5tr popcorn] into same ch sp, *[1ch, 5tr popcorn] twice into next ch sp; rep from * twice more, 1ch, sl st to top of first popcorn.
Cast off.

3rd round: Attach C in any ch sp between a pair of popcorns, [1sl st, 3tr, 2ch, 3tr, 1sl st] into same sp, *[1sl st, 3tr, 1sl st] into next ch sp, [1sl st, 3tr, 2ch, 3tr, 1sl st] into next ch sp; rep from * twice more, [1sl st, 3tr, 1sl st] into next ch sp, sl st to first sl st.
Cast off.

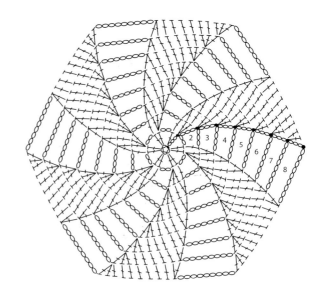

Water Wheel

Base ring: 4ch, join with sl st.

1st round: 3ch (count as 1tr), 1tr into ring, [2ch, 2tr into ring] 5 times, 2ch, sl st to top of 3ch.

2nd round: 3ch (count as 1tr), 2tr into same place as 3ch, 1tr into next tr, *3ch, miss 2ch, 3tr into next tr, 1tr into next tr; rep from * 4 more times, 3ch, miss 2ch, sl st to top of 3ch. (6 segments of 4 tr and 3 ch).

3rd round: 3ch (count as 1tr), 2tr into same place as 3ch, 1tr into next tr, tr2tog over next 2tr, *4ch, miss 3ch, 3tr into next tr, 1tr into next tr, tr2tog over next 2tr; rep from * 4 more times, 4ch, miss 3 ch, sl st to top of 3ch.

4th round: 3ch (count as 1tr), 2tr into same place as 3ch, 1 tr in each of next 2 tr, tr2tog over next 2 tr, *5ch, miss 4ch, 3tr into next tr, 1 tr in each of next 2 tr, tr2tog over next 2 tr; rep from * 4 more times, 5ch, miss 4ch, sl st to top of 3ch.

5th round: 3ch (count as 1tr), 2tr into same place as 3ch, 1 tr in each of next 3 tr, tr2tog over next 2 tr, *6ch, miss 5ch, 3tr into next tr, 1 tr in each of next 3 tr, tr2tog over next 2 tr; rep from * 4 more times, 6ch, miss 5ch, sl st to top of 3ch.

6th, 7th and 8th rounds: As 5th round, but adding 1 more single tr in each tr block and 1 more ch in each ch sp on each round.

Cast off.

Maui Orchid

Special Abbreviation: ttr (triple treble) = yo 4 times, insert hook in next st, yo, draw yarn through st, (yo, draw yarn through 2 loops on hook) 5 times.

Base ring: 8ch, join with sl st.

1st round: 3ch (count as 1tr), 19tr into ring, sl st to top of 3ch.

2nd round: [11ch, miss next tr, sl st into next tr] 9 times, 6ch, 1ttr into sl st at end of previous round.

3rd round: Sl st into loop just formed by ttr, 3ch, [2tr, 3ch, 3tr] into same loop, [3tr, 3ch, 3tr] into each of next 9 loops, sl st to top of 3ch.

Cast off.

Note: After working 3rd round it may be necessary to ease the shells of [3tr, 3ch, 3tr] to centre of loop formed in previous round.

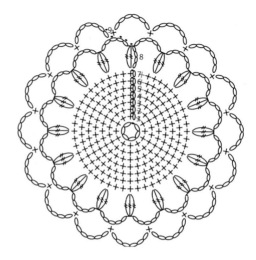

Sunflower

Special Abbreviations: 2dtr bobble = 2dtr into next dc until 1 loop of each remains on hook, yo and draw through all 3 loops on hook.

3dtr bobble = 3dtr into next dc until 1 loop of each remains on hook, yo and draw through all 4 loops on hook.

Base ring: 6ch, join with sl st.

1st round: 1ch, 12dc into ring, sl st to first dc.

2nd round: 1ch, [1dc into next dc, 2dc into next dc] 6 times, sl st to first dc. (18 dc made)

3rd round: 1ch, [1dc into each of next 2dc, 2dc into next dc] 6 times, sl st to first dc. (24 dc made)

4th round: 1ch, [1dc into each of next 3dc, 2dc into next dc] 6 times, sl st to first dc. (30 dc made)

5th round: 1ch, [1dc into each of next 4dc, 2dc into next dc] 6 times, sl st to first dc. (36 dc made)

6th round: 1ch, [1dc into each of next 5dc, 2dc into next dc] 6 times, sl st to first dc. (42 dc made)

7th round: 1ch, [1dc into each of next 6dc, 2dc into next dc] 6 times, sl st to first dc. (48 dc made)

8th round: 4ch, 2dtr bobble in same dc as last sl st, *5ch, miss 2dc, 3dtr bobble in next dc; rep from * 14 more times, 5ch, sl st to top of first bobble.

9th round: sl st to centre of 5ch, 7ch, [1dc in next 5ch sp, 6ch] 16 times, sl st to 1st of 7ch.

Cast off.

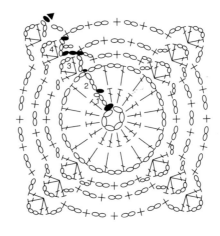

Nanna Square

Base ring: 6ch, join with sl st.

1st round: 3ch (count as 1tr), 15tr into ring, sl st to top of 3ch.

2nd round: 5ch (count as 1tr and 2ch), (1tr into next tr, 2ch) 15 times, sl st to 3rd of 5ch. (16 spokes)

3rd round: 3ch, [1tr, 3ch, 2tr] into first 2ch sp, *[2ch, 1dc into next 2ch sp] 3 times, 2ch**, [2tr, 3ch, 2tr] into next 2ch sp; rep from * twice more, then from * to ** again, sl st to top of 3ch.

4th round: Sl st into next 3ch sp, 3ch, [1tr, 3ch, 2tr] into same ch sp, *[2ch, 1dc into next 2ch sp] 4 times, 2ch ** [2tr, 3ch, 2tr] into next 2ch sp; rep from * twice more, then from * to ** again, sl st to top of 3ch.

5th round: Sl st into next 3ch sp, 3ch, [1tr, 3ch, 2tr] into same ch sp, *[2ch, 1dc into next ch sp] 5 times, 2ch** [2tr, 3ch, 2tr] into next 2ch sp; rep from * twice more, then from * to ** again, sl st to top of 3ch.

Cast off.

Old American Square

Base ring: 6ch, join with sl st.

1st round: 3ch (count as 1tr), 2tr into ring, [2ch, 3tr into ring] 3 times, 2ch, sl st to top of 3ch.

2nd round: Sl st into first 2ch sp, 3ch, [2tr, 2ch, 3tr] into same sp to form corner, *1ch, [3tr, 2ch, 3tr] into next 2ch sp to form corner; rep from * twice more, 1ch, sl st to top of 3ch.

3rd round: Sl st into first 2ch sp, 3ch, [2tr, 2ch, 3tr] into same sp to form corner, *[1ch, 3tr] into each 1ch sp along the side, [1ch, 3tr, 2ch, 3tr] into next 2ch sp to form corner; rep from * twice more, [1ch, 3tr] into each 1ch sp along the side, 1ch, sl st to top of 3ch.

Rep 3rd round for desired size.

Cast off.

Daisy Bloom

Base ring: 8ch, join with sl st.

1st round: 3ch (count as 1tr), 1tr into ring, [6ch, 3tr into ring] 5 times, 6ch, 1tr into ring, sl st to top of 3ch.

2nd round: *1ch, [1dc, 1htr, 7tr, 1htr, 1dc] into next 6ch sp, 1ch, miss 1tr, 1 sl st into next tr; rep from * 5 more times placing last sl st into top of 3ch at beg of previous round.

Cast off.

Springtime Blossom

Base ring: 6ch, join with sl st.

1st round: 3ch (count as 1tr), 15tr into ring, sl st to top of 3ch.

2nd round: 5ch (count as 1tr and 2ch), 1tr into same st as last sl st, *1ch, miss 1tr, [1tr, 2ch, 1tr] into next tr; rep from * 6 more times, 1ch, sl st to 3rd of 5ch.

3rd round: Sl st into first 2ch sp, 3ch (count as 1tr), [1tr, 2ch, 2tr] into same sp, *1ch, [2tr, 2ch, 2tr] into next 2ch sp; rep from * 6 more times, 1ch, sl st to top of 3ch.

4th round: Sl st into next tr and first 2ch sp, 3ch, 6tr into same sp as last sl st, 1dc into next ch sp, [7tr into next 2ch sp, 1dc into next ch sp] 7 times, sl st into top of 3ch.
Cast off.

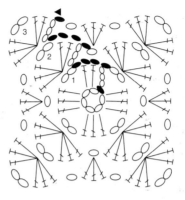

DAISY BLOOM

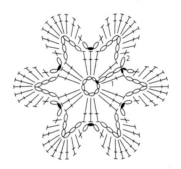

SPRINGTIME BLOSSOM

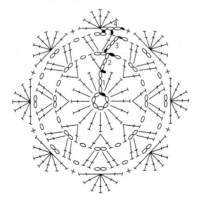

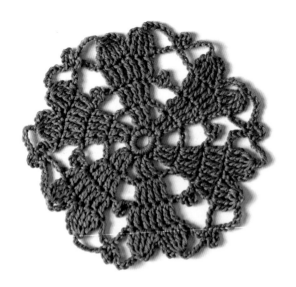

Six-Spoked Wheel

Special Abbreviations: Picot = 6ch, 1dc in 4th ch from hook.

3dtr cluster = yo twice, insert hook into same place as last sl st, yo and pull through, [yo and pull through 2 loops on hook] twice, [yo twice, insert hook into next dtr, yo and pull through, (yo and pull through 2 loops on hook) twice] twice, yo and pull through last 4 loops on hook.

Left cluster = [yo twice, insert hook into next dtr, yo and pull through, (yo and pull through 2 loops on hook) twice] 3 times, yo twice, insert hook into same dtr, yo and pull through, [yo and pull through 2 loops on hook] twice, yo and pull through last 5 loops on hook.

Right cluster = yo twice, insert hook into next dtr, yo and pull through, [yo and pull through 2 loops on hook] twice, yo twice, insert hook into same dtr, yo and pull through, [yo and pull through 2 loops on hook] twice, [yo twice, insert hook into next dtr, yo and pull through, (yo and pull through 2 loops on hook) twice], twice, yo and pull through last 5 loops on hook.

Base ring: 6ch, join with sl st.

1st round: 1ch, 12dc into ring, sl st to first dc.

2nd round: 4ch (count as 1dtr), 2dtr into same place as last sl st, [3ch, miss 1dc, 3dtr into next dc] 5 times, 3ch, sl st to top of 4ch.

3rd round: 4ch, 1dtr into same place as last sl st, [1dtr into next dtr, 2dtr into next dtr, picot, 2ch, 2dtr into next dtr] 5 times, 1dtr into next dtr, 2dtr into next dtr, picot, 2ch, sl st to top of 4ch.

4th round: 4ch, 1dtr into same place as last sl st, [1dtr into each of next 3dtr, 2dtr into next dtr, 9ch, 2dtr into next dtr] 5 times, 1dtr into each of next 3dtr, 2dtr into next dtr, 9ch, sl st to top of 4ch.

5th round: 4ch, 3dtr cluster *5ch, 1sl st into next dtr, 5ch, left cluster, 6ch, miss 4ch, [1dc, 4ch, 1dc] into next ch, 6ch, miss 4ch, right cluster; rep from * 4 more times, 5ch, 1 sl st into next dtr, 5ch, 1 left cluster over next 3dtr, 6ch, miss 4ch, [1dc, 4ch, 1dc] into next ch, 6ch, miss 4ch, sl st to top of first cluster.

Cast off.

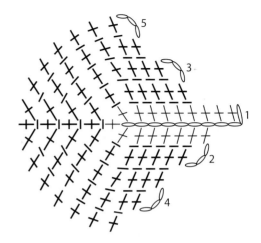

Leaf Over

Flower: 10ch, 1dc into 2nd ch from hook and into each of next 7 ch, 3dc into last ch, work on opposite side of ch, 1dc into each of next 6 chs, turn.

2nd row: 3ch, miss first st, working into back loops of sts, 1dc into each of next 6dc, 3dc into next dc, 1dc into each of next 6dc, turn.

Rep 2nd row 3 more times.

Cast off.

Maui Wheel

Work as given for Maui Orchid (see page 171) but working 1 round each in colours A, B and C.

Treasury

Base ring: Using A, 4ch, join with sl st.

1st round: 1ch, [1dc in ring, 10ch] 8 times, sl st to first dc. Fatsen off A.

2nd round: Join B at top of any 10ch sp, 3ch (count as 1tr), 2tr into same sp, *[3tr, 2ch, 3tr] into next sp for corner, 3tr into next sp; rep from * twice more, [3tr, 2ch, 3tr] into next sp, sl st to top of 3ch. Cast off B.

3rd round: Join C in 2ch of any corner, 3ch, 2tr into same 2ch sp, [1tr into each of next 9tr, 3tr into next 2ch sp] 3 times, 1tr into each of next 9tr; sl st to top of 3ch. Cast off.

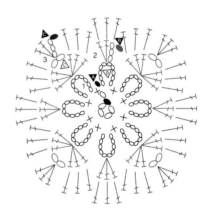

TREASURY

Fern Leaf

1st round: 18ch, sl st into 2nd ch from hook, 1dc into next ch, 1htr into next ch, 1tr into each of next 4 chs, 1dtr into each of next 5 chs, 1tr into each of next 2 chs, 1htr into next ch, 1dc in next ch, sl st into next ch. Cast off. Do not turn.

2nd round: Join yarn in first dc, 1dc into next st, 1htr into next st, 1tr into each of next 5 sts, 1htr into each of next 3 sts, 1dc into each of next 2 sts, sl st into each of next 3 sts.

Cast off.

FERN LEAF

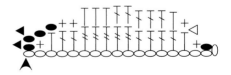

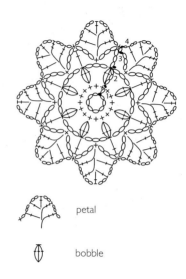

petal

bobble

Genesa Crystal

Special Abbreviations: Petal = 1ch, 1dtr into next dc, 2ch, 1dtr into stem of last dtr two thirds of the way down, 2ch, [1tr, 2ch] twice into stem of last dtr (two thirds of the way down as before), 1tr two thirds of the way down stem of first dtr, 1ch, 1dc into next tr.

Bobble = 3tr into next dc until 1 loop of each remains on hook, yo and through all 4 loops on hook.

Base ring: 8ch, join with sl st.

1st round: 1ch, 16dc into ring, sl st to first dc.

2nd round: 3ch, 2tr into same place as last sl st until 1 loop of each tr remains on hook, yo and draw through all 3 loops, (1 bobble made at beg of round), [3ch, miss next dc, 1 bobble into next dc] 7 times, 3ch, sl st to top of 3ch at beg of round.

3rd round: 6ch (count as 1tr and 3ch), 1dc into next 3ch sp, 3ch, [1tr into next bobble, 3ch, 1dc to next 3ch sp, 3ch] 7 times, sl st into 3rd of 6ch.

4th round: 1ch, 1dc into same place as last sl st, work 8 petals omitting dc at end of last petal, sl st to first dc. Cast off.

Astro Motif

Base ring: Using A, 4ch, join with sl st.

1st round: 3ch (count as 1tr), 17tr into ring, sl st to top of 3ch.

2nd round: 1ch, 1dc into same place as last sl st, [5ch, miss 2tr, 1dc into next tr] 5 times, 5ch, sl st to first dc. (6 loops).
Drop A, draw B through loop on hook.

3rd round: Sl st into first 5ch sp, 3ch (count as 1tr), 6tr into same 5ch sp, [7tr into next 5ch sp] 5 times, sl st to top of 3ch.
Draw A through loop on hook, tighten B, Cast off.

4th round: *Yo twice, insert hook from right to left behind next dc of 2nd round, yo and draw up loop to height of tr of 3rd round, [yo and draw through 2 loops] 3 times (first dtr made), 1dc into each of next 7tr through back loops; rep from * 5 more times, sl st to top of first dtr.

5th round: 1ch, 1dc into same place as last sl st, [5ch, miss 3 sts, 1dc in next st] 11 times, 5ch, sl st to first dc. (12 loops)
Drop A, draw C through loop on hook.

6th round: Sl st into first 5ch sp, 3ch, 5tr into same 5ch sp, [6tr into next 5ch sp] 11 times, sl st to top of 3ch, draw A through loop on hook, tighten C and Cast off.

7th round: 1ch, yo 3 times, insert hook under tr of 4th round, yo and draw up long loop, [yo and through 2 loops] 4 times (trtr worked around dtr), 2ch, trtr around same dtr, miss 1 st, *working through back loops, 1dc into each of next 10 sts, (1trtr, 2ch, 1trtr) around next dtr of 4th round, miss 2 sts; rep from * 4 more times, 1dc into back loop of each of next 10 sts, sl st to first trtr.

8th round: 1ch, *yo, insert hook behind first trtr, yo and draw up loop, yo and draw through 3 loops on hook (1htr worked around trtr), 3dc into next 2ch sp, 1htr around next trtr, 1dc into back loop of each of next 10 sts; rep from * 5 more times, sl st to first htr.
Cast off.

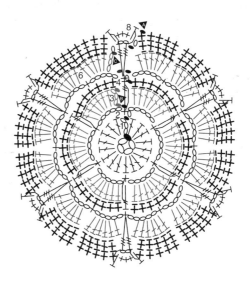

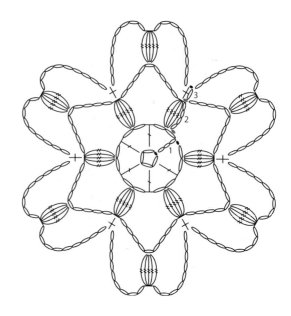

Webbed Flower

Special Abbreviation: Bobble = holding back last loop of each dtr, 5dtr into next sp, yo and draw through all 6 loops on hook.

Base ring: 4ch, join with sl st.

1st round: 5ch (count as 1tr and 2ch), [1tr, 2ch] 5 times into ring, sl st to 3rd of 5ch.

2nd round: Sl st into next sp, 4ch, holding back last loop of each dtr, 4dtr into same sp, yo and draw through all 5 loops on hook, *9ch, bobble in next sp; rep from * 4 more times, 9ch, sl st to top of first bobble.

3rd round: 1ch, 1dc into same place as last sl st, *9ch, miss 4ch, work bobble into next ch of 9ch, 9ch, 1dc into top of next bobble; rep from * 5 more times missing 1dc at end of last rep, sl st to first dc. Cast off.

Give your project a fresh look by mixing knitting and crochet techniques together. Designs often look more contemporary, refined and interesting with simple adornments such as contrasting knitted rib trims or welts.

Framed Star

Base ring: 5ch, join with sl st.

1st round: 6ch (count as 1tr and 3ch), [1tr into ring, 3ch] 7 times, sl st to 3rd of 6ch. (8tr)

2nd round: 3ch (count as 1tr), [4tr into next 3ch sp, 1tr into next tr] 7 times, 4tr into last 3ch sp, sl st to top of 3ch (40 tr made). Cast off.

3rd round: Working behind all tr of 2nd round, attach yarn to top of any tr of 1st round, *8ch (count as 1 long dc and 6ch), 1dc into 2nd ch from hook, 1htr into next ch, 1tr into next ch, 1dtr into next ch, 1trtr into last ch, [1 long dc into top of next tr of 1st round, 6ch, 1dc into 2nd ch from hook, 1htr into next ch, 1tr into next ch, 1dtr into next ch, 1trtr into last ch] 7 times, sl st to 2nd of first 8ch. Cast off.

4th round: Attach yarn to turning ch of any star point, 4ch [1dtr, 3ch, 2dtr] into same ch, *6ch, 1dc into turning ch of next star point, 6ch, [2dtr, 3ch, 2dtr] into turning ch of next star point (corner made); rep from * twice more, 6ch, 1dc into turning ch of next star point, 6ch, sl st to top of 4ch.

5th round: 3ch (count as 1tr), 1tr into next dtr, [5tr into next 3ch sp (corner made), 1tr into each of next 2dtr, 6tr into next 6ch sp, 1tr into next dc, 6tr into next 6ch sp, 1tr into each of next 2dtr] 4 times missing 2tr at end of last rep, sl st to top of 3ch.

6th round: 4ch (count as 1tr and 1ch), miss 1tr, 1tr into next tr, 1ch, miss 1tr, *[1tr, 3ch, 1tr] into next tr (corner made), [1ch, miss 1tr, 1tr into next tr] 10 times, 1ch, miss 1tr; rep from * twice more, [1tr, 3ch, 1tr] into next tr, [1ch, miss 1tr, 1tr into next tr] 8 times, 1ch, miss 1tr, sl st to 3rd of 4ch.

Cast off.

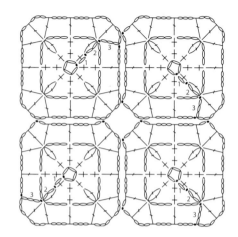

Solidarity Plaque

1st motif

Base ring: 4ch, join with sl st.

1st round: 1ch, 8dc into ring, sl st to first dc.

2nd round: 2ch, 1tr into same place as sl st, *3ch, 1dc into next dc, 3ch, tr2tog in next dc; rep from * twice more, 3ch, 1dc into next dc, 3ch, sl st to top of 3ch.

3rd round: 6ch (count as 1tr and 3ch), [1tr, 3ch] twice into same place as last sl st, 1tr into next dc, 3ch, *[1tr, 3ch] 3 times into top of next tr2tog, 1tr into next dc, 3ch; rep from * 2 twice more, sl st to 3rd of 6ch.

2nd motif:

Follow pattern for 1st motif through round 2.

3rd round: 5ch (count as 1tr and 2ch), sl st in 3ch sp of 1st motif corner group, 1ch, [1tr, 3ch] twice into same place as last sl st from prev rnd, 1tr into next dc, 3ch, *[1tr, 3ch] 3 times into top of next tr2tog, 1tr into next

dc, 3ch; rep from * once more, (1tr, 3ch, 1tr) in next tr2tog, 2ch, sl st in 3ch sp of corresponding corner of 1st motif, (1ch, 1tr) in same tr2tog, 3ch, 1tr in next dc, 3ch, sl st to 3rd of 6ch.

Join 3rd motif to bottom edge of 1st motif as for 2nd motif. Join 4th motif as for 2nd motif except also join corresponding corner sps to 2nd motif.

Cast off.

.

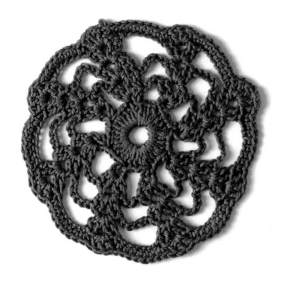

Ripples

Base ring: 8ch, join with sl st.

1st round: 8ch, sl st into 5th ch from hook (picot), *4tr into ring, 5ch, sl st into top of last tr made (picot); rep from * 6 more times, ending 3tr into ring, sl st to 3rd of 8ch.

2nd round: Sl st into centre of first picot, 3ch (count as 1tr), [1tr, 2ch, 2tr] into same picot, *4ch, [2tr, 2ch, 2tr] into next picot (shell); rep from * 6 more times, 4ch, sl st to top of 3ch.

3rd round: Sl st into next tr and into next 2ch sp, 3ch (count as 1tr), [1tr, 2ch, 2tr] into same sp, *6ch, shell into 2ch sp of next shell; rep from * 6 more times, 6ch, sl st to top of 3ch.

4th round: Sl st into next tr and into next 2ch sp, 3ch, [1tr, 2ch, 2tr] into same ch sp, *8ch, shell into 2ch sp of next shell; rep from * 6 more times, 8ch, sl st to top of 3ch.

5th round: Sl st into next tr and into next 2ch sp, 3ch, 3tr into same sp, *1dc into each ch of next 8ch, 4tr into next 2ch sp; rep from * 6 more times, ending 1dc into each ch of next 8ch, sl st to top of 3ch.

Cast off.

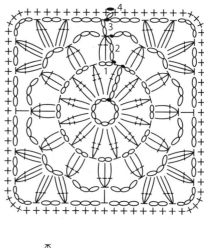

 3tr

 dtr2tog

Doily Square

Special Abbreviations: Dtr2tog = 2dtr into ring until 1 loop of each remains on hook, yo and draw through all 3 loops on hook.

Bobble = work 3tr into sp until 1 loop of each remains on hook, yo and draw through all 4 loops on hook.

Base ring: 10ch, join with sl st.

1st round: 4ch, 1dtr into ring, 2ch, [dtr2tog, 2ch] 11 times into ring, sl st to first dtr.

2nd round: Sl st into next 2ch sp, 3ch, into same 2ch sp as sl st, work 2tr until 1 loop of each remains on hook, yo and draw through all 3 loops on hook (first bobble made), 3ch, [1 bobble into next 2ch sp, 3ch] 11 times, sl st to top of first bobble.

3rd round: 5ch (count as 1htr and 3ch), miss first 3ch sp, [1 bobble, 2ch, 1 bobble, 4ch, 1 bobble, 2ch, 1 bobble] into next 3ch sp, 3ch, *miss next 3ch sp, 1htr into top of next bobble, 3ch, miss next 3ch sp, [1 bobble, 2ch, 1 bobble, 4ch, 1 bobble, 2ch, 1 bobble] into next 3ch sp, 3ch; rep from * twice more, sl st to 2nd of 5ch.

4th round: 1ch, 1dc into same place as last sl st, *3dc into next 3ch sp, 1dc into next bobble, 2dc into next 2ch sp, 1dc into next bobble, 5dc into next 4ch sp, 1dc into next bobble, 2dc into next 2ch sp, 1dc into next bobble, 3dc into next 3ch sp, 1dc into next htr; rep from * 3 more times missing 1dc at end of last rep, sl st to first dc. Cast off.

Tunisia Flower

Base ring: Using A, 4ch, join with sl st.

1st round: 3ch (count as 1tr), 9tr into ring, sl st to top of 3ch.

2nd round: 1ch, 1dc into same place as last sl st, 2dc into next tr, [1dc into next tr, 2dc into next tr] 4 times, sl st to first dc.

3rd round: 1ch, 1dc into same place as last sl st, 1dc into next dc, 2dc into next dc, [1dc into each of next 2dc, 2dc into next dc] 4 times, sl st to first dc. (20 dc)

4th round: [7ch, 1dc into 2nd ch from hook and into each of next 5ch, sl st into next dc, 1dc into next dc] 10 times, missing 1dc at end of last rep, sl st to dc of first point, turn.

5th round: *Miss sl st and next dc, 1dc into back loop of each of next 6 dc, [1dc, 1ch, 1dc] into top of point, 1dc into each of next 6ch on other side of ch; rep from * 9 more times, sl st to sl st between points, draw B through loop, Cast off A, turn.

6th round: Miss first dc, *1dc into back loop of each of next 6 dc, [1dc, 2ch, 1dc] into 1ch of point, 1dc into back loop of each of next 6dc, miss next 2 dc; rep from * 9 more times missing 1dc at end of last rep, sl st to first dc, turn.

7th, 8th, and 9th rounds: Work as 6th round, through back loops of 6 sts at each side of points with [1dc, 2ch, 1dc] into 2ch sp at each point.

Cast off.

Ringlet

Base ring: 8ch, join with sl st.
1st round: 3ch, 20tr into ring, sl st to top of 3ch.
Cast off.

Aquarius Stitch

Base ring: 8ch, join with sl st.
1st round: 1ch, 16dc into ring, sl st to first dc.
2nd round: 4ch (count as 1dtr), 2dtr into first dc, 3dtr into next dc, 5ch, [miss 2dc, 3dtr into each of next 2dc, 5ch] 3 times, sl st to top of 4ch.
3rd round: 1ch, 1dc into same place as last sl st, *[1htr, 1tr] into next dtr, 2dtr into each of next 2dtr, [1tr, 1htr] into next dtr, 1dc into next dtr, 1dc into each of next 2ch, 3dc into next ch, 1dc into each of next 2ch, 1dc into next dtr; rep from * 3 more times missing 1dc at end of last rep, sl st to first dc.
Cast off.

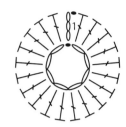

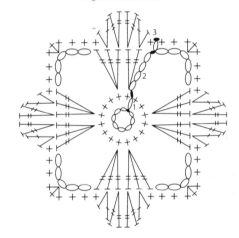

AQUARIUS STITCH

Shell Cluster

Special Abbreviation: Picot = 3ch, sl st into top of last st.
Base ring: 4ch, join with sl st.
1st round: *3ch, 2tr into ring, picot, 1tr into ring, 3ch,
sl st into ring (petal made), 3ch, 3tr into ring, 3ch, sl st into
ring; rep from * once more.
Cast off.

SHELL CLUSTER

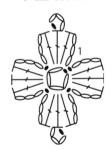

To join a new yarn, start the final stitch and begin to draw
in the new yarn through the last loop of the stitch. Leave
long loose ends to weave in later or work over the ends for
several stitches before snipping them off.

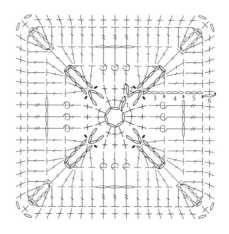

Starburst

Base ring: Using A, 6ch, join with sl st.

1st round: 1ch, [3dc into ring, 4ch] 4 times, sl st to first dc.

2nd round: 1ch, 1dc into same place as last sl st, 1dc into each of next 2dc, [sl st into next 4ch sp, 9ch, sl st into same 4ch sp, 1dc into each of next 3dc] 3 times, sl st into next 4ch sp, 9ch, sl st into same 4ch sp, sl st to first dc. Cast off A.

3rd round: Holding 9ch loop in front, join B in any 4ch sp of 1st round, 3ch (count as 1tr), [1tr, 2ch, 2tr] into same sp, *1tr into each of next 3dc, holding 9ch loop in front, [2tr, 2ch, 2tr] into next 4ch sp of 1st round; rep from * twice more, 1tr into each of next 3dc, sl st to top of 3ch.

4th round: 3ch (count as 1tr), 1tr into next tr, *2tr into next 2ch sp, 1tr into next 9ch loop, 9ch, sl st into top of last tr made, 2tr into same 2ch sp, 1tr into each of next 2tr, 3ch, miss 3 tr, 1tr into each of next 2tr; rep from * 3 more times missing 2tr at end of last rep, sl st to top of 3ch, draw C through loop, tighten B, Cast off.

5th round: 3ch, 1tr into each of next 3tr, *holding 9ch loop to front, in tr where 9ch loop was started work [2tr, 1ch, 2tr], 1tr into each of next 4tr, 1dtr around post of each of next 3tr of 3rd round, 1tr into each of next 4tr; rep from * 3 more times missing 4tr at end of last rep, sl st to top of 3ch.

6th round: 1ch, [1dc in each st to corner 1ch sp, 1ch, 1dc into 9ch loop, 1ch] 4 times, sl st to first dc. Cast off.

Daisy Motif

Base ring: 6ch, join with sl st.
1st round: 1ch, 15dc into ring, sl st to first dc.
2nd round: 1ch, 1dc into same place as last sl st, *[2tr, 1dtr, 2tr] into next dc, 1dc into each of next 2dc; rep from * 4 more times missing 1dc at end of last rep, sl st to first dc. Cast off.

Mandala

Work as given for Six-Point Motif (see page 149) but working 1st and 2nd rounds in A, 3rd round in B, and 4th round in C.

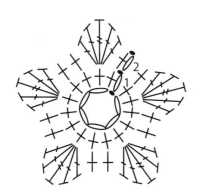

Orchid Blossom

Base ring: 6ch, join with sl st.
Petal: [6ch, 1dc into 2nd ch from hook, 1htr into next ch, 1tr into next ch, 1htr into next ch, 1dc into next ch, sl st into ring] 8 times.
Cast off.

Popcorn Cluster

Base ring: 6ch, join with sl st.
1st round: 5ch (count as 1tr and 2ch), [1tr into ring, 2ch] 7 times, sl st to 3rd of 5ch.
2nd round: 3ch, holding back last loop of each tr; *[3tr, yo and draw through all loops on hook] into next 2ch sp, 1ch; rep from * 7 more times, sl st top of 3ch.
Cast off.

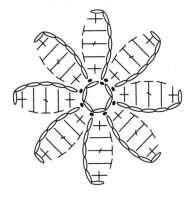

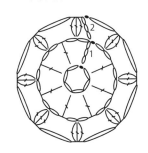

Swirl Motif

Note: This motif is worked as a continuous spiral, the size can therefore be increased or decreased as required.

1st round: 2ch, 6dc into 2nd ch from hook, sl st to first dc. Continue in a spiral as follows:

1ch, 1dc into same st as last sl st, 3ch, [1dc into next dc, 3ch] 5 times, [1dc into next dc, 1dc into next sp, 3ch] 6 times, [miss 1dc, 1dc into next dc, 2dc into next sp, 3ch] 6 times, [miss 1dc, 1dc into each of next 2dc, 2dc into next sp, 4ch] 6 times, [miss 1dc, 1dc into each of next 3dc, 2dc into next 4ch sp, 4ch] 6 times, [miss 1dc, 1dc into each of next 4dc, 2dc into next 4ch sp, 5ch] 6 times, [miss 1dc, 1dc into each of next 5dc, 2dc into next 5ch sp, 5ch] 6 times, [miss 1dc, 1dc into each of next 6dc, 2dc into next 5ch sp, 6ch] 6 times, [miss 1dc, 1dc into each of next 7dc, 2dc into next 6ch sp, 6ch] 6 times, [miss 1dc, 1dc into each of next 8dc, 2dc into next 6ch sp, 7ch] 6 times, miss 1dc, sl st to next dc.

Cast off.

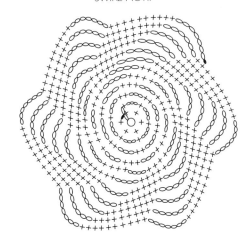

SWIRL MOTIF

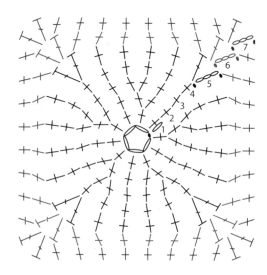

Kerala Stitch

Base ring: Using A 5ch, join with sl st.

1st round: 10dc into ring. Place marker to indicate end of rounds.

2nd round: [1dc into next dc, 2dc into next dc] 5 times. (15 dc)

3rd round: [1dc into each of next 2dc, 2dc into next dc] 5 times. (20 dc)

4th round: 1dc into each dc around, sl st to first dc, draw B through loop on hook, tighten A, Cast off A.

5th round: 3ch (count as 1tr), 1tr into same place as last sl st, 1dc into each of next 4dc, [2tr into next dc, 1dc into each of next 4dc] 3 times, sl st to sp between 3ch and next tr.

6th round: 3ch (count as 1tr), 1tr into same sp as last sl st, [1dc into next tr, 1dc into each of next 4dc, 1dc into next tr, 2tr into sp between 2tr of last round] 3 times, 1dc into next tr, 1dc into each of next 4dc, 1dc into base of 3ch, sl st to sp between 3ch and next tr. Cast off B.

7th round: Attach C between 2tr at any corner, 3ch (count as 1tr), 1tr into same sp, [1dc into each st to next corner, 2tr between corner trs] 3 times, 1dc into each of next 7sts, 1dc into base of 3ch, sl st to sp between 3ch and next tr.
Cast off.

Ring Square

Base ring: Using A, 5ch, join with sl st.

1st round: *[1dc, 1tr, 1dc] into next ch; rep from * 3 more times. (4 petals)

2nd round: *2ch, from wrong side sl st to base of 2nd dc of next petal; rep from * 3 more times.

3rd round: *4tr and 1 sl st into next 2ch sp; rep from * 3 more times, draw B through loop on hook, tighten and Cast off A.

4th round: *3ch, sl st to base of next sl st of previous round; rep from * 3 more times.

5th round: *8tr and 1 sl st into next 3ch sp; rep from * 3 more times.

6th round: Rep 4th round.

7th round: *10tr and 1sl st into next 3ch sp; rep from * 3 more times, draw C through loop, tighten and cast off B.

8th round: 3ch (count as 1tr), 2tr into sl st just made, *2ch, (3tr, 1 ch, 3tr) into 5th tr of next petal, 1ch, 3tr into same tr, 2ch, 3tr into sp before next petal; rep from * 3 times more missing 3tr at end of last rep, sl st to top of first tr. Cast off C.

9th round: Attach D into any corner ch (between two 3tr groups), 3ch (count as 1tr) and in same sp work [2tr, 1ch, 3tr], 2ch, *[3tr into next sp, 2ch] twice, [3tr, 1ch, 3tr] into next sp, 2ch; rep from * twice more, [3tr into next sp, 2ch] twice, sl st to top of 3ch.

Cast off.

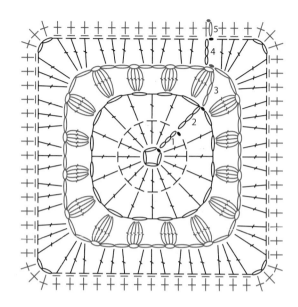

Granny Anne

Special Abbreviations: 4tr Popcorn = 3ch, 4tr into next sp, drop loop from hook, insert hook from front to back through top of 3ch and through dropped loop, draw loop through.

5tr Popcorn = 5tr into next sp, drop loop from hook, insert hook in top of first of 5tr group and through dropped loop, draw loop through.

Base ring: Using A, 4ch, join with sl st.

1st round: 3ch (count as 1tr), 15tr into ring, sl st to top of 3ch. (16 tr in ring)

2nd round: 4ch (count as 1tr, 1ch), [1tr into next tr, 1ch] 15 times, sl st to 3rd of 4ch, draw B through loop on hook, tighten A, break A, and cast off.

3rd round: 4tr popcorn in 1ch sp, 2ch, [5tr popcorn, 2ch] 15 times, sl st to top of 3ch of first popcorn, draw A through loop on hook, tighten B, break B, and Cast off.

4th round: 3ch, 2tr into next 2ch sp, *[3tr into next 2ch sp] twice, [3tr, 2ch, 3tr] into next 2ch sp for corner, 3tr into next 2ch sp; rep from * 3 more times missing 3tr at end of last rep, sl st to top of 3ch, draw B through loop on hook, tighten A, break A, and Cast off.

5th round: Working through back loops, 1ch, 1dc into same place as last sl st, 1dc into each tr round, working 3dc into each 2ch sp at corners, sl st to first dc. Cast off.

 3-picot cluster

Granny Mae

Special Abbreviation: 3-Picot cluster = 4ch, sl st into first ch, [3ch, sl st into same ch as first sl st] twice.

Base ring: 6ch, join with sl st.

1st round: 1ch, 12dc into ring, sl st to first dc.

2nd round: 3ch (count as 1tr), 1tr into same place as last sl st, 2tr into each of next 11 dc, sl st to top of 3ch.

3rd round: 1ch, 1dc into same place as last sl st, 1dc into each of next 23 tr, sl st to first dc.

4th round: 1ch, 1dc into same place as last sl st, 5ch, miss 2 dc, [1dc into next dc, 5ch, miss 2dc] 7 times, sl st to first dc.

5th round: 1ch, 1dc into same place as last sl st, *[1htr, 3tr, 3-picot cluster, 3tr, 1htr] into next 5ch sp, 1dc into next dc; rep from * 7 more times missing 1dc at end of last rep, sl st to first dc.

6th round: 1ch, 1dc into same place as last sl st, *7ch, 1dc into centre picot of 3-picot cluster, 7ch, 1dc into next dc; rep from * 7 more times missing 1dc at end of last rep, sl st to first dc.

7th round: Sl st into next 7ch sp, 1ch, [8dc into next 7ch sp, 3-picot cluster, 8dc into next 7ch sp] 8 times, sl st to first dc.

Cast off.

Posey

Base ring: 6ch, join with sl st.

1st round: 1ch, 24dc into ring, sl st to first dc.

2nd round: 5ch (count as 1tr and 2ch), 1tr into next tr, [1ch, miss 1tr, 1tr into next tr, 2ch, 1tr into next tr] 7 times, 1ch, skip 1tr, sl st to 3rd of 5ch.

3rd round: Sl st into first 2ch sp, 2ch (count as 1htr), [1htr, 2ch, 2htr] into same 2ch sp, 1dc into next 1ch sp, *[2htr, 2ch, 2htr] into next 2ch sp, 1dc into next 1ch sp; rep from * 6 more times, sl st to top of 2ch.

4th round: Sl st into next tr and into next 2ch sp, 3ch, [2tr, 1ch, 3tr] into same 2ch sp, 1dc on each side of next dc, *[3tr, 1ch, 3tr] into next 2ch sp, 1 dc on each side of next dc; rep from * 6 more times, sl st to top of 3ch. Cast off.

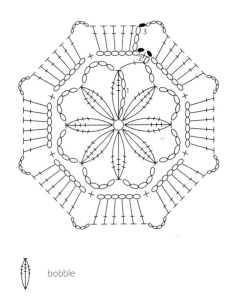

 bobble

African Violet

Special Abbreviation: Bobble = 3trtr into ch until 1 loop of each remains on hook, yo and draw through all 4 loops on hook.

1st round: 6ch, trtr2tog into first ch (count as first bobble), [5ch, 1 bobble] 7 times into same ch, 2ch, 1tr into top of first bobble.

2nd round: 1ch, 1dc into sp just formed, 6ch, [1dc into next 5ch sp, 6ch] 7 times, sl st to first dc.

3rd round: Sl st into first 6ch sp, 3ch (count as 1tr), 5tr into same sp, 3ch, [6tr into next 6ch sp, 3ch] 7 times, sl st to top of 3ch at beg of round.

Cast off.

Brighten up simple knitting with your favourite crochet. Adding a crochet trim or motif section to a piece of plain stocking-stitched background or other basic knit stitch can be extremely effective.

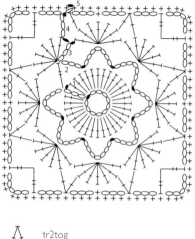

$\bigwedge$ tr2tog

Floral Lace

Special Abbreviation: Tr2tog = 1tr into next tr until 2
loops remain on hook, miss 2tr, 1tr into next tr until 3
loops remain on hook, yo and draw through all 3 loops
on hook.

Base ring: 10ch, join with sl, st.

1st round: 3ch (count as 1tr), 31tr into ring, sl st to top of
3ch.

2nd round: [7ch, miss 3tr, sl st into next tr] 7 times, 3ch,
1dtr into same st as last sl st of previous round.

3rd round: 3ch (count as 1tr), 6tr into top of dtr, [7tr into
4th ch of next 7ch sp] 7 times, sl st to top of 3ch.

4th round: Sl st into next tr, 6ch (count as 1tr and 3ch),

*miss 1tr, [1dtr, 5ch, 1dtr] into next tr, 3ch, miss 1tr, tr2tog,
3ch, miss 1tr, 1dc into next tr, 3ch, miss 1tr, tr2tog, 3ch; rep
from * 3 more times missing 1tr2tog and 3ch at end of
last rep, miss 1tr, 1tr into next tr, sl st to 3rd of 6ch.

5th round: 1ch, 1dc into same place as last sl st, *3dc into
next 3ch sp, 1dc into next dtr, 6dc into 5ch sp, 1dc into
next dtr, 3dc into next 3ch sp, 1dc into top of next tr2tog,
3dc into next 3ch sp, 1dc into next dc, 3dc into next 3ch
sp, 1dc into top of next tr2tog; rep from * 3 more times
missing 1dc at end of last rep, sl st to first dc.

Cast off.

Bull's Eye

Special Abbreviation: Bobble = leaving last loop of each tr on hook, 3tr in same sp, yo and draw through all 4 loops on hook.

Base ring: Using A, 8ch, join with sl st.

1st round: 1ch, 20dc into ring, sl st to first dc.

2nd round: Working through front loops only, 1dc into same place as last sl st, [3ch, 1dc into next dc] 19 times, 3ch, sl st to first dc.

Cast off.

3rd round: Attach B behind A to any dc on first round. Working through back loops only of each dc in first round, holding the 3ch loops forward, 4ch (count as 1tr, 1ch), [1tr into next dc, 1ch] 19 times sl st to 3rd of 4ch.

4th round: Sl st in next 1ch sp, 3ch, tr2tog in same sp (count as first bobble), 5ch, bobble in same ch sp, *bobble in next sp, (bobble, 3ch, bobble) in next sp, bobble in next sp**, (bobble, 5ch, bobble) in next sp; rep from * 3 more times and from * to ** once more, sl st to top of first bobble.

Cast off.

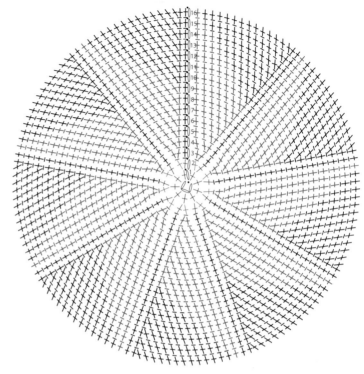

Lotus Circle

Note: Begin with 3rd round, work each stitch in back loop only.

Base ring: Using A, 3ch, join with sl st.

1st round: 1ch, 9dc into ring, sl st to first dc.

2nd round: 1ch, 1dc into same place as last sl st, join B, 1dc in B into same place, [1dc in A and 1dc in B into next st] 8 times, sl st in A to first dc.

3rd round: 1ch in A, 1dc in A into same place as last sl st, [2dc in B into next dc, 1dc in A into next dc] 8 times, 2dc in B into next dc, sl st in A to first dc.

4th round: 1ch in A, 1dc in A into same place as last sl st, [2dc in B into next dc, 1dc in B into next dc, 1dc in A into next dc] 8 times, 2dc in B into next dc, 1dc in B into next dc, sl st in A to first dc.

5th round: 1ch in A, 1dc in A into same place as last sl st, [2dc in B into next dc, 1dc in B into each of next 2dc, 1dc

in A into next dc] 8 times, 2dc in B into next dc, 1dc in B into each of next 2dc, sl st in A to first dc. Cont in this way, working 1 more st in B in each group on every round until there are 8 sts in B in each group (81sts in round).

10th round: 1ch in A, 1dc in A into same place as last sl st, [2dc in A into next dc, 1dc in B into each of next 7dc, 1dc in A into next dc] 9 times missing last dc in A at end of last rep, sl st in A to first dc.

11th round: 1ch in A, 1dc in A into same place as last sl st, [2dc in A into next dc, 1dc in A into each of next 2dc, 1dc in B into each of next 6dc, 1dc in A into next dc] 9 times missing last dc in A at end of last rep, sl st in A to first dc. Cont in this way, still inc 9 sts in every round, but working 1 st less in B in each group on every round until only 1 st in B remains. (144 sts in round)

Cast off.

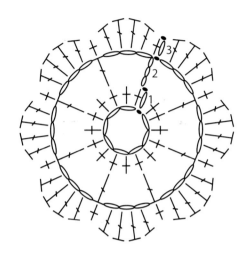

Gemini Spoke

Base ring: 8ch, join with sl st.

1st round: 1ch, 16dc into ring, sl st to first dc.

2nd round: 6ch (count as 1tr and 3ch), miss next dc, [1tr into next dc, 3ch, miss 1dc] 7 times, sl st to 3rd of 6ch.

3rd round: 1ch, 1dc into same place as last sl st, [4tr into next 3ch sp, 1dc into next tr] 7 times, 4tr into next 3ch sp, sl st to first dc.

Cast off.

Don't save the worst until last – work in any ends as you go. This will make finishing a much less arduous task at the end of all your crocheting!

Five-Point Starfish

Base chain: 2ch.

1st round: 5dc into 2nd ch from hook, sl st to first dc.

2nd round: 1ch, 3dc into each dc, sl st to first dc. (15dc)

3rd round: 1ch, 1dc into same place as last sl st, [6ch, sl st into 2nd ch from hook, 1dc into next ch, 1htr into next ch, 1tr into next ch, 1dtr into next ch, 1dtr into base of last dc worked into circle, miss 2dc, 1dc into next dc] 5 times missing 1dc at end of last rep, sl st to first dc. Cast off.

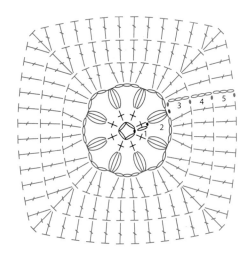

Libra Square

Special Abbreviation: Puff = yo, insert hook into next st, yo and draw up 2.5-cm (1-in.) loop, [yo, insert hook in same st, yo and draw up 2.5-cm (1-in.) loop] 3 times, yo and draw through 9 loops on hook.

Base ring: Using A, 4ch, join with sl st.

1st round: 1ch, 8dc into ring, sl st to first dc, draw B through loop on hook.
Cast off A.

2nd round: Draw B up to 2.5-cm (1-in.) puff in same sp as last sl st, 3ch, [puff in next dc, 3ch] 7 times, sl st to top of first puff.
Cast off B.

3rd round: Attach C in any 3ch sp, 3ch (count as 1tr), 4tr into same sp, [4tr into next 3ch sp, 5tr into next 3ch sp] 3 times, 4tr into last 3ch sp, sl st to top of 3ch.

4th round: 3ch (count as 1tr), 1tr into next tr, [3tr into next tr, 1tr into each of next 8 tr] 3 times, 3tr into next tr, 1tr into each of last 6 tr, sl st to top of 3ch.

5th round: 3ch (count as 1tr), 1tr into each of next 2 tr, [3tr into next tr, 1tr into each of next 10 tr] 3 times, 3tr into next tr, 1tr into each of last 7 tr, sl st to top of 3ch.
Cast off.

Flower In Hexagon

Special Abbreviation: Puff st = [yo, insert hook from the front and from right to left around post of next dtr, yo and pull up a long loop] 5 times, yo and pull through 11 loops on hook, 1ch to tighten.

Base ring: 6ch, join with sl st.

1st round: 4ch, 23dtr into ring, sl st to top of 4ch.

2nd round: 5ch, [yo, insert hook from the front and from right to left around 4ch of previous round, yo and pull up a long loop] 4 times, yo and pull through 9 loops on hook, 1ch, *miss 1dtr, (2tr, 1dtr, 2tr) into next dtr; miss 1

dtr, puff st in next dtr; rep from * 4 more times, miss 1dtr, (2tr, 1dtr, 2tr) into next dtr, miss 1 dtr, sl st to top of first puff st. (6 puff sts).

3rd round: 1 ch, *1dc into each of next 2tr, 3dc into next dtr (corner made), 1dc into each of next 2tr, 1dc into top of next puff st; rep from * 5 more times, sl st to first dc. Cast off.

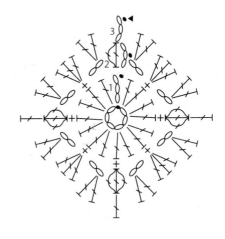

Circle Of Life

Special Abbreviation: Bobble = 3tr into next tr (leaving last loop of each tr on hook), yo and draw through all 4 loops on hook.

Base ring: 6ch, join with sl st.

1st round: 3ch, (count as 1tr), 15tr into ring, sl st to top of 3ch.

2nd round: 3ch, tr2tog in same place as last sl st (count as first bobble), [2ch, miss 1tr, 1dc into next tr, 2ch, miss 1tr, bobble into next tr] 3 times, 2ch, miss 1 tr, 1dc into next tr, 2ch, miss 1tr, sl st to top of 3ch.

3rd round: 3ch, [2tr into next 2ch sp, 3tr into next dc, 2tr into next 2ch sp, 1tr into next bobble] 4 times missing 1 tr at end of last rep, sl st to top of 3ch.

Cast off.

bobble

fan

Granny Jane

Special Abbreviations: Bobble = 3tr into next st until 1 loop of each remains on hook, yo and draw through all 4 loops on hook.

Fan = [1htr, 3tr, 1htr] into next tr.

1st round: 5ch, [1tr, 1ch] 7 times into first ch, sl st to 4th of 5ch.

2nd round: 4ch (count as 1tr and 1ch), 1tr into first ch sp, 1ch, [1tr into next tr, 1ch, 1tr into next ch sp, 1ch] 7 times, sl st to 3rd of 4ch.

3rd round: 3ch (count as 1tr), tr2tog in same place as last sl st (count as bobble), 2ch, [1 bobble into next tr, 2ch] 15 times, sl st to top of first bobble.

4th round: 3ch (count as 1tr), 3tr into first 2ch sp, [1tr into next bobble, 3tr into next 2ch sp] 15 times, sl st to top of 3ch.

5th round: 3ch, [1tr, 1htr] into same place as last sl st, miss 1tr, 1dc into next tr, [miss 1tr, 1 fan into next tr, miss 1tr,

1dc into next tr] 15 times, miss last tr, [1htr, 1tr] into same place as sl st at end of previous round, sl st to top of 3ch.

6th round: 1ch, 1dc into same place as last sl st, 5ch, [1dc into centre tr of next fan, 5ch] 15 times, sl st into first dc.

7th round: Sl st into first 5ch sp, 3ch, 6tr into same sp as sl st, 7tr into each of next 15 5ch sps, sl st to top of 3ch.

8th round: Sl st into each of first 6tr, 1ch, 1dc between last tr worked into and next tr, 6ch, [miss 7tr, 1dc between last tr skipped and next tr, 6ch] 14 times, miss 7tr, 1dc between last tr skipped and 3-ch at beg of previous round, 6ch, sl st into first dc.

9th round: 1ch, 1dc into same place as last sl st, [2ch, 1tr into next 6ch sp] twice 2ch, 2dc into next dc; rep from * 15 more times missing 1dc at end of last rep, sl st to first dc.
Cast off.

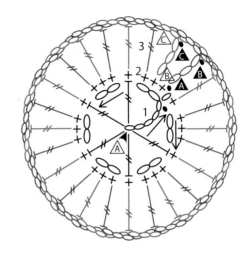

Mediterranean Circle

1st round: Using A, 7ch (count as 1dtr and 2ch), [1dtr, 2ch] 5 times into 7th ch from hook, sl st into 4th ch of 7ch, turn.

2nd round: 1ch, 1dc into same place as last sl st, *[3dc into next 2ch sp, 1dc into next dtr] 5 times, 3dc into next 2ch sp, sl st to back loop of first dc, draw B through loop. Cast off A.

3rd round: 8ch, drop B from hook, join C in next dc, 8ch, *drop C loop, pick up B loop in back of C, 1dtr into next dc, 5ch, drop B, pick up C loop in back of B, 1dtr into next dc, 5ch; rep from * around, ending with first B ch in front, first C ch in back, join last C 5ch with sl st to 3rd ch of first C 8ch and cast off C, keeping first B ch at back, join last B 5ch with sl st to 3rd ch of first B 8ch.
Cast off.

Dahlia

Base ring: 5ch, join with sl st.

1st round: 1ch, 12dc into ring, sl st to first dc.

2nd round: Working into back loop only of each dc, 12ch, sl st into first dc, *sl st into next dc, 12ch, sl st into same dc; rep from * to end.

3rd round: Work as for 2nd round, but into the front loop only of each dc and 8ch only between sl sts. Cast off.

The beauty of crochet is that it is a multi-dimensional medium and thinking in 3-D will help you elevate your designs to new heights! Add crochet motifs, flowers, leaves and outlines of raised double crochet to your knitted or crochet cushion and accessory projects.

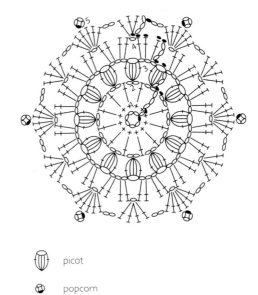

picot

popcorn

Waterwheel Motif

Special Abbreviations: Popcorn = 5tr into next st, drop loop from hook, insert hook into top of first of these tr, pick up dropped loop and draw through, 1ch to secure popcorn.

Picot = 3ch, sl st into first of these ch.

Base ring: 6ch, join with sl st.

1st round: 1ch, 12dc into ring, sl st into first dc.

2nd round: 5ch (count as 1tr and 2ch), miss first dc, [1tr into next dc, 2ch] 11 times, sl st to 3rd of 5ch.

3rd round: Sl st into first 2ch sp, 3ch, 4tr into same sp as sl st, drop loop from hook, insert hook into top of 3ch, pick up dropped loop and draw through, 1ch to secure (1 popcorn made at beg of round), 3ch, [1 popcorn into next 2ch sp, 3ch] 11 times, sl st to top of first popcorn.

4th round: Sl st into first 3ch sp, 3ch (count as 1tr), 3tr into same sp as last sl st, 1ch, [4tr into next 3ch sp, 1ch] 11 times, sl st to top of 3ch.

5th round: Sl st into each of next 3tr and into ch sp, 3ch (count as 1tr), 3tr into same sp as last sl st, 2ch, [3tr, 1 picot, 3tr] into next ch sp, *2ch, 4tr into next ch sp, 2ch, [3tr, 1 picot, 3tr] into next ch sp; rep from * 4 more times, 2ch, sl st to top of 3ch

Cast off.

Orient Motif

Special Abbreviation: Puff = [yo, insert hook, yo and draw up loop] twice, yo and draw through all 5 loops on hook.

Base ring: 4ch, join with sl st.

1st round: 3ch (count as 1tr), 1tr into ring, [1ch, 2tr into ring] 4 times, 1ch, sl st to top of 3ch.

2nd round: Sl st into next tr and next ch sp, puff into same ch sp, [4ch, puff into next ch sp] 4 times, 4ch, sl st to top of first puff.

3rd round: 1ch, 1dc into same place as last sl st, [5dc into next 4ch sp, 1dc into top of next puff] 4 times, 5dc into next 4ch sp, sl st to first dc.

Cast off.

Druid Motif

Base ring: Using A, 6ch, join with sl st.

1st round: 2ch, 1htr into ring (count as htr2tog), [3ch, htr2tog into ring] 7 times, 3ch, sl st to first htr2tog.

2nd round: Sl st into each of next 2ch, 1ch, 1dc into same ch sp, [5ch, 1dc into next 3ch sp] 7 times, 5ch, sl st to first dc.

3rd round: 1ch, [5dc into next 5ch sp] 8 times, sl st to first dc. Cast off.

4th round: Join B to 3rd of next 5dc, 1ch, 1dc into same place as 1ch, *7ch, miss 4dc, 1dc into next dc; rep from * 7 more times missing dc at end of last rep, sl st to first dc.

5th round: 1ch, *[4dc, 3ch, 4dc] all into next 7ch sp; rep from * 7 more times, sl st to first dc.

Cast off.

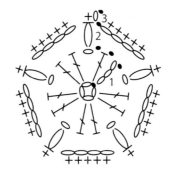

ORIENT MOTIF

Catherine Medallion

Base ring: 6ch, join with sl st.

1st round: 5ch (count as 1tr and 2ch), [1tr into ring, 2ch] 7 times, sl st to 3rd of 5ch.

2nd round: 3ch (count as 1tr), [2tr into next 2ch sp, 1tr into next tr] 7 times, 2tr into next 2ch sp, sl st to top of 3ch.

3rd round: 3ch (count as 1tr), 2tr in next tr, 1 tr in next tr, [1tr in next tr, 2tr in next tr, 1tr in next tr] 7 times, sl st to top of 3ch.

Cast off.

DRUID MOTIF

CATHERINE MEDALLION

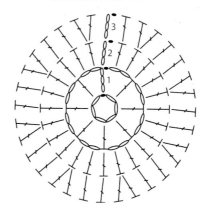

cluster

Star To Star

Special Abbreviation: Cluster = 1dtr into each of next 6tr until 1 loop of each remains on hook, yo and draw through all 7 loops on hook.

Base ring: 6ch, join with sl st.

1st round: 3ch (count as 1tr), 15tr into ring, sl st to top of 3ch.

2nd round: 3ch (count as 1tr), 2tr into next tr, [1tr into next tr, 2tr into next tr] 7 times, sl st to top of 3ch.

3rd round: 3ch (count as 1tr), 2tr into each of next 23tr, 1tr into same place as sl st at end of previous round, sl st to top of 3ch.

4th round: 4ch, 1dtr into each of next 5tr until 1 loop of each remains on hook, yo and draw through all 6 loops on hook (1 cluster made at beg of round), 13ch, [1 cluster over next 6tr, 13ch] 7 times, sl st to top of first cluster.

5th round: 1ch, 1dc into same place as last sl st, *1dc into each of next 6ch, 3dc into next ch, 1dc into each of next 6ch, 1dc into top of next cluster; rep from * 7 more times missing 1dc at end of last rep, sl st into first dc.

6th round: 1ch, miss first dc, 1dc into each of next 7dc, 3dc into next dc, 1dc into each of next 7dc, [miss 1dc, 1dc into each of next 7dc, 3dc into next dc, 1dc into each of next 7dc] 7 times, sl st to first dc.

7th round: 1ch, miss first dc, 1dc into each of next 7dc, 3dc into next dc, 1dc into each of next 7dc, [miss 2dc, 1dc into each of next 7dc, 3dc into next dc, 1dc into each of next 7dc] 7 times, miss next dc, sl st to first dc.

8th round: As 7th round.

Cast off.

Rose

Wind the yarn 3 or 4 times around a finger, remove the loop from finger and fasten with a sl st.

1st round: 1ch, 24dc into ring, sl st to first dc.

2nd round: 6ch, miss next dc, 1htr into next dc, [4ch, miss 2dc, 1htr into next dc] 6 times, 4ch, sl st to 2nd of 6ch.

3rd round: Ch 4, working in dc in 1st round, in front of sts in 2nd round, * miss next 2dc, 1htr into next dc; rep from * 6 times more, 4ch, sl st into 2nd of first 4ch.

4th round: [1dc, 1htr, 3tr, 1htr, 1dc] into each 4ch sp from round 3, sl st to first dc.

5th round: Sl st into back of htr on 2nd round, [5ch, keeping yarn at back of work 1 sl st into back of next htr on 2nd round] 7 times, 5ch, sl st to same htr as first sl st.

6th round: [1dc, 1htr, 5tr, 1htr, 1dc] into each 5ch sp, sl st to first dc.

7th round: Sl st into back of sl st of 4th round, [6ch, keeping yarn at back of work 1sl st into next sl st on 4th round] 8 times.

8th round: [1dc, 1htr, 7tr, 1htr, 1dc] into each 6ch sp, end with a sl st into first dc.

Cast off.

Snowflake Picot

Special Appreviations: Picot = 4ch, sl st into 4th ch from hook.

Dtr-rice stitch = 5ch, 2 dtr into 5th ch from hook whilst holding back last loop of each dtr; yo and pull through all 3 loops on hook.

Base ring: 6 ch, join with sl st.

1st round: 7 ch (count as 1tr and 4ch), *1 tr into ring, 4ch; repeat from * 4 more times, join with sl st to 3rd of 7ch.

2nd round: 1ch, 1 dc into same st, *7dc into next 4-ch sp, 1 dc into next tr; repeat from * 5 times more omitting last dc from last rep, join with sl st to first dc.

3rd round: 1ch, 1dc into same st, 5ch, *sk 3 dc, 1 dc into next dc, 5ch; rep from * around, join with sl st to first dc (12 loops).

4th round: 1ch, 1dc into same st, *7dc into next 5-ch sp, 1dc into next dc; rep from * 10 times more ending with 7 dc into last 5-ch sp, join with sl st to first dc.

5th round: *5 ch, dtr-rice st, 2ch, sk 7 dc, dtr into next dc, 2ch, 3 picots, 3ch, 3 picots, sl st on top of trtr just made, 2ch, dtr-rice st, sk 7dc, 1dc between 7th and 8th dc of round 4, 2ch, 2 picots, 3ch, 2 picots, 2ch, sl st on top of dc just made; rep from * around, join with sl st to first of first 5ch. Cast off.

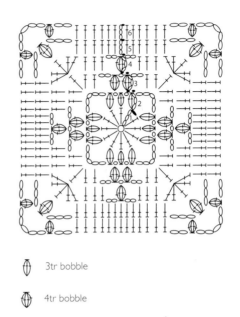

 3tr bobble

 4tr bobble

Bobble Square

Special Abbreviation: 3tr bobble or 4tr bobble = 3 (or 4) tr into st indicated until 1 loop of each remains on hook, yo and draw through all 4 (or 5) loops on hook.

1st round: 4ch, 11tr into first of these ch, sl st into 4th of 4ch.

2nd round: 3ch, 2tr into same place as last sl st until 1 loop of each remains on hook, yo and through all 3 loops on hook (3tr bobble made at beg of round), [1ch, 3tr bobble into next tr] twice, 5ch, *3tr bobble into next tr, [1ch, 3tr bobble into next tr] twice, 5ch; rep from * twice more, sl st to top of first bobble.

3rd round: Sl st into first ch sp, 3ch, into same ch sp as last sl st work 3tr bobble (4tr bobble made at beg of round), *1ch, 4tr bobble into next ch sp, 2ch, 5tr into 5ch sp, 2ch, 4tr bobble into next ch sp; rep from * 3 more times missing bobble at end of last rep, sl st to top of first bobble.

4th round: Sl st into first ch sp, 3ch then complete first 4tr bobble as on 3rd round, *2ch, 1tr into next 2ch sp, 1tr into each of next 2tr, 5tr into next tr, 1tr into each of next 2tr, 1tr into next 2ch sp, 2ch, 4tr bobble into next ch sp; rep from * 3 more times missing bobble at end of last rep, sl st to top of first bobble.

5th round: 3ch, *2tr into next 2ch sp, 1tr into each of next 4tr, 3ch, miss 1tr, 4tr bobble into next tr, 3ch, miss 1tr, 1tr into each of next 4tr, 2tr into next 2ch sp, 1tr into top of next bobble; rep from * 3 more times missing 1tr at end of last rep, sl st to top of 3ch.

6th round: 3ch, 1tr into each of next 6tr, *2ch, miss 2ch, 4tr bobble into next ch, 5ch, 4tr bobble into next ch, 2ch, 1tr into each of next 13tr; rep from * 3 more times missing 7tr at end of last rep, sl st to top of 3ch.
Cast off.

Shells And Popcorns

Special Abbreviation: Popcorn = 5tr into next st, withdraw hook from working loop and insert through top of first of 5tr, insert hook back into working loop and draw through first of 5tr.

Base ring: 6ch, join with sl st.

1st round: 3ch (count as 1tr), 1tr into ring, [3ch, 3tr into ring] 3 times, 3ch, 1tr into ring, sl st to top of 3ch. (4 3tr blocks)

2nd round: 3ch, popcorn into next tr, *[5tr into next 3ch sp, popcorn into next tr, 1tr into next tr, popcorn into next tr] 3 times, 5tr into next 3ch sp, popcorn into next tr, sl st to top of 3ch.

3rd round: 5ch, *miss popcorn, popcorn into next tr, 1tr into next tr, 3tr into next tr, 1tr into next tr, popcorn into next tr, 2ch, miss popcorn, 1tr into next tr, 2ch; rep from * 3 more times missing sl st to 3rd of 5ch.

4th round: Sl st into next 2ch sp, 5ch, *miss popcorn, popcorn into next tr, 1tr into next tr, 3tr into next tr, 1tr into next tr, popcorn into next tr, 2ch, miss next popcorn, 1tr into next 2ch sp, 2ch, 1tr into next 2ch sp, 2ch; rep from * three more times missing 1tr and 2ch at end of last rep, sl st to 3rd of 5ch.

5th round: Sl st into next 2ch sp, 5ch, *miss popcorn, popcorn into next tr, 1tr into next tr, 3tr into next tr, 1tr into next tr, popcorn into next tr, 2ch, [1tr into next 2ch sp, 2ch] 3 times; rep from * 3 more times missing 1tr and 2ch at end of last rep, 5ch.

6th round: Work as 5th round, but working section in brackets 4 times instead of 3.

7th round: As 5th round, but working section in brackets 5 times instead of 3.

Cont working in this way until motif is required size. Cast off.

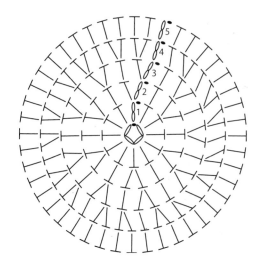

Viking Medallion

Base ring: 4ch, join with sl st.

1st round: 2ch (count as 1htr), 11 htr into ring, sl st to top of 2ch. (12 htr)

2nd round: 2ch (count as 1htr), 1htr into same place as last sl st, 1htr into next htr, [2htr into next htr, 1 htr into next htr] 5 times, sl st to top of 2ch. (18htr)

3rd round: 2ch (count as 1htr), 1htr into same place as last sl st, 1htr into next htr, [2htr into next htr, 1 htr into next htr] 8 times, sl st to top of 2ch. (27htr)

4th round: 2ch (count as 1htr), [2htr into each of next 2 htr, 1htr into next htr] 8 times, 2 htr into next 2htr, htr, 1htr into next htr, sl st to top of 2ch. (44htr)

5th round: 2ch, 1htr into each htr around, sl st to top of 2ch.

Cast off.

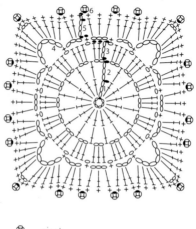

$\oplus$ picot

Reign Of Fire Motif

Special Abbreviation: Picot = 3ch, sl st into side of last dc worked.

Base ring: 6ch, join with sl. st.

1st round: 3ch (count as 1tr), 15tr into ring, sl st to top of 3ch.

2nd round: 5ch (count as 1tr and 2ch), [1tr into next tr, 2ch] 15 times, sl st to 3rd of 5ch.

3rd round: Sl st into first 2ch sp, 3ch (count as 1tr), 2tr into first 2ch sp, 1ch, [3tr into next 2ch sp, 1ch] 15 times, sl st to top of 3ch.

4th round: Sl st into each of next 2tr, 1ch, 1dc into first ch sp, 3ch, 1dc into next ch sp, 6ch, *1dc into next ch sp, [3ch, 1dc into next ch sp] 3 times, 6ch; rep from * twice more, [1dc into next ch sp, 3ch] twice, sl st to first dc.

5th round: Sl st into first 3ch sp, 3ch, 2tr into first 3ch sp, [5tr, 2ch, 5tr] into next 6ch sp, *3tr into each of next 3 3ch sps, [5tr, 2ch, 5tr] into next 6ch sp; rep from * twice more, 3tr into each of last 2 3ch sps, sl st to top of 3ch.

6th round: 1ch, 1dc into same st as last sl st, 1dc into each of next 2tr, 1 picot, 1dc into each of next 5tr, [1dc, 1 picot, 1dc] into next 2ch sp, 1dc into each of next 5tr, *1 picot, [1dc into each of next 3tr, 1 picot] 3 times, 1dc into each of next 5tr, [1dc, 1 picot, 1dc] into next 2ch sp, 1dc into each of next 5tr; rep from * twice more, 1 picot, [1dc into each of next 3tr, 1 picot] twice, sl st to first dc.
Cast off.

Openwork Popcorn Motif

Special Abbreviations: 3dtr bobble = leaving last loop of each st on hook work 3dtr into ring, yo and draw through all loops on hook.

4dtr bobble = leaving last loop of each st on hook work 4dtr into ring, yo and draw through all loops on hook.

Popcorn = 5tr into next st, withdraw hook from working loop and insert into first of 5tr, then back into working loop and draw loop through first of 5tr.

Base ring: 8ch, join with sl st.

1st round: 3ch, [3dtr bobble, 3ch, 4dtr bobble] into ring, *5ch, [4dtr bobble, 3ch, 4dtr bobble] into ring; rep from * twice more, 5ch, sl st to top of first bobble. (8 bobbles)

2nd round: Sl st to 2nd ch of 3 ch sp, 1ch, 1dc into same place, [9dtr into next 5ch sp, 1dc into next 3ch sp] 3 times, 9dtr into next 5ch sp, sl st to first dc.

3rd round: 3ch, popcorn into st at base of 3ch, *2ch, miss 2dtr, 1tr into next dtr, 2ch, miss 1dtr, [2tr, 3ch, 2tr] into next dtr, 2ch, miss 1dtr, 1tr into next dtr, 2ch, popcorn into

next dc; rep from * three more times missing popcorn at end of last rep, sl st to top of first popcorn.

4th round: 3ch, *[2tr into next 2ch sp, 1tr into next tr] twice, 1tr into next tr, [2tr, 3ch, 2tr] into next 3ch sp, 1tr into next tr, [1tr into next tr, 2tr into 2ch sp] twice, 1tr into top of next popcorn; rep from * three more times, missing 1tr at end of last rep, sl st to top of 3ch.

5th round: 6ch, 1tr into st at base of 6ch, *miss 2tr, 1tr into each of next 3 tr, popcorn into next tr, 1tr into each of next 3 tr, [2tr, 3ch, 2tr] into next 3ch sp, 1tr into each of next 3 tr, 1popcorn into next tr, 1tr into each of next 3 tr, miss 2tr, [1tr, 3ch, 1tr] into next tr; rep from * 3 more times, missing [1tr, 3ch, 1tr] at end of last rep, sl st to 3rd of 6ch.

6th round: Sl st to 2nd ch of first 3ch sp, 4ch, *miss next tr, 1tr into next tr, [1ch, miss next st, 1tr into next st] 4 times, [2tr, 3ch, 2tr] into next 3ch sp, 1tr into next tr, [1ch, miss next st, 1tr into next st] 4 times, 1ch, 1tr into 2nd ch of next 3ch sp, 1ch; rep from * 3 more times missing 1tr and 1ch at end of last rep, sl st to 3rd of 4ch.

Cast off.

Embossed Motif

Base ring: 6ch, join with sl st.

1st round: 3ch (count as first tr), 15tr into ring, sl st to top of 3ch. (16 tr)

2nd round: 4ch, [5tr into next tr, 1ch, 1tr into next tr, 1ch] 7 times, 5tr into next tr, 1ch, sl st to 3rd of 4ch.

3rd round: 4ch, 1tr into same place as last sl st, 1ch, [2tr into each of next 5tr, 1ch, 1tr into next tr, 1ch, 1tr into same place as last tr, 1ch] 7 times, 2tr into each of next 5 tr, 1ch, sl st to 3rd of 4ch.

4th round: 3ch, 1tr into same place as last sl st, 1ch, 2tr into next tr, 1ch, [tr2tog 5 times over next 10tr, 1ch, 2tr into next tr, 1ch, 2tr into next tr, 1ch] 7 times, tr2tog 5 times over next 10 tr, 1ch, sl st to top of 3ch.

5th round: 4ch, [1tr into next tr, 1ch] 3 times, *work tr5tog over next 5 tr, 1ch, [1tr into next tr, 1ch] 4 times; rep from * 6 more times, work tr5tog over next 5 tr, 1ch sl st to 3rd of 4ch.

6th round: 4ch, *1tr into next tr, 1ch, [2dtr, 3ch, 2dtr] into next 1ch sp, [1ch, 1tr into next tr] twice, 1ch, 1htr into top of next cluster, [1ch, 1dc into next tr] 4 times, 1ch, 1htr into top of next cluster, 1ch, 1tr into next tr, 1ch; rep from * three more times missing 1tr and 1ch at end of last rep, sl st to 3rd of 4ch.

7th round: 3ch, *1tr into next ch sp, 1tr into next tr, 1tr into next ch sp, 1tr into each of next 2dtr, [2tr, 2ch, 2tr] into next 3ch sp, 1tr into each of next 2dtr, [1tr into next ch sp, 1tr into next tr] twice, 1tr into next ch sp, 1tr into next htr, [1tr into next ch sp, 1tr into next dc] 4 times, 1tr into next ch sp, 1tr into next htr, 1tr into next ch sp, 1tr into next tr; rep from * 3 more times missing 1tr at end of last rep, sl st to top of 3ch.

8th round: 4ch, miss next tr, 1tr into next tr, [1ch, miss next tr, 1tr into next tr] twice, *1ch, miss next tr, [2tr, 2ch, 2tr] into 2ch sp, [1ch, miss next tr, 1tr into next tr] 14 times; rep from * three more times working [1ch, miss next tr, 1tr into next tr] 10 times, 1ch at end of last rep, sl st to 3rd of 4ch.

Cast off.

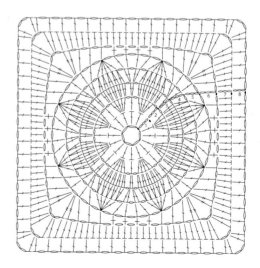

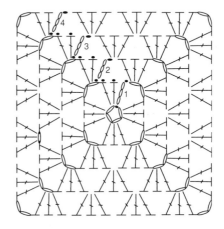

Textured Tile

Base ring: 4ch, join with sl st.

1st round: 3ch (count as 1tr), 2tr in ring, [2ch, 3tr into ring] 3 times, 2ch, sl st to top of 3ch.

2nd round: Sl st into each of next 2tr and next 2ch sp, 3ch, [2tr, 2ch, 3tr] into same sp, [3tr, 2ch, 3tr] into each of next 3 2ch sps, sl st to top of 3ch.

3rd round: Sl st into each of next 2tr and next 2ch sp, 3ch, [2tr, 2ch, 3tr] into same sp, * miss 3tr, 3tr between last tr skipped and next tr, miss 3tr, [3tr, 2ch, 3tr] into next 2ch sp; rep from * twice more, miss 3tr, 3tr between last tr skipped and next tr, sl st to top of 3ch.

4th round: Work as for 3rd round, having 2 groups of 3 tr between corners.

Cast off.

Try using a crochet hook for embroidery. You can easily create simple surface and Aran-effect stitches with basic surface treble crochet.

Six-Point Snowflake

Special Abbreviations: Picot = 4ch, sl st into 4th ch from hook.

Tr rice stitch = 3ch, 2 tr into indicated base st whilst holding back last loop of each tr, yo and pull through all 3 loops on hook, 3ch, sl st into same base st.

Trtr rice stitch = 5ch, 2 trtr into indicated base st whilst holding back last loop of each trtr, yo and pull through all 3 loops on hook, 5ch, sl st into same base st..

Base ring: 6 ch, join with sl st..

1st round: 1 ch, 12 dc into ring, join with sl st to first dc.

2nd round: trtr rice st in same place as sl st, sl st into next dc, *tr rice st in next dc, sl st in next dc, trtr rice st in next dc, sl st in next dc; repeat from * 4 more times, tr rice st in next dc.

3rd round: 5 sl sts to top of trtr rice st, 1ch, 1dc into same st, *7ch, 1dc on top of next trtr rice st; repeat from * 4 times more, 7ch, join with sl st to first dc.

4th round: 6ch (count as 1tr, 3ch), 1tr into same st, *7tr into next 7-ch sp, [1tr, 3ch, 1tr] into next dc; repeat from * 4 times more ending with 7tr into last 7-ch sp, join with sl st to 3rd of 6ch.

5th round: Sl st into 3-ch sp, 3 ch (count as 1tr), *1 trtr into 3ch sp, 1 picot, 8ch, sl st into 8th ch from hook, 10ch, sl st into 10th ch from hook, 14ch, sl st into 14th ch from hook, 3 picots, 4ch, (from now on work on the other side of the picots just made and slip stitch into base ch of respective picot of the other side after completing each one), 3 picots, 14ch, sl st into 14th ch from hook, 10ch, sl st into 10th ch from hook, 8ch, sl st into 8th ch from hook, 1 picot, sl st on top of trtr just made, 1 tr into same 3-ch sp, 1 tr into next tr, 1dc into each of next 3 tr, into next dc work 4tr whilst holding back last loop of each tr, yo and and pull through all 5 loops on hook, 1dc into each of next 3tr, 1tr into next tr, 1 tr into next 3-ch sp; repeat from * 5 times more omitting last tr, end with sl st into 3rd of first 3ch. Cast off.

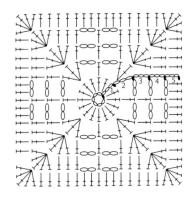

Openwork Cross

Base ring: 6ch, join with sl st.

1st round: 3ch (count as 1tr), 15tr into ring, sl st to top of 3ch.

2nd round: 3ch (count as 1tr), 2tr into same place as last sl st, 2ch, miss 1tr, 1tr into next tr, 2ch, miss 1tr, *3tr into next tr, 2ch, miss 1tr, 1tr into next tr, 2ch, miss 1tr; rep from * twice more, sl st to top of 3ch.

3rd round: 3ch (count as 1tr), 5tr into next tr, *1tr into next tr, [2ch, 1tr into next tr] twice, 5tr into next tr; rep from * twice more, [1tr into next tr, 2ch] twice, sl st to top of 3ch.

4th round: 3ch, 1tr into each of next 2tr, 5tr into next tr, *1tr into each of next 3tr, 2ch, 1tr into next tr, 2ch, 1tr into each of next 3tr, 5tr into next tr; rep from * twice more, 1tr into each of next 3tr, 2ch, 1tr into next tr, 2ch, sl st to top of 3ch.

5th round: 3ch, 1tr into each of next 4tr, 5tr into next tr, *1tr into each of next 5tr, 2tr into next 2-ch sp, 1tr into next tr, 2tr into next 2ch sp, 1tr into each of next 5 tr, 5tr into next tr; rep from * twice more, 1tr into each of next 5 tr, 2tr into next 2ch sp, 1tr into next tr, 2tr into last 2ch sp, sl st to top of 3ch.

Cast off.

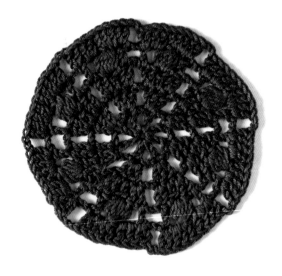

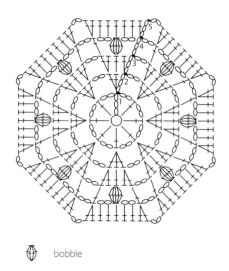

 bobble

Shitake Motif

Special Abbreviation: Bobble = 5tr into next st until 1 loop of each remains on hook, yo and draw through all 6 loops on hook.

1st round: 6ch, into first of these ch [1tr, 2ch] 7 times, sl st to 4th of 6ch.

2nd round: 3ch (count as 1tr), 2tr into same place as last sl st, 2ch, [3tr into next tr, 2ch] 7 times, sl st to top of 3ch.

3rd round: 3ch, 1tr into same place as last sl st, 1tr into next tr, 2tr into next tr, 2ch, [2tr into next tr, 1tr into next tr, 2tr into next tr, 2ch] 7 times, sl st to top of 3ch.

4th round: 5ch (count as 1tr and 2ch), miss next tr, 1 bobble into next tr, 2ch, miss 1tr, 1tr into next tr, 2ch, [1tr into next tr, 2ch, miss 1tr, 1 bobble into next tr, 2ch, miss 1tr, 1tr into next tr, 2ch] 7 times, sl st to top of 5ch.

5th round: 3ch, 1tr into same place as last sl st, 2tr into first 2ch sp, 1tr into top of next bobble, 2tr into next 2ch sp, 2tr into next tr, 2ch, [2tr into next tr, 2tr into next 2ch sp, 1tr into top of next bobble, 2tr into next 2ch sp, 2tr into next tr, 2ch] 7 times, sl st to top of 3ch.
Cast off.

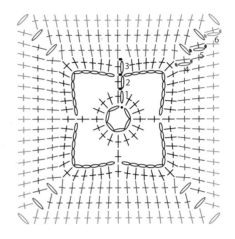

Alpine Square

Base ring: Using A, 6ch, join with sl st.

1st round: 1ch, 16dc into ring, sl st to first dc.

2nd round: 1ch, 1dc into same place as last sl st, 10ch, *miss next 3dc, 1dc into next dc, 10ch; rep from * twice more, sl st to first dc.

3rd round: 1ch, 1dc into same place as last sl st, [11dc into 10ch sp, 1dc into next dc;] 4 times missing dc at end of last rep, sl st to first dc. Cast off.

4th round: Join B to 6th of 11dc in any loop, 1ch, [1dc, 1ch, 1dc] into same place, 1dc into each dc all around and [1dc, 1ch, 1dc] into each corner, sl st to first dc. Cast off.

5th round: Join C to any corner space and work as 4th round. Cast off.

6th round: Join D to any corner space and work as 4th round. Cast off. Cont in the same way, working 1 round in C, then 2 rounds in A.

Cast off.

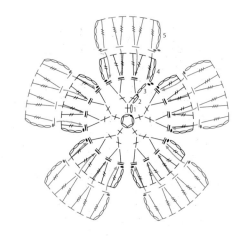

Magnolia

Base ring: Using A, 5ch join with sl st.

1st round: 1ch, 5dc into ring, sl st to first dc.

2nd round: 1ch, 2dc into same place as last sl st, 2dc into each of next 4dc, sl st to first dc.

3rd round: 2ch (count as 1htr), 1htr into same place as last sl st, 2htr into each of next 9dc, sl st to 2nd of 2ch.

4th round: Inserting hook into front loop only of each st, *3ch, 1dtr into same place, 2dtr into each of next 2htr; [1dtr, 3ch, 1 sl st] into next htr; sl st into next htr; rep from * 4 more times.
Cast off.

5th round: Join B behind the centre of one petal, then inserting hook into back loop only of each st of 4th round, work as 4th round but working trtr instead of dtr.
Cast off.

6th round: Join C from front of work, inserting hook from right to left around dc of first round, [3ch, 1dc into next dc] 4 times, 3ch, sl st to same place as join.
Cast off.

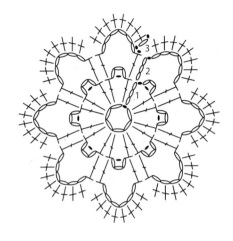

Garden Party

Special Abbreviation: Picot = 3ch, sl st in 3rd ch from hook.

Base ring: 6ch, join with sl st.

1st round: 3ch (count as 1tr), 1 tr into ring, [picot 2tr into ring] 7 times, picot, sl st to top of 3ch.

2nd round: 3ch (count as 1tr), 1tr into next tr, [6ch, 1tr into each of next 2tr] 7 times, 6ch, sl st to top of 3ch.

3rd round: Sl st into next tr and into next 6ch sp, 1ch, 8dc into same 6ch space, [8dc into next 6ch sp] 7 times, sl st to first dc.

Cast off.

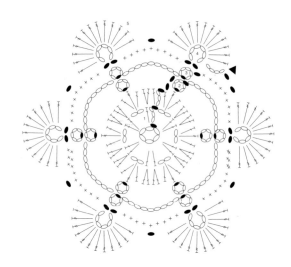

Fanning Points Motif

Special Abbreviation: Picot = 5ch, sl st into top of dtr just made.

Base ring: 6 ch, join with sl st to form a ring

1st round: 3 ch (count as 1tr), 1 tr into ring, *2ch, 2tr; repeat from * 4 more times, 2ch, join with sl st to 3rd of first 3ch.

2nd round: 3 ch (count as 1tr), 1tr into same st, 2tr into next tr, *(1tr, 1dtr, picot, 1tr) into 2ch sp, 2tr into each of next 2tr; repeat from * 4 times more, (1tr, 1dtr, picot, 1tr) into last 2ch sp, join with sl st to 3rd of first 3ch, turn.

3rd round: Sl st to 3rd ch of last picot of previous round, turn, *5ch, sl st into same ch as before, 9ch, sl st to 3rd ch of next picot; repeat from * around.

4th round: *sl st into 5ch loop, 6ch, sl st into same loop, 9dc into 9ch sp; repeat from * around, join with sl st into first 5ch loop.

5th round: 4ch (count as 1dtr), 12dtr into 6ch sp, *sk 4dc, sl st in next dc, sk 4dc, 13dtr into next 6ch sp; repeat from * around skipping 13dtr of last repeat, join with sl st to 4th of first 4ch.

Cast off.

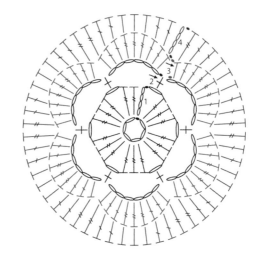

Star Hexagon

Base ring: Using A, 6ch, join with sl st.

1st round: 4ch (count as 1dtr), 2dtr into ring, [1ch, 3dtr into ring;] 5 times, 1ch, sl st to top of 4ch, turn.

2nd round: [1dc into next 1ch sp, 6ch] 6 times, sl st to first dc. Cast off.

3rd round: Join B to a 7ch sp, [1htr, 2tr, 3dtr, 2tr, 1htr] into each 7ch sp, sl st to first htr (6 petals). Cast off.

4th round: Turn, join C to first htr of a petal, 4ch (count as 1dtr), *1tr into each of next 2tr, 1htr into each of next 3dtr, 1tr into each of next 2tr, 1dtr into each of next 2htr; repeat from * around skipping last htr, sl st to top of 4ch. Cast off.

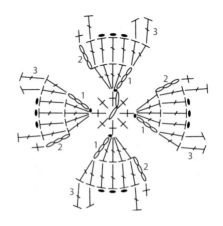

Shamrock Motif

Base ring: 2ch, 8dc into first ch, sl st to first dc, turn.

1st Petal: 3ch (count as 1tr), 4tr into same place as last sl st, turn.

1st row: 3ch (count as 1tr), 1tr into same tr, 1tr into each of next 3tr, 2tr into top of 3ch, turn.

2nd round: 1tr into first tr, 1htr into next tr, sl st into each of next 3tr, 1tr into next tr, 1dc into top of 3ch. Cast off.

2nd Petal: Skip 1dc of first row, join yarn in next st, work same as first petal.

Work 2 more petals in same manner.

When working with yarn, always keep a crochet hook nearby for those tricky little moments when all seems lost! They are especially useful for times like picking up stitches when you need to be nimble-fingered.

Feathered Snowflake

Special Abbreviations: Dtr-rice stitch = 5ch, 2 dtr into 5th ch from hook whilst holding back last loop of each dtr, yo and pull through all 3 loops on hook.

Picot = 4ch, sl st in top of dtr just made.

Base ring: 6ch, join with sl st to form a ring.

1st round: 1ch, 12 dc into ring, join with sl st to first dc.

2nd round: 1ch, 1dc into each dc, join with sl st to first dc.

3rd round: 2 ch (count as 1htr), sk 1dc, 2htr into each of next 11dc, 1htr into first dc, join with sl st to 2nd of 2ch.

4th round: *2ch, (work into front loop in this round) 2tr into each of next 3htr, 2ch, sl st into next htr; rep from * 5 times more with last sl st into 2nd of 2ch from 3rd round. (6 petals)

5th round: (work behind petals and into back loop of each htr of round 3) sl st into first 2 htr, *4ch, 2trtr into each of next 3htr, 4ch, sl st into next htr; rep from * 4 more times, 4ch, 2trtr into next htr, 2trtr into 2nd of 2ch at beginning of round 3, 2trtr into next htr, 4ch, sl st into next htr.

6th round: 4 sl sts over 4ch until top of first trtr, 1ch, * [1dc into next trtr, 4ch, 1dtr on top of dc just made, picot, 4ch, sl st on top of same dc] 4 times, 1ch, dtr-rice st, 1ch, sk 2trtr; rep from * around, join with sl st to first dc. Cast off.

Water Garden

Base ring: 10ch, join with sl st.

1st round: 3ch (count as 1tr), 23tr into ring, sl st to top of 3ch.

2nd round: 6ch (count as 1tr, 3ch), [skip 1tr, 1tr into next tr, 3ch] 11 times, sl st to 3rd ch of 6ch.

3rd round: 8ch (count as 1tr, 5ch), [1tr into next tr, 5ch] 11 times, sl st to 3rd of 8ch.

4th round: 10ch (count as 1tr, 7ch), [1tr into next tr, 7ch] 11 times, sl st to 3rd of 10ch.

5th round: 6ch (count as 1tr, 3ch), 1tr into same place as last sl st, *8tr into next 7ch sp, 1tr into next tr, 8tr into next 7ch sp, [1tr, 3ch, 1tr] into next tr; rep from * 5 more times skipping [1tr, 3ch, 1tr] at end of last rep, sl st to 3rd of 6ch.

6th round: Sl st into first 3ch sp, 6ch (count as 1tr, 3ch), 1tr into same 3ch sp, *2ch, skip next 2tr, 1tr into each of next 15tr, 2ch, [1tr, 3ch, 1tr] into next 3ch sp; rep from * 5 more times, skipping [1tr, 3ch, 1tr] at end of last rep, sl st to 3rd of 6ch.

7th round: 7ch (count as 1tr, 4ch), *1tr into next tr, 2ch, 1tr into next tr, 2ch, skip next 2tr, 1tr into each of next 9tr, 2ch, skip next 2tr, 1tr into next tr, 2ch, 1tr into next tr, 4ch; rep from * 5 more times skipping 1tr and 4ch at end of last rep, sl st to 3rd of 7ch.

8th round: 8ch (count as 1tr, 5ch), *1tr into next tr, [2ch, 1tr into next tr] twice, 2ch, skip next 2tr, 1tr into each of next 3tr, 2ch, skip next 2tr, 1tr into next tr, [2ch, 1tr into next tr] twice, 5ch; rep from * five more times skipping 1tr and 5ch at end of last rep, sl st to 3rd of 8ch.

9th round: 3ch (count as 1tr), *[3tr, 5ch, 3tr] into next 5ch sp, 1tr into next tr, [2ch, 1tr into next tr] 3 times, 2ch, skip 1tr, 1tr into next tr, [2ch, 1tr into next tr] 3 times; rep from * 5 more times skipping 1tr at end of last rep, sl st to top of 3ch.

10th round: 3ch (count as 1tr), *1tr into each of next 3tr, [3tr, 5ch, 3tr] into next 5ch sp, 1tr into each of next 4tr, [2ch, 1tr into next tr] 3 times, 2tr into next 2ch sp, 1tr into next tr, [2ch, 1tr into next tr] 3 times; rep from * 5 more times skipping 1tr at end of last rep, sl st to top of 3ch.
Cast off.

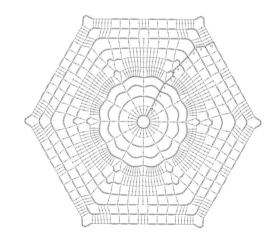

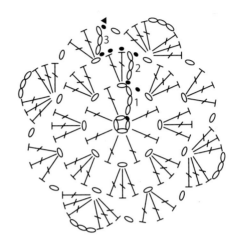

Desert Garden

Base ring: 4ch, join with sl st.

1st round: 4ch (count as 1tr and 1ch), [1tr into ring, 1ch] 7 times, sl st to 3rd of 4ch.

2nd round: Sl st into first 1ch sp, 3ch, 2tr into same 1ch sp, 1ch, [3tr into next 1ch sp, 1ch] 7 times, sl st to top of of 3ch.

3rd round: Sl st into each of next 2tr and next 1ch sp, 3ch, 2tr into same ch sp, 1ch, *[3tr, 3ch, 3tr] into next 1ch sp, 1ch, 3tr into next 1ch sp, 1ch; rep from * twice more, [3tr, 3ch, 3tr] into next 1ch sp, 1ch, sl st to top of 3ch. Cast off.

American Square

Base ring: Using A, 6ch, join with sl st.
1st round: 3ch (count as 1tr), 2tr into ring, [3ch, 3tr into ring] 3 times, 3ch, sl st to top of 3ch. Cast off.
2nd round: Join B to any 3ch sp, 3ch (count as 1tr), [2tr, 3ch, 3tr] into same 3ch sp, *1ch, [3tr, 3ch, 3tr] into next 3ch sp; rep from *twice more, 1ch, sl st to top of 3ch. Cast off.
3rd round: Join A to any 3ch sp, 3ch (count as 1tr), [2tr, 3ch, 3tr] into same 3ch sp, *1ch, 3tr into next 1ch sp, 1ch, [3tr, 3ch, 3tr] into next 3ch sp; rep from * twice more, 1ch, 3tr into next 1ch sp, 1ch, sl st to top of 3ch. Cast off.
4th round: Join B to any 3ch sp, 3ch (count as 1tr), [2tr, 3ch, 3tr] into same 3ch sp, *[1ch, 3tr into next 1ch sp] twice, 1ch, [3tr, 3ch, 3tr] into next 3ch sp; rep from * twice more, [1ch, 3tr into next 1ch sp] twice, 1ch, sl st to top of 3ch. Cast off.
Cast off.

Pinwheel

Base ring: 6ch, join with sl st.
1st round: 1ch, [1dc, 12ch] 12 times into ring, sl st to first dc.
Cast off.

Easy Polygon

Base ring: 3ch, join with sl st.

1st round: 3ch (count as 1tr), 23tr into ring, sl st to top of 3ch.

2nd round: 3ch, [1tr, 2ch, 2tr] into same place as last sl st, *skip next 3tr, [2tr, 2ch, 2tr] into next tr; rep from * 4 more times, skip next 3tr, sl st to top of 3ch.

Cast off.

PINWHEEL

EASY POLYGON

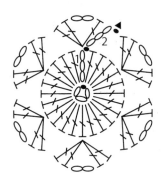

Wheel Square

Base ring: Using A, 8ch, join with sl st.

1st round: 6ch (count as 1tr and 3ch), [1tr into ring, 3ch] 7 times, sl st to 3rd of 6ch. Cast off.

2nd round: Join B to any 3ch sp, 3ch (count as 1tr), 3tr into same 3ch sp, [2ch, 4tr into next 3ch sp] 7 times, 2ch, sl st to top of 3ch. Cast off.

3rd round: Join A to any 2ch sp, 3ch, 5tr into same 2ch sp, [1ch, 6tr into next 2ch sp, 3ch, 6tr into next 2ch sp] 3 times, 1ch, 6tr into next 2ch sp, 3ch, sl st to top of 3ch. Cast off.

4th round: Join B to 1ch sp, 1ch, 1dc into same 1ch sp, *3ch, 1dc between 3rd and 4th tr of next tr group, 3ch, [2tr, 3ch, 2tr] into next 3ch sp, 3ch, 1dc between 3rd and 4th tr of next tr group, 3ch, 1dc into next 1ch sp; rep from * 3 more times skipping last dc, sl st to first dc. Cast off.

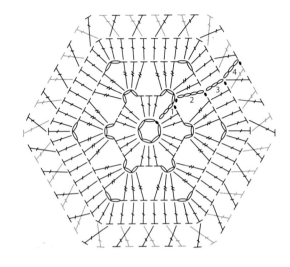

Polyfleur

Base ring: 6ch, join with sl st.

1st round: 6ch (count as 1tr and 3ch), [3tr into ring, 3ch] 5 times, 2tr into ring, sl st to 3rd of 6ch.

2nd round: Sl st into first 3ch sp, 4ch, [2dtr, 2ch, 3dtr] into same 3ch sp, *[3dtr, 2ch, 3dtr] into next 3ch sp; rep from * 4 more times, sl st to top of 4ch.

3rd round: 3ch (count as 1tr), 1tr into each dtr; 3tr into each 2ch sp around, sl st to top of 3ch.

4th round: 3ch (count as 1tr), *miss 1tr, 1tr into next tr, 1tr into the skipped tr; rep from * to end, sl to top of 3ch.

Cast off.

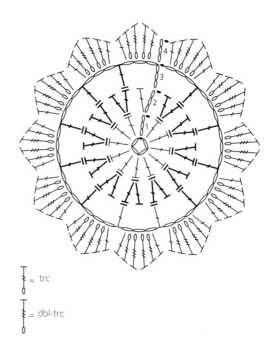

= trc

= dbl-trc

Twelve-Petal Flower

Special Abbreviations: Trc = yo twice, insert hook as indicated, yo and pull through, yo and pull through 2 loops on hook, yo and pull through last 3 loops on hook.
Dbl-trc = yo 3 times, insert hook as indicated, yo and pull through, (yo and pull through 2 loops on hook) twice, yo and pull through last 3 loops on hook.
Base ring: 4ch, join with sl st.
1st round: 3ch (count as 1tr), 11tr into ring, sl st to top of 3ch. (12 tr)

2nd round: 3ch (count as 1tr), 1tr into same place as last sl st, [2tr through back loop only of next tr] 11 times, sl st to top of 3ch. (24 tr)
3rd round: 6ch (count as 1tr, 3ch), [miss 1tr, 1tr through back loop only of next tr, 3ch;] 11 times, sl st to 3rd of 6ch. (12 3ch sps)
4th round: 3ch (count as 1tr), [1dtr, 2dtrc, 1trc, 1tr] into next 3ch sp, *[1tr, 1trc, 2dtrc, 1trc, 1tr] into next 3ch sp; rep from * 10 more times, sl st to top of 3ch.
Cast off.

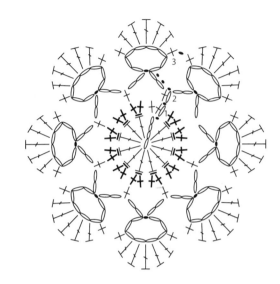

Morning Glory

Base ring: 4ch (count as 1tr), 11tr in first ch, sl st to 3rd of 4ch. (12 tr)

1st round: 1ch, 2dc into same place as last sl st, working through back loops 2dc in each tr around, sl st to first dc. (24 dc)

2nd round: 1ch, 1dc into same place as last sl st *10ch, sl st into 8th ch from hook (forming an 8ch loop), 2ch, miss next 2dc, 1dc in next dc; rep from * 7 more times, missing 1dc at end of last rep, sl st to first dc.

3rd round: Sl st into each of first 2ch, [1dc, 5tr, 1dc] into first 8ch loop, *[1dc, 5tr, 1dc] into next 8ch loop; rep from * 6 more times, sl st to first dc.

Cast off.

Don't be afraid to try something dramatic – contrast pretty stitches with a more unexpected or exciting technique.

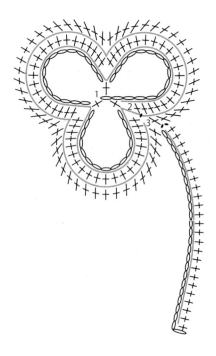

Shamrock 1

1st round: 16ch, 1dc into first of these 16ch to make 1 loop, [15ch, 1dc into same ch as before] twice. (3 loops now made)

2nd round: Lay a length of yarn along the work, then working over this thread, 1ch, 21dc into each 15ch loop, sl st into first dc.

3rd round: Working over length of yarn, miss next dc, *1dc into each of next 19dc, miss 2dc (1dc of this loop and 1dc of next loop); rep from * twice more, sl st into first dc, 25ch, turn.

Stalk: 1dc into 2nd ch from hook, then over length of yarn work 1dc into each ch, then work 1sl st into first dc of shamrock.

Cast off.

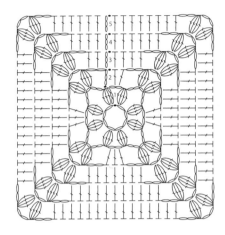

Double-Eyelet Square

Special Abbreviation: Bobble = 4tr until 1 loop of each remains on hook, yo and pull through all 5 loops on hook.
Base ring: 8ch, join with sl st.
1st round: 3ch, 3tr into ring until 1 loop of each remains on hook, yo and pull through all 4 loops on hook (count as 1st bobble), [5ch, bobble into ring, 2ch, bobble into ring] 3 times, 5ch, bobble into ring, 2ch, sl st to top of first bobble.
2nd round: 5ch (count as 1tr and 2ch), *[bobble, 2ch, bobble] into next 5ch sp, 2ch, 3tr into next 2ch sp, 2ch; rep from * 3 more times missing 1tr and 2ch at end of last rep, sl st to 3rd of 5ch.
3rd round: 3ch (count as 1tr), *2tr into next 2ch sp, 2ch, [bobble, 2ch, bobble] into corner 2ch sp, 2ch, 2tr into next 2ch sp, 1tr into each of next 3tr; rep from *3 more times, missing 1tr at end of last rep, sl st to top of 3ch.
4th round: 3ch (count as 1tr), 1tr into each of next 2tr, *2tr into next 2ch sp, 2ch, [bobble, 2ch, bobble] into corner 2ch sp, 2ch, 2tr into next 2ch sp, 1tr into each of next 7tr; rep from * 3 more times missing 3tr at end of last rep, sl st to top of 3ch.
5th round: 3ch (count as 1tr), 1tr into each of next 4tr, *2tr into next 2ch sp, 2ch, [bobble, 2ch, bobble] into corner 2ch sp, 2ch, 2tr into next 2ch sp, 1tr into each of next 11tr; rep from * 3 more times missing 5tr at end of last rep, sl st to top of 3ch.
Cast off.

Spoked-Wheel Eyelet Square

Base ring: 8ch, join with sl st.

1st round: 3ch (count as 1tr), 15tr into ring, sl st to top of 3ch.

2nd round: 5ch (count as 1tr, 2ch), [1tr into next tr, 2ch] 15 times, sl st to 3rd of 5ch. (16 spokes)

3rd round: 3ch (count as 1tr), 2tr into first 2ch sp, 1ch, [3tr into next 2ch sp, 1ch] 15 times, sl st to top of 3ch.

4th round: Sl st into each of next 2tr and next 1ch sp, 1ch, 1dc into same 1ch sp, *[3ch, 1dc into next 1ch sp] 3 times, 6ch, 1dc into next 1ch sp; rep from * 3 more times missing 1dc at end of last rep, sl st to first dc.

5th round: 3ch (count as 1tr), 2tr into first 3ch sp, [3tr into next 3ch sp] twice, *[5tr, 2ch, 5tr] into next 6ch sp, [3tr into next 3ch sp] three times; rep from * twice more, [5tr, 2ch, 5tr] into next 6ch sp, sl st to top of 3ch.

6th round: 3ch (count as 1tr), work 1tr into each tr around and [1tr, 1dtr, 1tr] into each 2ch sp at corners, sl st to top of 3ch.

Cast off.

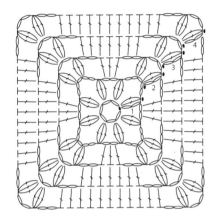

Squared Eyelet

Special Abbreviations: 2tr cluster = [yo, insert hook as indicated, yo and draw up loop, yo and draw through 1 loop, yo and draw through 2 loops] twice, yo and draw through all loops on hook.

3tr cluster = [yo, insert hook as indicated, yo and draw up loop, yo and pull through 1 loop on hook, yo and pull through 2 loops on hook] 3 times, yo and pull through last 4 loops on hook.

Base ring: 6ch, join with sl st.

1st round: 2ch, 2tr cluster into ring (count as 1st cluster) *5ch, 3tr cluster into ring, 2ch, 3tr cluster into ring; rep from * twice more, 5ch, 3tr cluster into ring, 2ch, sl st to top of 2ch.

2nd round: Sl st into next st, sl st into next 5ch sp, 2ch, 2tr cluster into same 5ch sp, *2ch, 3tr cluster into same 5ch sp, 2ch, 3tr into next 2ch sp, 2ch, 3tr cluster into next 5ch sp; rep from * twice more, 2ch, 3tr cluster into same 5ch sp, 2ch, 3tr into next 2ch sp, 2ch, sl st to top of 2ch.

3rd round: Sl st into next st, sl st into next 2ch sp, 2ch 2tr cluster into same 2ch sp, *2ch, 3tr cluster into same 2ch sp, 2ch, 2tr into next 2ch sp, 1tr into each tr of next tr-group, 2tr into next 2ch sp, 2ch, 3tr cluster into next 2ch sp; rep from * twice more, 2ch, 3tr cluster into same 2ch sp, 2ch, 2tr into next 2ch sp, 1tr into each tr of next tr-group, 2tr into next 2ch sp, 2ch, sl st to top of 2ch.

4th round: Rep 3rd round.

Cast off.

Granny Wheel Square

Base ring: 6ch, join with sl st.
1st round: 6ch (count as 1tr and 3ch), [1tr into ring, 3ch] 5 times, sl st to 3rd of 6ch.
2nd round: Sl st into first 3ch sp, 3ch (count as 1tr), 3tr into same 3ch sp, 2ch, [4tr into next 3ch sp, 2ch] 5 times, sl st to top of 3ch.
3rd round: Sl st into each of next 3tr and into next 2ch sp, 3ch, [3tr, 2ch, 4tr] into same 2ch sp, [(4tr, 2ch, 4tr) into next 2ch sp] 5 times, sl st to top of 3ch.
Cast off.

Paddle Wheel

Notes: Do not join rounds.
Base ring: 5ch, join with sl st.
1st round: [6ch, 1dc into ring] 6 times.
2nd round: Sl st in each of first 3ch and ch sp of first 6ch loop, [4ch, 1dc into next sp] 6 times.
3rd round: [4ch, 1dc into next sp, 1dc into next dc] 6 times.
4th round: [4ch, 1dc into next sp, 1dc into each of next 2 dc] 6 times.
5th round: [4ch, 1dc into next sp, 1dc into each of next 3dc] 6 times.
Rep for as many rounds as desired, making 1 extra dc in each group on each round and beg with 10th round working 5ch in each sp instead of 4ch.
Cast off.

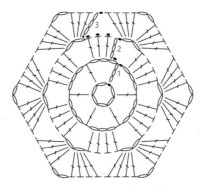

PADDLE WHEEL

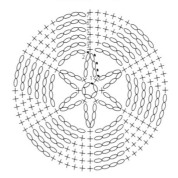

FRAMED ETOILE

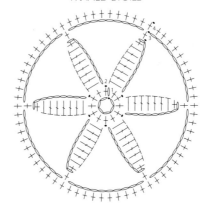

Framed Etoile

Base ring: 6ch, join with sl st.

1st round: 1ch, 12dc into ring, sl st to first dc.

2nd round: [9ch, 1dc into 2nd ch from hook, 1htr into next ch, 1tr into each of next 5ch, 1htr into next ch, miss next dc of 1st round, sl st into next dc of 1st round] 6 times. Cast off.

3rd round: Attach thread to tip of any petal with a sl st, 1dc into same place, [10ch, join to tip of next petal with 1dc] 5 times, 10ch, sl st to first dc.

4th round: 1dc into each ch and dc of prev round, sl st to first dc.

Cast off.

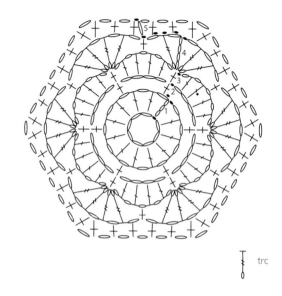

$\perp$ trc

Lacy Hexagon

Special Abbreviation: Trc = yo twice, insert hook as indicated, yo and draw through, yo and draw through 2 loops on hook, yo and draw through last 3 loops on hook.

Base ring: 8ch, join with sl st.

1st round: 4ch (count as 1tr and 1ch), [1tr into ring, 1ch] 11 times, sl st to 3rd of 4ch. (12tr)

2nd round: 1dc into first 1ch sp, 4ch, *miss [1tr, 1ch sp, 1tr], 1dc into next 1ch sp, 4ch; rep from * 4 more times, sl st to first dc. (6 4ch sps)

3rd round: 1dc into same place as last sl st *1ch, [1tr, 1ch] 4 times into next 4ch sp, 1dc into next dc; rep from * 4 more times, 1ch, [1tr, 1ch] 4 times into next 4ch sp, sl st to first dc.

4th round: 5ch (count as 1trc, 1ch), 1trc into same place as last sl st, 1ch, *miss [1ch sp, 1tr] twice, 1dc into next 1ch sp, 1ch, miss [1tr, 1ch sp] twice, [1trc, 1ch] 4 times into next dc; rep from * 4 more times, miss [1ch sp, 1tr] twice, 1dc into next 1ch sp, 1ch, [1trc, 1ch] twice into same place as last sl st of previous round, sl st to 4th of 5ch.

5th round: Sl st into each of next 2 1ch sps, sl st into next dc, 1ch, 1dc into next 1ch sp, 1ch, 1dc into next 1ch sp, *1ch, [1dc, 1ch, 1dc] into next 1ch sp, [1ch, 1dc into next 1ch sp] 4 times; rep from * 4 more times, 1ch, [1dc, 1ch, 1dc] into next 1ch sp, [1ch, 1dc into next 1ch sp] twice, 1ch, sl st to first dc.

Cast off.

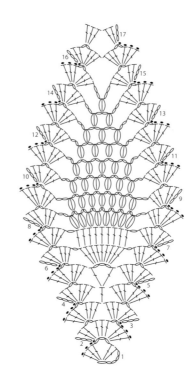

Grape Leaf

Special Abbreviations: Shell = [3tr, 2ch, 3tr] into next 2ch sp.
Puff st = yo, insert hook in sp indicated, yo and draw through, [yo, insert hook into same sp, yo and pull through] twice, yo and draw through all loops on hook.

Base chain: 5ch.

1st row: 2tr into 5th ch from hook, 3ch, 3tr into same ch, turn.

2nd row: Sl st into each of first 3 tr, [sl st, 3ch, 2tr] into next 3ch sp, [2ch, 3tr into same 3ch sp] twice, turn.

3rd row: Sl st into each of first 3 tr, [sl st, 3ch, 2tr, 2ch, 3tr] into next 2ch sp, miss 3tr, 1 shell, turn.

4th row: Sl st into each of first 3tr, [sl st, 3ch, 2tr, 2ch, 3tr] into next 2ch sp, miss 3tr, 1tr into sp before next tr, miss 3 tr, 1 shell, turn.

5th row: Sl st into each of first 3 tr, [sl st, 3ch, 2tr, 2ch, 3tr] into next 2ch sp, miss 3 tr, [1tr, 3ch, 1tr] into next tr, miss 3tr, 1 shell, turn.

6th row: Sl st into each of first 3 tr, [sl st, 3ch, 2tr, 2ch, 3tr] into next 2ch sp, 1ch, miss 4tr, 9tr in next 3ch sp, 1ch, miss 4tr, 1 shell, turn.

7th row: Sl st into each of first 3tr, [sl st, 3ch, 2tr, 2ch, 3tr] into next 2ch sp, 1ch, miss [3tr, 1ch], 1tr into each of next 9tr, 1ch, miss [1ch, 3tr], 1 shell, turn.

8th row: 8th row: Sl st into each of first 3tr, [sl st, 3ch, 2tr, 2ch, 3tr] into next 2ch sp, 2ch, miss [3tr, 1ch], [puff st in sp between next 2tr, 2ch] 8 times, miss [1ch, 3 tr], 1 shell, turn.

9th row: Sl st into each of first 3tr, [sl st, 3ch, 2tr, 2ch, 3tr] into next 2ch sp, 2ch, miss [3tr, 2ch], [1 puff st, 2ch] into each 2ch sp between 2 puff sts of previous row, miss (last puff st, 2ch, 3tr], 1 shell, turn.

10th to 15th rows: Work as 9th row working 1 less puff on each row.

16th row: Sl st into each of first 3tr, [sl st, 3ch, 2tr, 2ch, 3tr] into next 2ch sp, miss [3tr, 2ch, 1 puff st, 2 ch, 3 tr], 1 shell, turn.

17th row: Sl st into each of first 3tr, [sl st, 3ch, 2tr] into next 2ch sp, miss 6tr, 3tr into next 2ch sp.
Cast off.

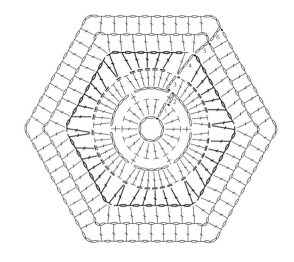

Spoked Hexagon

Base ring: 8ch, join with sl st.

1st round: 3ch (count as 1tr), 17tr into ring, sl st to top of 3ch.

2nd round: 1ch, 1dc into same place as last sl st, [5ch, miss next 2tr, 1dc into next tr] 5 times, 5ch, miss next 2tr, sl st to first dc.

3rd round: Sl st into first 5ch sp, 3ch, 7tr into same 3ch sp, [8tr into next 3ch sp] 5 times, sl st to top of 3ch. (48tr)

4th round: Working through back loops of sts only, 3ch (count as 1tr), 1tr into same place as last sl st, *miss 1tr, [1ch, 1tr into next tr] 5 times, 1ch, miss 1 tr, 2tr into next tr; rep from * 4 more times, miss 1tr, [1ch, 1tr into next tr] 5 times, 1ch, sl st to top of 3ch.

5th round: 6ch (count as 1tr and 3ch), 1tr into same place as last sl st (first corner), *[1ch, 1tr into next tr] 6 times, 1ch, [1tr, 3ch, 1tr] into next tr (corner made); rep from * 4 more times, [1ch, 1tr into next tr] 6 times, 1ch, sl st to 3rd of 6ch.

6th round: sl st into 3ch sp, 6ch (count as 1tr and 3ch), 1tr into same place as last sl st *[1ch, miss 1tr, 1tr into next 1ch sp] 7 times, 1ch, [1tr, 3ch, 1tr] into corner 3ch sp; rep from * 4 more times, end with [1ch, miss 1 tr, 1tr into next 1ch sp] 7 times, 1ch, sl st to 3rd 6ch.
Cast off.

Six-Point Snowflake

Base ring: 15ch, join with sl st.

1st round: [4ch, 1dtr into ring, 4ch, sl st into ring] 12 times.

2nd round: Sl st into each of first 4ch at beg of round, 1dc into dtr, [11ch, miss next dtr, 1dc into next dtr] 5 times, 11ch, miss next dtr, sl st into first dc.

3rd round: 1ch, *[1dc into each of the first 5ch sts, 3dc into next ch st, 1dc into each of next 5ch sts] of next 11ch loop; rep from * 5 more times, sl st to first dc.

4th round: 1ch, 1dc into same place as last sl st, 1dc into each of next 5dc, 3dc into next dc (centre dc of the 3dc group), 1dc into each of next 6dc, [1dc into each of next 6dc, 3dc into next dc, 1dc into each of next 6dc] 5 times, sl st into first dc.

5th round: 1ch, 1dc into same place as last sl st, 1dc into each of next 6dc, 3dc into next dc, 1dc into each of next 7dc, [1dc into each of next 7dc, 3dc into next dc, 1dc into each of next 7dc] 5 times, sl st to first dc.

6th round: 1ch, 1dc into same place as last sl st, *6ch, miss 7dc, [1dtr into same dc, 5ch, sl st into 3rd ch from hook, 2ch] 4 times into centre dc of 3dc group, 1dtr into same dc, 6ch, miss 7dc, 1dc into each of next 2dc; rep from * 5 more times missing 1dc at end of last rep, sl st to first dc. Cast off.

Wreath

Special Abbreviation: 2dtr cluster = [yo twice, pull up a loop in next tr; yo, pull through 2 loops on hook, yo, pull through 2 loops on hook] twice, yo, pull through all 3 loops on hook.

3dtr cluster = [yo twice, pull up a loop in next tr; yo, pull through 2 loops on hook, yo, pull through 2 loops on hook] 3 times, yo, pull through all 4 loops on hook.

Base ring: 48ch, join with sl st.

1st round: 5ch (count as 1tr and 2ch), miss 1 ch, 1tr into next ch, [2ch, miss 1ch, 1tr into next ch] 22 times, 2ch, miss 1 ch, sl st to 3rd of 5ch.

2nd round: Sl st into first 2ch sp, 3ch (count as 1tr), 2tr into same 2ch sp, 2ch [3tr into next 2ch sp, 2ch] 23 times, sl st to top of 3ch.

3rd round: 4ch, 2dtr cluster in next 2tr, 4ch, 1dc into next 2ch sp, *4ch, 3dtr cluster in next 3tr, 4ch, 1dc into next 2ch sp; rep from *22 more times, 4ch, sl st to top of first cluster.

4th round: [6ch, sl st into top of next dtr cluster] 23 times, 6ch, sl st to top of first cluster.

5th round: Sl st into first 2ch of next 6ch sp, [7ch, sl st into next 6ch sp] 23 times, 7ch, sl st to 3rd sl st at beg of round. Cast off.

= trc

Five-Point Snowflake

Special Abbreviations: 5dtr cluster = dtr into each of next 5tr leaving the last loop of each dtr on hook, yo and draw through all 6 loops on hook.

6dtr cluster = dtr into each of next 6tr leaving the last loop of each dtr on hook, yo and draw through all 7 loops on hook.

3 picot = 3ch, sl st into 3rd ch from hook.

4 picot = 4ch, sl st into 4th ch from hook.

Base chain: 2ch.

1st round: 10dc in first ch from hook, sl st in first dc.

2nd round: 6ch (count as 1dtr and 2ch) [1dtr into next dc, 2ch] 9 times, sl st to 4th of 6ch.

3rd round: 3ch (count as 1tr) 2tr into first 2ch sp, 1tr into next dtr, 2tr into next 2ch sp, 3ch, [1tr into next dtr, 2tr into next 2ch sp, 1tr into next dtr, 2tr into next 2ch sp, 3ch] 4 times, sl st to top of 3ch.

4th round: 4ch (count as 1dtr), 5dtr cluster, 15ch, *6dtr cluster, 15ch; rep from * 3 more times, sl st to top of first cluster.

5th round: [2dc, 3tr, 2dtr, 3ch, 2dtr, 3tr, 2dc, 1ch] into each 15ch sp, sl st to top of first dc.

6th round: Sl st into last 1ch sp made, 4ch (count as 1dtr), 8ch, 5dtr into next 3ch sp, 8ch, [1dtr into next 1ch sp, 8ch, 5dtr into next 3ch sp, 8ch] 4 times, sl st to top of 4ch.

7th round: *[2ch, 3 picot, 2ch, sl st into 8ch sp] twice, 5ch, 5trc cluster into next 5dtr, 4 picot, 5ch, [sl st into 8ch sp, 2ch, 3 picot, 2ch] twice, sl st into next trc; rep from * 4 more times working last sl st to top of 4ch at beg of previous round.

Cast off.

Eight-Point Snowflake

Special abbreviation: Trc = yo twice, insert hook as indicated, yo and pull through a loop, yo and pull through 2 loops on hook, yo and pull through last 3 loops on hook.

4dtr cluster = dtr into each of next 4tr leaving the last loop of each dtr on hook, yo and draw through all 5 loops on hook.

5dtr cluster = dtr into each of next 5tr leaving the last loop of each dtr on hook, yo and draw through all 6 loops on hook.

Base ring: 12ch, join with sl st.

1st round: 3ch (count as a 1tr), 23tr into ring, sl st to top of 3ch. (24 tr)

2nd round: 3ch (count as 1tr), 1tr into each of next 4tr, 6ch [miss 1tr, 1tr into each of next 5tr, 6ch] 3 times, sl st to top of 3ch.

3rd round: Sl st into next tr, 3ch, (count as 1tr), 1tr into each of next 2tr, 5ch, 1dc into next 6ch sp, 5ch [miss next tr, 1tr into each of next 3tr, 5ch, 1dc into next 6ch sp, 5ch] 3 times, sl st to top of 3ch.

4th round: Sl st into next tr, 9ch (count as 1tr and 6ch), 1tr into same place as last sl st, 4ch, 1dc into next 5ch sp, 6ch, 1dc into next 5ch sp, 4ch, [miss 1tr, (1tr, 6ch, 1tr) into next tr, 4ch, 1dc into next 5ch sp, 6ch, 1dc into next 5ch sp, 4ch] 3 times, sl st to 3rd of 9ch.

5th round: Sl st into first 2ch and into ch sp of 6ch sp, 3ch (count as 1tr), 4tr into same 6ch sp, 8ch, (2tr, 3ch, 2tr) into next 6ch sp, 8ch, [5tr into next 6ch sp, 8ch, (2tr, 3ch, 2tr) into next 6ch sp, 8ch] 3 times, sl st to top of 3ch.

6th round: 3ch (count as 1tr), 1tr into each of next 4tr, 8ch, [2tr, 3ch, 2tr] into next 3ch sp, 8ch, *1tr into each of next 5tr, 8ch, [2tr, 3ch, 2tr] into next 3ch sp, 8ch; rep from * twice more, sl st to top of 3ch.

7th round: 4ch (count as 1dtr), [yo, 4dtr cluster, 8ch, 1dc over next 2 8ch sps below on 5th and 6th rounds, 8ch, [2trc, 3ch, 2trc] into next 3ch sp, 8ch, 1dc over next 2 8ch sps, 8ch, *5dtr cluster, 8ch, 1dc over next 2 8ch sps, 8ch, [2trc, 3ch, 2trc] into next 3ch sp, 8ch, 1dc over next 2 8ch sps, 8ch; rep from * twice more, sl st to first cluster.

8th round: Sl st into next 8ch sp, 1ch, 8dc into same 8ch sp, *8dc into next 8ch sp, [2dc, 3ch, 2dc] into next 3 ch sp, 8dc into each of next 2 8ch sps, 4ch, 8dc into next 8ch sp; rep from * twice more, 8dc into next 8ch sp, [2dc, 3ch, 2dc] into next 3ch sp, 8dc into each of next 2 8ch sps, 4ch, sl st to first dc.

9th round: Sl st into next dc, [3ch, miss 1dc, sl st into next dc] 8 times, *[2dc, 6ch, sl st into 4th ch from hook, 2ch, 2dc] into next 3ch sp, [3ch, miss 1dc, sl st into next dc] 9 times; [3dc, 4ch, sl st into 4th ch from hook, 3dc] into next 4ch sp, [3ch, miss 1dc, sl st into next dc] 9 times; rep from * twice more, [2dc, 6ch, sl st into 4th ch from hook, 2ch, 2dc] into next 3ch sp, [3ch, miss 1dc, sl st into next dc] 9 times, [3dc, 4ch, sl st into 4th ch from hook, 3dc] into next 4ch sp, 3ch, sl st to first sl st.

Cast off.

Experiment with fine, delicate crochet to create something beautiful and unique. Use 2- and 3-ply yarns for gossamer-like cobweb stitches and fabrics.

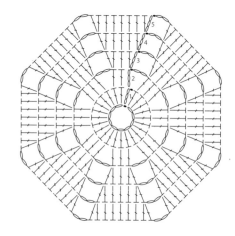

Plain Octagon

Base ring: 10ch, join with sl st.

1st round: 3ch (count as 1tr), 23tr into ring, sl st to top of 3ch. (24 tr)

2nd round: 3ch (count as 1tr), 1tr into each of next 2tr, [2ch, 1tr into each of next 3tr] 7 times, 2ch, sl st to top of 3ch. (8 groups)

3rd round: 3ch (count as 1tr), 1tr into same place as last sl st, tr into next tr, 2tr into next tr, [2ch, 2tr into next tr, 1tr into next tr, 2tr into next tr] 7 times, 2ch, sl st to top of 3ch.

4th round: 3ch (count as 1tr), 1tr into same place as last sl st, 1tr into each of next 3tr, 2tr into next tr, [2ch, 2tr into next tr, 1tr into each of next 3tr, 2tr into next tr] 7 times, 2ch, sl st to top of 3ch.

5th round: 3ch (count as 1tr), 1tr into same place as last sl st, tr into each of next 5tr, 2tr into next tr, [2ch, 2tr into next tr, 1tr into each of next 5tr, 2tr into next tr] 7 times, 2ch, sl st into top of 3ch.
Cast off.

It is usually very important to check yarn tension when working from a pattern. When making throws and cushions, use the opportunity to be experimental with yarns, stitches and patterns.

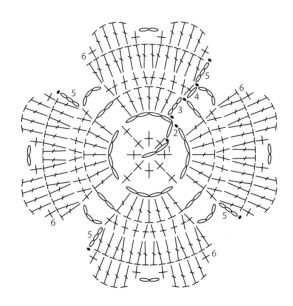

Dogwood

Base chain: 2ch.

1st round: 8dc in 2nd ch from hook, sl st to first dc.

2nd round: 5ch (count as 1dc, 4ch), miss 2dc, 1dc into next dc, [4ch, miss 1dc, 1dc into next dc] twice, 4ch, sl st to first of 5ch.

3rd round: Sl st into next ch sp, 3ch (count as 1tr), 6tr into same sp as last sl st, [2ch, 7tr] into each of next 3 4ch sps, 2ch, sl st to top of 3ch.

4th round: 1ch, 2dc into same place as last sl st [1dc into each of next 2trs, 2dc into next tr] twice, 3ch, *[2dc into next tr, 1dc into each of next 2trs] twice, 2dc into next tr, 3ch; rep from * twice more, sl st to first dc.

5th row: 3ch (count as 1tr), 1tr into same place as last sl st, 1tr into next dc, 2tr into next dc, 1tr into next dc, [2tr into next dc] twice, [1tr into next dc, 2tr into next dc] twice, turn.

6th row: *1dc into next tr, 1tr into each of next 4tr, 1dc into next tr * 2ch, miss 2tr, rep from * to *, sl st to top of 3ch. Cast off. (1 petal made)

With right side facing, miss next 3ch sp of 4th round, rejoin yarn to next dc and work 5th and 6th rows for next petal.

Work 2 more petals in the same way.

Summer Garden Motif

Base ring: 10ch, join with sl st.

1st round: 1ch, 24dc in ring, sl st to first dc.

2nd round: 12ch (count as 1dtr, 8ch), **miss next dc, 1dc into next dc, 1ch, turn, 1dc into each of next 8ch, 1ch, turn, *1dc into each dc across, 1ch, turn; rep from * until there are 6 rows of dc, miss next dc of ring, 1dtr into next dc, 8ch; rep from ** 5 more times ending last rep after 6th row of dc, sl st to 4th of 12ch.

3rd round: 12ch (count as 1dtr, 8ch), [1dc into free tip of next dc-block, 8ch, 1dtr into next dtr, 8ch] 5 times, 1dc into free tip of next dc-section, 8ch, sl st to 4th of 12ch.

4th round: 3ch, [1tr into each ch of next 8ch, 1tr into next dc, 1tr into each ch of next 8ch, 1tr into next dtr] 6 times missing 1tr at end of last rep, sl st to top of 3ch. Cast off.

Leafy Pinwheel

Base ring: 10ch, join with sl st.

1st round: 1ch, 16dc into ring, sl st to first dc. Cast off.

2nd round: 9ch, sl st into any dc on ring, hold chain to left, 1ch to right of ch, across ch work 1dc, 1htr, 5tr, 1htr, ending 1dc into last ch, *17ch, turn, miss 1dc on ring, sl st into next dc, 1ch, turn, across half of ch work 1dc, 1htr, 5tr, 1htr, 1dc; rep from * 6 more times, 8ch, turn, sl st to end of first petal.

3rd round: 1ch, turn, [2dc, 2htr, 7tr, 2htr, 2dc] into each 8ch sp around, sl st to first dc. Cast off.

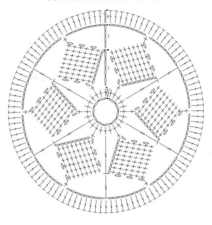

LEAFY PINWHEEL

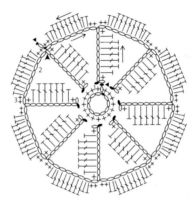

Shamrock II

Special Abbreviation: Picot loop = 4ch, 1dc into 3rd ch from hook, 5ch, 1dc into 3rd ch from hook, 1ch.

Base chain: 16ch.

1st round: 1dc into first ch to form a loop, [15ch, 1dc into same first ch as before] twice. (3 loops formed)

2nd round: 24dc into each loop formed in first round, sl st to first dc.

3rd round: 1dc into each dc around all 3 petals, sl st to first dc.

4th round: Sl st into each of next 3dc, 1dc into next dc, *[picot loop, miss 4dc, 1dc into next dc], 3 times, picot loop, 1dc into 5th dc of next petal; rep from * twice more missing 1dc at end of last rep, sl st to first dc.

5th round: 4sl st along edge of first picot loop, *5dc across picot loop from picot to picot, 4ch; rep from * 11 more times, end with sl st to 4th sl st at beg of round.

6th round: *8ch, 1dc into next 4ch sp; rep from * 11 more times, sl st into each of next 2ch of last 4ch sp. Cast off.

SHAMROCK II

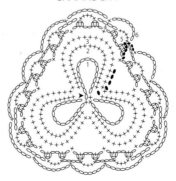

Textured Popcorn Motif

Special Abbreviation: Popcorn = 5tr into next tr, drop loop from hook, insert hook in top of first tr of 5tr group, catch dropped loop and draw through and tighten.

Base ring: 6ch, join with sl st.

1st round: 3ch (count as 1tr), 19tr into ring, sl st to top of starting 3ch. (20tr)

Note: In the following rounds, work through back loop only of each tr.

2nd round: 3ch (count as 1tr), 1tr in same place as last sl st, 1tr into next tr, [2tr into next tr, 1tr into next tr] 9 times, sl st to top of 3ch. (30 tr)

3rd round: 3ch (count as 1tr), 1tr into same place as last sl st, [1tr into each of next 3tr, 2tr into next tr, 1ch, 2tr into next tr] 5 times, 1tr into each of next 3tr, 2tr into last tr, 1ch, sl st to top of 3ch. (6 groups of 7 tr with 1ch between groups)

4th round: 3ch (count as 1tr), 1tr into same place as last sl st, 1tr into each of next 2tr, popcorn into next tr, 1tr into each of next 2tr, 2tr into next tr, [2ch, 2tr into first tr of next group, 1tr into each of next 2 tr, popcorn into next tr, 1tr into each of next 2tr, 2tr into next tr] 5 times, 2ch, sl st to top of 3ch.

5th round: 3ch (count as 1tr), 1tr into same place as last sl st, [1tr into each of next 3tr, 1tr into popcorn, 1tr into each of next 3tr, 2tr into next tr, 2ch, 2tr into first tr of next group] 6 times missing 2tr at end of last rep, sl st to top of 3ch.

6th round: 3ch (count as 1tr), 1tr into same place as last sl st, [1tr into each of next 2tr, popcorn into next tr, 1tr into each of next 3tr, popcorn into next tr, 1tr into each of next 2tr, 2tr into last tr of group, 3ch, 2tr into first tr of next group] 6 times missing 2tr at end of last rep, sl st to top of 3ch.

7th round: 3ch (count as 1tr), 1tr into same place as last sl st, [1tr into each of next 11 sts, 2tr into last tr of group, 3ch, 2tr into first tr of next group, 1tr in each of next 11 tr, 2tr in last tr of group] 6 times missing 2tr at end of last rep, sl st to top of 3ch.

8th round: 3ch (count as 1tr), 1tr into same place as last sl st, [1tr into each of next 2tr, popcorn into next tr, [1tr into each of next 3tr, popcorn into next tr] twice, 1tr into each of next 2tr, 2tr into last tr of group, 4ch, 2tr into first tr of next group] 6 times missing 2tr at end of last rep, sl st to top of 3ch.

9th round: 3ch (count as 1tr), 1tr into same place as last sl st, [1tr into each of next 15sts, 2tr into last tr of group, 4ch, 2tr into first tr of next group] 6 times missing 2tr at end of last rep, sl st to top of 3ch.

Cast off.

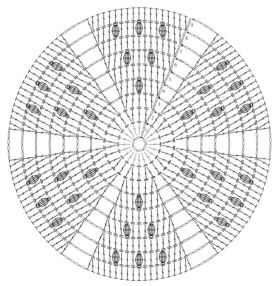

Decorative Button

Base ring: 6ch, join with sl st.

1st round: 3ch (count as 1tr), 2tr into ring, 7ch, [3tr into ring, 7ch] 3 times, sl st to top of 3ch.

2nd round: Sl st into each of next 2tr and into next 7ch, sp, 3ch, [2tr, 3dtr, 5dtr, 3dtr, 3tr] into same 7ch sp, [3tr, 3dtr, 5dtr, 3dtr, 3tr] into each of next 3 7ch sps, sl st to top of 3ch.

3rd round: 1ch, working through back loops only 1dc in each st around, sl st to first dc.

Cast off.

DECORATIVE BUTTON

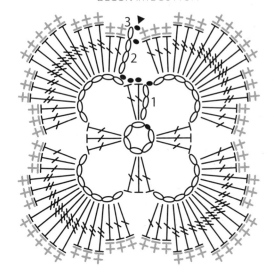

Grape Eyelet Square

Special Abbreviations: Popcorn = 5tr into next st, drop loop from hook, insert hook in top of first tr of 5tr group, catch dropped loop and draw through and tighten.

Trc = yo twice, insert hook in joining sp, yo and pull through, yo and pull through 2 loops on hook, yo and pull through last 3 loops on hook.

Base ring: 10ch, join with sl st.

1st round: 3ch, 4tr into ring, take loop off hook, insert hook into top of 3ch, pull loop of 4th tr through, [3ch, popcorn into ring] 7 times, 3ch, sl st to top of first popcorn. (8 popcorns made)

2nd round: [1sl st, 6ch (count as 1tr, 3ch), 1tr] into next 3ch sp, *3ch, [1tr, 3ch, 1tr] into next 3ch sp; rep from * around, 3ch, sl st to 3rd of 6ch.

3rd round: [1sl st, 3ch, 4tr] into next 3ch sp, take loop off hook, insert hook into top of 3ch, pull loop of 4th tr through, *3ch, popcorn into next 3ch sp; rep from *

around, 3ch, sl st to top of first popcorn.

4th round: Rep 2nd round.

5th round: Rep 3rd round. (32 popcorns)

6th round: Sl st into next 3ch sp, 1dc into same 3ch sp [8ch, miss next 3ch sp, 1dc into next 3ch sp] 15 times, 8ch, sl st to first dc.

7th round: 3ch, *[popcorn, 2ch] 3 times into each of next 2 8ch sps, 8trc into each of next 2 8ch sps, 2ch; rep from * 3 more times sl st to top of first popcorn.

8th round: [1sl st, 3ch, popcorn] into next 2ch sp, *[2ch, popcorn into next 2ch sp] 4 times, 5ch, miss popcorn, 1dc into next trc, [5ch, miss 1trc, 1dc into next trc] twice, 5ch, miss 1trc, 1trc into each of next 4 trc, [5ch, miss 1trc, 1dc into next trc] 3 times, 5ch, miss popcorn, popcorn into next 2ch sp; rep from * 3 more times missing popcorn at end of last rep, sl st to top of first popcorn.

9th round: [1sl st, 3ch, popcorn] into next 2ch sp, *[2ch, popcorn into next 2ch sp] 3 times, miss popcorn, [5ch, 1dc into next 5ch sp] 3 times, 5ch, miss next 5ch sp, 1trc into next trc, [2ch, 1trc into next trc] 3 times, 5ch, miss next 5ch sp, 1dc into next 5ch sp, [5ch, 1dc into next 5ch sp] twice, 5ch, miss popcorn, popcorn into next 2ch sp; rep from * 3 more times missing popcorn at end of last rep, sl st to top of first popcorn.

10th round: [1sl st, 3ch, 1 popcorn] into next 2ch sp, *[2ch, popcorn into next 2ch sp] twice, miss popcorn, [5ch, 1dc into next 5ch sp] 3 times, 5ch, miss next 5ch sp, 2tr into next trc, [3ch, 2tr into next trc] 3 times, 5ch, miss next 5ch sp, 1dc into next 5ch sp, [5ch, 1dc into next 5ch sp] twice, 5ch, miss popcorn, popcorn into next 2ch sp; rep from * 3 more times missing popcorn at end of last rep, sl st to top of first popcorn.

11th round: [1sl st, 3ch, popcorn] into next 2ch sp, *2ch, popcorn into next 2ch sp, miss popcorn, [5ch, 1dc into next 5ch sp] 3 times, 5ch, miss next 5ch sp, [1tr into each of next 2tr, 4ch] twice, popcorn into next 3ch sp, [4ch, 1tr into each of next 2tr] twice, 5ch, miss next 5ch sp, 1dc into next 5ch sp, [5ch, 1dc into next 5ch sp] twice, 5ch, miss popcorn, popcorn into next 2ch sp; rep from * 3 more times missing popconr at end of last rep, sl st to top of first popcorn.

12th round: [1sl st, 3ch, popcorn] into next 2ch sp, *miss popcorn, [5ch, 1dc into next 5ch sp] 3 times, 5ch, miss next 5ch sp, [1tr into each of next 2tr, 4ch] twice, popcorn into next 4ch sp, 2ch, miss popcorn, popcorn into next 4ch sp, [4ch, 1tr into each of next 2tr] twice, 5ch, miss next 5ch sp, 1dc into next 5ch sp, [5ch, 1dc into next 5ch sp] twice, 5ch, miss popcorn, popcorn into next 2ch sp;

rep from * 3 more times missing popcorn at end of last rep, sl st to top of first popcorn.

13th round: [1sl st, 1dc] into next 5ch sp, 5ch, 1dc into next 5ch sp, *7ch, 1dc into next 5ch sp, 5ch, miss next 5ch sp, [1tr into each of next 2tr, 4ch] twice, popcorn into next 4ch sp, 2ch, popcorn into next 2ch sp, 2ch, popcorn into next 4ch sp, [4ch, 1tr into each of next 2tr] twice, 5ch, miss next 5ch sp, 1dc into next 5ch sp, 7ch, 1dc into next 5ch sp, [5ch, 1dc into next 5ch sp] 3 times; rep from * 3 more times, missing [1dc into next 5ch sp, 5ch, 1dc into next 5ch sp] at end of last rep, sl st to first dc.
Cast off.

$\updownarrow$ = Trc

key

Stitch diagrams are detailed 'maps' of fabric showing the right side uppermost. They enable you to see what you are going to do before you start and also where you are at any moment.

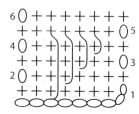

Spikes: The stitch symbol is extended downward to show where the hook is to go through the fabric.

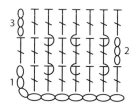

Raised (relief) stitches: When a stitch is to be worked by inserting the hook behind a stem (instead of under the top two loops), the stitch symbol ends in a 'crook' around the appropriate stem. The direction of the crook indicates which side of the fabric the hook is to be inserted. On a RS row, work a raised stitch with a RS crook at the front and one with a left crook at the back.

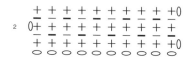

Back/front loop: Stitches that are to be made by inserting the hook under only one of the top two loops are indicated by heavy and lightweight stitch symbols with underlining. A lightweight symbol in conjunction with an underline means pick up the loop nearest the right side of the fabric, i.e. front loop on right-side rows, but back loop on wrong-side rows. A heavyweight symbol with an underline means pick up the loop nearest the wrong side, i.e. back loop on right-side rows, but front loop on wrong-side rows.

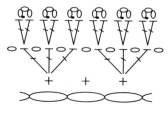

Distortion: The stitch symbols are drawn and laid out realistically, but are distorted for the sake of clarity. Sometimes, for example, single crochet stitches may look extra long. This is only to show clearly where they go and you should not to make artificially long stitches.

When the diagram represents a fabric that is not intended to lie flat – for instance, a 'gathered' or frilled edging – since the drawing itself has to remain flat, the stitch symbols have to be stretched.

○

Chain

●

Slip Stitch

+

Double Crochet

Half Treble Crochet

Treble Crochet

Double Treble

Triple Treble

Quadruple Treble

Quintuple Treble

Sextuple Treble

Bullion Stitch

Lace Loop

Solomon's Knot

Single Crochet

Half Double Crochet

Double Crochet

Treble

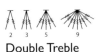

Double Treble

Marguerites = the individual parts of the marguerite clusters have barbs.

Popcorns: Half Double Treble

Popcorns: Double Crochet

Popcorns: Treble

Crossed Stitches

'X' Shape

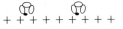

Picots = when a single picot loop occurs after a solid stitch, note the usual method of working the closing slip stitch.

Figures = figures indicate round (or row) numbers.

Motifs = when the base ring of a motif is drawn as a plain circle, make it by looping the yarn around a finger.

Colour = letters A, B, etc and also light and heavy stitch symbols confirm changes of colour.

Arrows = once you are familiar with the basic fabric-making procedures, it is usually clear where a stitch pattern diagram begins and ends, which direction a row goes (Hint: Look for the turning chain), etc. If there is any doubt, additional directions are given with the help of various arrows.

Commence

Re-join yarn

Bind off

Direction of row

Five Treble Group = work five treble crochet into one stitch.

2, 3 and 4 Half Treble Group = work 2 (3, 4) half treble into same place.

2, 3, 4 and 5 Treble Crochet Group = work 2 (3, 4, 5) **treble** into same place.

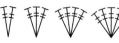

2, 3, 4 and 5 Double Group = work 2 (3, 4, 5) double into same place.

Three Tr Cluster = (Worked over adjacent stitches). Work a treble crochet into each of the next three stitches leaving the last loop of each treble crochet on the hook. Yarn over and draw through all four loops on the hook. On diagrams each 'leg' of the cluster will be positioned above the stitch where the hook is to be inserted.

3, 4 and 5 Treble Crochet Cluster = work a treble crochet into each of the next 3 (4, 5) stitches leaving the last loop of each on the hook. Yarn over and draw through all loops on hook.

3, 4 and 5 Double Treble Cluster = work a double treble into each of the next 3 (4, 5) stitches leaving the last loop of each on the hook. Yarn over and draw through all

Five Tr Bobble = work five treble crochet into one stitch leaving the last loop of each on the hook. Yarn over and draw through all the loops on the hook. More bulky bobbles can be secured with an extra chain stitch. If this is necessary it would be indicated within the pattern.

3, 4 and 5 Treble Crochet bobble = follow instructions as if working a cluster but for each 'leg' insert the hook into the same stitch or space.

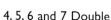

4, 5, 6 and 7 Double Treble Bobble = follow instructions as if working a cluster but for each 'leg' insert the hook into the same stitch or space.

Five Tr Popcorn = work five treble crochet into one stitch. Take the hook out of the working loop and insert it into the top of the first treble crochet made, from front to back. Pick up the working loop and draw this through to close the popcorn. If required work one chain to secure the popcorn. On diagrams the point at the base of the popcorn will be positioned above the space or stitch where it is to be worked.

3 and 4 Treble Crochet Popcorn = work 3 (4) half treble crochet into the same place, drop loop off hook, insert hook into first half treble crochet, pick up dropped loop and draw through.

3, 4 and 5 Double Crochet Popcorn = work 3 (4, 5) treble crochet into the same place, drop loop off hook, insert hook into first treble crochet, pick up dropped loop and draw through.

3, 4 and 5 Double **Popcorn** = work 3 (4, 5) double treble into the same place, drop loop off hook, insert hook into first double treble, pick up dropped loop and draw through.

Three Half Trreble Puff Stitch = (Worked into one stitch).

Four Chain Picot = (Closed with a slip stitch). Work four chain. Into fourth chain from hook work a slip stitch to close. Continue working chain or required stitch.

Crossed Double Treble = skip two stitches and work the first double treble into next stitch. Work one chain then work second double treble into first of skipped stitches taking the hook behind the first double treble before inserting. See individual pattern instructions for variations on crossed stitch.

5dc bobble into a stitch or space

abbreviations

Most crochet pattern instructions are written out in words. In order to follow these, you must be able to understand the simple jargon, abbreviations and standard conventions.

You are expected to know how to make the basic stitches and to be familiar with basic fabric-making procedures; anything more advanced or specialised is always spelled out in individual pattern instructions.

Important terms and abbreviations with which you should be familiar include:

alt = alternate

approx = approximate(ly)

beg = begin(ning)

ch sp = chain space

ch(s) = chain(s)

CL = cluster

cm = centimeter(s)

cont = continue

dc = double crochet

dec = decrease

folls = follows

gr = group

htc = half treble crochet

inc = increase

quin tr = quintuple treble

rem = remaining

rep = repeat

sext tr = sextruple treble

sl st = slip stitch

st(s) = stitch(es)

stch = starting chain

tch = turning chain

tog = together

yo = yarn over

Jargon Busting

Base (Foundation) chain = the length of chain made at the beginning of a piece of crochet as a basis for constructing the fabric.

Turning/starting chain = one, or more chains, depending upon the length of stitch required, worked at the beginning of a row (or end of the previous row) as preparation for the new row; sometimes counts as the first stitch in the new row. Called 'starting chain' when working 'in the round.'

Group = several stitches worked into the same place; sometimes called 'shell,' 'fan,' etc.

Picot = a run of chain stitches normally brought back on itself and fixed into a decorative loop with a slip stitch, or single crochet.

Note: Terms such as 'group', 'cluster', 'picot', and even 'shell', 'fan', 'flower', 'petal', 'leaf', 'bobble', etc, do not denote a fixed arrangement of stitches. Exactly what they mean may be different for each pattern. The procedure is therefore always spelled out at the beginning of each set of instructions and is valid only for that set, unless stated otherwise.

Yarn over = the stitch-making instruction to wrap the yarn from the ball over the hook (or manipulate the hook around the yarn) in order to make a new loop; always done in an anti-clockwise direction, unless otherwise stated.

Work straight = work over an existing row of stitches without 'increasing' (i.e. adding stitches and so making the fabric wider), or 'decreasing' (i.e. reducing the number of stitches and so making the fabric narrower). Precise methods of increasing and decreasing vary according to each stitch pattern and circumstances and are detailed in pattern instructions.

Right/wrong side (RS/WS) = the 'right side' is the surface of the fabric intended to be the outside of the finished article and therefore shown in the photographs; the 'wrong side' is the inside. If there is a difference, the instructions state which side is facing you as you work the first row and that surface of the fabric is identified and fixed from then on.

Hint: crochet stitches are not the same back and front and so the two sides of a fabric may well be quite different. Even when a stitch pattern has no particular 'right side', however, it is wise to make a positive decision in respect of all separate pieces of the same article, so that the 'grain' of the rows can be matched exactly, when you join the pieces

together.

Front/back = 'front' and 'back' mean the front and back surfaces of a fabric for the time being as you hold and look at it; these change over every time you turn the work.

Note: In garment pattern instructions the terms 'front' and 'back' denote the different pieces of the garment.

Multiple = all but the simplest crochet stitch patterns are built around repeated sequences of stitches. In order to make sense of the instructions you must have exactly the right number of stitches in your base row. This number is a multiple of the number of stitches required for one complete sequence – sometimes plus an extra edge stitch, or two – and is given at the beginning of each set of instructions.

The number of chains you need for the base chain in order to be able to create the appropriate number of stitches in the base row is also given. For example, 'Multiple of 2 sts + 1, (add 1 for base chain)' = make 4, 6, 8, etc chains for a base row of 3, 5, 7, etc stitches; or 'Multiple of 8 sts + 3, (add 2 for base chain)' = make 13, 21, 29, etc chains for a base row of 11, 19, 27, etc stitches.

Colour note = capital letters A, B, C, D, etc, are used to indicate different yarn colours; when only two colours are involved and one of these is intended to dominate, the terms 'main (M)' and 'contrast (C)' may be used instead.

Asterisks (*) and brackets [] = these are used to simplify repetition. Instructions are put inside brackets and these are to be worked the number of times stated, for example: '[1ch, skip 1ch, 1dc into next st] 5 times.'

A sequence of stitches after an asterisk means that the whole sequence between that asterisk and the next semi-colon is to be repeated as many times as necessary to reach the end of the row, for example:

'*1ch, skip 1ch, 1dc into next st, 1ch, skip 1ch, 1dc into each of next 3 sts; rep from * to end, turn.'

If no further details are given, as in this case, the end of the sequence will coincide exactly with the end of the row. If there are stitches remaining unworked after the last complete repeat sequence, details of how to complete the row are given, for example: 'Rep from * to last 4 sts, ending 1ch, skip 1ch, 1dc into each of last 3 sts, turn.' 'Rep from * 4 more times' means work that sequence 5 times in all.

Charts = Filet crochet patterns, which are based on a regular grid of double crochet and chain stitches, are much easier to follow from a squared chart, when you understand the basic procedures. This type of chart is also used to indicate different colours in Jacquard and Fair Isle patterns, which are usually based on a plain single crochet fabric.

Stitch diagrams = accurate stitch diagrams show the overall picture at a glance and at the same time indicate precisely every detail of construction. To follow them you need to be familiar with the symbols which represent each individual stitch.

index

resources

Rowan
Green Lane Mill
Holmfirth
HD9 2DX
England
www.knitrowan.com

Other titles currently available in the Harmony Guides series:

KNITTING   CROCHET

Publisher's Acknowledgements

First and foremost, we'd like to thank Rowan Yarns for suppplying all the yarns used throughout this book. We would like to thank all those who helped recreate the swatches: Heather Stephenson, Melina Kalatzi, Sharon Brant and her team of crocheters. Lastly, we would like to thank all past and present editors who have contributed to the series. All photography by Michael Wicks.